The Evolution of Justice, Equity, and Equality

This book presents a comprehensive exploration of historical perspectives on justice, equity, and equality, which have been, and still are, considered as the core values of any balanced political system. Combining historical methodology with wider philosophical and ethical insights, the volume offers a unique contribution to the fields of legal history, legal heritage, and legal culture. Bringing together scholars who specialise in different historical periods, the book covers a variety of concepts and practices, but also identifies some universal ideas about justice, equity, and equality that have been stimulating the development of the European political and legal tradition throughout the ages. In this way, it provides a multidisciplinary approach that advances the field of legal studies. By bridging the disciplines of history, law, and philosophy, the book demonstrates the interconnectedness of these fields and highlights how historical legal concepts can inform contemporary discussions. As such, it will be a valuable resource for academics and researchers working in these and related areas.

Iwona Barwicka-Tylek (Jagiellonian University in Kraków, Poland) is an associate professor in the Chair of the History of Political and Legal Doctrines. Her main academic interests include the evolution of fundamental ethical concepts (freedom, justice), in Western and Central European culture, with a particular focus on the Aristotelian heritage.

Jan Halberda (Jagiellonian University in Kraków, Poland) is an associate professor in the Chair of General History of the State and Law. His recent research was conducted as a visiting researcher at Yale Law School (Spring Term 2024). He is an attorney-at-law and an expert witness (in the field of foreign law – common law jurisdictions).

Maciej Mikuła (Jagiellonian University in Kraków, Poland) is a professor at the Jagiellonian University, author and editor of several monographs on late medieval law in Central Europe. He is also a principal investigator of numerous projects, including "IURA. Sources of Law of the Past" (https://iura.uj.edu.pl).

Routledge Studies in Comparative Legal History

This series covers the general area of comparative legal history, including contributions focusing on both 'internal' legal history, i.e., doctrinal and disciplinary developments in the law, and 'external' legal history, i.e., legal ideas and institutions in wider contexts. Considering the various legal traditions worldwide, the series also welcomes works dealing with other laws and customs from around the globe. Temporal or geographical in approach, the series will consider both legal and similar law-like normative traditions. Works encompassing views from different schools of thought and contributions from comparative and transnational historiography, including interdisciplinary approaches, are encouraged. With a focus on higher level research in the form of monographs and edited collections, proposals for supplementary reading and textbooks are also welcomed.

Titles in this series:

Borders of the Early Modern Ius Commune
England, Venice and Scandinavia
Edited by Dolores Freda, Mario Piccinini, Heikki Pihlajamäki, and Chiara Maria Valsecchi

Framing Devices and Global Legal Traditions
From the Ancient World to the Modern Nation State
Edited by Laura Culbertson and Susan Longfield Karr

The Evolution of Justice, Equity, and Equality
Practical Wisdom from the Past
Edited by Iwona Barwicka-Tylek, Jan Halberda, Maciej Mikuła

For more information about this series, please visit:
https://www.routledge.com/Routledge-Studies-in-Comparative-Legal-History/book-series/COMPLEGHIST

The Evolution of Justice, Equity, and Equality

Practical Wisdom from the Past

Edited by Iwona Barwicka-Tylek, Jan Halberda, and Maciej Mikuła

Routledge
Taylor & Francis Group
LONDON AND NEW YORK

First published 2026
by Routledge
4 Park Square, Milton Park, Abingdon, Oxon OX14 4RN

and by Routledge
605 Third Avenue, New York, NY 10158

Routledge is an imprint of the Taylor & Francis Group, an informa business

British Library Cataloguing-in-Publication Data
A catalogue record for this book is available from the British Library

ISBN: 978-1-041-10253-3 (hbk)
ISBN: 978-1-041-10260-1 (pbk)
ISBN: 978-1-003-65413-1 (ebk)

DOI: 10.4324/9781003654131

The research for this publication has been supported by a grant from the Priority Research Area Heritage under the Strategic Programme Excellence Initiative at Jagiellonian University.

The Open Access version of Chapters 1 and 9 was funded by Jagiellonian University in Krakow.

For Product Safety Concerns and Information please contact our EU representative: GPSR@taylorandfrancis.com
Taylor & Francis Verlag GmbH, Kaufingerstraße 24, 80331 München, Germany

Contents

List of Contributors

Francisco J. Andrés Santos (University of Valladolid, Spain) is a full professor of Roman law. His research concerns Roman law, legal history in Europe and Latin America, European private law, and legal theory. He teaches Roman law, comparative private law, and legal argumentation. Currently he is a researcher in the Max-Planck-Institut für Rechtsgeschichte und Rechtstheorie (Frankfurt am Main, Germany).

Iwona Barwicka-Tylek (Jagiellonian University in Kraków, Poland) is an associate professor in the Chair of the History of Political and Legal Doctrines. Her main academic interests include the evolution of fundamental ethical concepts (freedom, justice), in Western and Central European culture, with a particular focus on the Aristotelian heritage.

Tomáš Gábriš https://orcid.org/0000-0002-6862-2688 (Trnava University in Trnava, Slovakia) is a full professor and head of the Department of Historical Law and Legal Methodology. He is a researcher at the Slovak Academy of Sciences (Institute of State and Law) and at the Palacky University in Olomouc, Faculty of Law (Czechia).

Jan Halberda (Jagiellonian University in Kraków, Poland) is an associate professor in the Chair of General History of the State and Law. His recent research was conducted as a visiting researcher at Yale Law School (Spring Term 2024). He is an attorney-at-law and an expert witness (in the field of foreign law - common law jurisdictions).

Maciej Mikuła (Jagiellonian University in Kraków, Poland) is a professor at the Jagiellonian University, author and editor of several monographs on late medieval law in Central Europe. He is also a principal investigator of numerous projects, including "IURA. Sources of Law of the Past" (https://iura.uj.edu.pl).

Guido Rossi (University of Edinburgh, United Kingdom) is a reader in European Legal History at Edinburgh University.

Adrian Schmidt-Recla (Friedrich Schiller-Universität Jena, Germany) is an extraordinary professor of German civil law, German and European legal history and medical law at the Faculty of Law of the Friedrich Schiller-University Jena. He graduated in law at the University of Leipzig in 1995 and has since been researching medieval inheritance law.

Kamila Staudigl-Ciechowicz (University of Vienna, Austria) is an assistant professor at the Department of Legal and Constitutional History at the Vienna Faculty of Law and research fellow at the University of Regensburg.

Norbert Varga (University of Szeged, Hungary) is a professor and head of the Hungarian Legal History Department at the Faculty of Law. His recent research concerned cartel law in interwar Hungary. He was either visiting fellow or professor in Cambridge, Oxford, Frankfurt am Main, Heidelberg, Amsterdam, Zagreb, Trnava, Kraków, Bloomington, Hong Kong, and Beijing.

Introduction. Kaleidoscope

Iwona Barwicka-Tylek, Jan Halberda, and Maciej Mikuła

The present volume is the result of two international workshops organised in 2023 at the Faculty of Law and Administration of the Jagiellonian University in Kraków. These were the milestones of the project entitled "Hector: Heritage, Culture, Norms,"[1] which was funded by the Jagiellonian University in the framework of the Initiative of Excellence – Research University programme: "Research Platforms in the Heritage Priority Research Area (2nd edition)" (2022–2024). The sequel to this project is the research group "Hector. Heritage, Culture, Norms 2.0" (2024–2026) operating within the Critical Heritage Studies Hub, another part of the Initiative of Excellence – Research University programme.[2]

The "Hector" initiative was an innovative, interdisciplinary, international research platform. It brought together researchers from different disciplines (lawyers, legal historians, general historians, historians of art, sociologists, philosophers, and political scientists) and from various countries (predominantly Central and Eastern Europe, but also Belgium, France, Norway, Scotland, Spain, Switzerland, and the United States). The project was aimed at providing a proper venue for academic discussion on a wide range of topics on legal heritage, from transforming fundamental and universal values into norms through the consolidation of norms into artefacts to their presence in the present as well as their role in the future.

From the very beginning, the two Kraków workshops[3] were meant as experiments, born out of a rather pessimistic observation that being a legal historian in a Central and Eastern Europe law school condemns one to becoming less and less visible. Legal historians are perceived by scholars conducting research

1 The project's official webpage can be found under the following link: https://lhlab.wpia.uj.edu.pl/.

2 Cf. the link: https://crihestu.id.uj.edu.pl/en_GB/hector.

3 The first workshop, entitled "Law/Justice/Equity. Historical Perspective," took place on 29 June 2023, and gathered scholars from Austria, France, Germany, Hungary, Poland, Scotland, and Slovakia. The second one, entitled "Freedom/Equality/Law. Historical Perspective," was organised on 20 October 2023, with participants coming from Hungary, Lithuania, Poland, and Spain.

DOI: 10.4324/9781003654131-1

in other legal sciences as experts in ancient facts who need to be consulted only if one is interested in showing that some contemporary legal doctrine, regulation, or concept is deeply embedded (for better or worse) in the constantly developing legal tradition. This propaedeutic role of legal history falls woefully short of the potential of this discipline, but it is not at all easy for legal historians to justify a claim that they deserve to be assigned a more important role. The decades of specialisation have done their job. Multiple divisions wedge seemingly insurmountable obstacles between particular legal subdisciplines, setting them apart. Researchers in legal sciences, in general, and legal historians, in particular, feel comfortable only within the well-defined limits of their own disparate research, scattered across time and space so they hardly see one another in everyday academic work. Thus, Roman historians prefer talking to Roman historians, and those who specialise in canon law feel more comfortable in the presence of other canonists.

The "Hector" initiative attempted a different approach, more attuned to the changes in contemporary social science, which advocates leaving one's "comfort zone" and engaging in a dialogue that goes well beyond traditional (sub)disciplinary divisions, as its main concern is to get as close as possible to the dynamic and complex human experience to provide knowledge that helps one act and make conscious choices, and not only know and understand a given subject. The idea was to invite scholars who work in different parts of the "quarry" of the past, ask them to dig up some interesting facts as solid as rocks, and then grind those "rocks" according to our standards so they all became gems that could attract the attention of everybody and not only fellow "historian-geologists." In this case, the standard method was to narrate the past in such a manner that the spotlight would be on the language of human values, especially the concepts of justice, equity, equality, and freedom.

Under the auspices of the "Hector" project, we wanted to investigate whether a topic that is at the same time both specific and universal would encourage invited scholars to use their expertise to contribute to a more general and synthetising discussion on the topic itself, or, on the contrary, would make them try to parcel the topic into smaller subtopics so it could be analysed within the modest limits of their own historical knowledge. One goal was to demonstrate, as stated by Russell Sandberg, that "we are all legal historians"[4] and that a historical approach should be "at the beating heart of the Law School."[5] We also wanted to show that, in practice, legal historians themselves are capable of and willing to make use of the assumed potential of their discipline.

The results of the "Hector" initiative's experiment were frustrating at first, but it was a kind of a frustration that soon led to enthusiasm rather than

4 Russell Sandberg, *Subversive Legal History: A Manifesto for the Future of Legal Education* (London–New York: Routledge 2021), 198.

5 Sandberg, *Subversive Legal History*, 223–224.

despair. The dynamics of both workshops were in many ways analogous to the process described by Sandberg in his *Subversive Legal History: A Manifesto for the Future of Legal Education*. In the afterword to that book, he wrote:

> This book develops an argument that is the exact opposite to that developed in my previous two sole-authored books. In those two books I explored and argued for the development of Law and Religion as a subdiscipline in its own right. [...] [H]ere I have argued against the development of legal history as a sub-discipline in its own right. Indeed, this book applies this not only to legal history but also calls for a re-construction of legal education generally. The argument developed here is that legal history is more important than it is commonly assumed to be. [...] My critique here comes from a position of frustration. I am frustrated that the potential of legal history and of law as an academic discipline is not being fully realised.[6]

Analogously, the participants of the workshops were at first rather hesitant about having to confront presenters with a background much different from theirs and an audience that, while admittedly engaged, was hardly interested in the particular area of their historical knowledge. It soon turned out, however, that, in spite of the initial hesitation and the fears of anachronisms which impeded making too far-reaching historical parallels, diverse presentations set side by side triggered questions and remarks that allowed a broader picture to emerge. Separately, each of them was just a small piece of glass, different in shape and colour from all the others. Assembled together, they created unexpected images like those in a child's kaleidoscope. These are frustrating in that they change with a twist of the hand, which makes them difficult to present to others. This also applied to the results of both workshops.

Just as with a kaleidoscope, the difficulty with showing the image produced is no obstacle to handing it over to others to let them see for themselves some new images constructed with the same pieces of glass. The same is true of this monograph, and so it applies what is called in literature the episodic approach.[7] It is composed of texts which seem to be objectively distant from one another, but they are focused upon the same general subject. They are compounded in order to present the argument, humble as it may be in one book, that history, including legal history, can be practiced in such a manner that it becomes practical. Just as authorities such as Marc Bloch[8] and Frederic Maitland[9] argued,

6 Sandberg, *Subversive Legal History*, 225–226.

7 See: Gábor Gángó and Knud Haakonssen, "Preface," in *Early-Modern Natural Law in East-Central Europe*, ed. Gábor Gángó (Leiden–Boston: Brill, 2023), VII.

8 Marc Bloch, *The Historian's Craft*, trans. P. Putnam (New York: Vintage Books, 1964).

9 Frederic W. Maitland, *The Collected Papers of Frederic William Maitland*, vol. 3, ed. Herbert A. L. Fisher (Cambridge: Cambridge University Press, 1911).

it provides knowledge that is much more useful in the present than other possible narratives about the past. To quote Sandberg once again, it helps in purifying the field of law from deeply sown grains of progressivism:

> The existence of the progress narrative in law (in judgments and in works on the law) is [...] so endemic that it is hidden. It masks how law is contingent, authored and contestable. It results in legal conservatism. Legal change is constrained within narrow parameters. Presenting the past not only as a foreign country but also as a primitive and barbarous one and hiding the historical fact that different and often still feasible approaches have been available means that it is not realised that different options and realities are possible and may be desirable.[10]

This book is divided into three parts preceded by texts authored by Iwona Barwicka-Tylek and Tomáš Gábriš. These three parts revolve around the relationship between law and fundamental values, such as justice, equity, and equality.

In her chapter ("The Historian's Craft and Ethical Values: A Lesson from Aristotle"), Iwona Barwicka-Tylek of the Jagiellonian University in Kraków argues that both history and law, being generally crafts employing productive knowledge (*poiesis*), should encourage their practitioners to also develop "practical wisdom" (*phronesis*). The difference between *poiesis* and *phronesis* is discussed in the context of Aristotle's practical philosophy (*Nicomachean Ethics, Politics*) and his aesthetics (*Poetics*). Arguments for introducing *phronesis* into the field of law are provided. It is emphasised that *phronesis* (translated into Latin as *prudentia*) involves internal limitations on action, guiding experts in some areas (including lawyers) to act in ways that embody universal human values (justice, equality, freedom). Equally important are temporal aspects of this kind of practical wisdom, which are briefly discussed with the help of two symbolic representations of *phronesis/prudentia*: Titian's *Allegory of Prudence* and Cesare Ripa's description from his *Iconologia*. The relevance of history in understanding and guiding human actions in a complex and value-oriented world of human affairs is defended. Ultimately, it is suggested that the legal curriculum should balance the knowledge of law with ethical engagement to promote a more humane and adaptable legal practice, which means that history deserves to be recognised as a source of practical wisdom that should be part of legal education.

The following chapter is authored by Tomáš Gábriš of the Trnava University ("Justice as an *Empty Principle* in Post-Structuralist Legal Thought. Towards Neohistorical Jurisprudence?"). It argues that since the end of the 20th century structuralism in legal scholarship has come under attack in Continental Europe and is being replaced by post-structuralist thought. Instead of trust

10 Sandberg, *Subversive Legal History*, 201.

in immutable structures, the ever-changing and fluid nature of "structures" is being accepted. As a litmus test, this chapter examines the changing idea of justice and confirms that there is indeed a shift from methodological collectivism to methodological individualism. In structuralist thought, there are "empty points" or "empty principles," through which static inner structures are connected to outer structures, just as law is connected to society and the economy via the "empty principle" of justice. Law is thus influenced by the general driving forces of history. This was, paradoxically, accepted in the same manner even by Marxist-Leninist legal thought. Nowadays, in contrast, methodological individualism has resurfaced instead, stressing the role of independent actors. Individual perceptions of justice come into play, just like individual preferences and interests come into play in the overall development of law. This is a major revelation to lawyers, meaning in fact the emergence of a renewed historical school of law – albeit in the greatly modernised form of "recent legal history" (*Juristische Zeitgeschichte*) or "neohistorical jurisprudence." The methodological individualism of historical scholarship is particularly apt at explaining the sometimes haphazard changes in legal systems and in the perception of justice, which cannot be explained by the traditional theories of grand narratives.

The first part of the book is entitled "Law and Justice." It starts with a chapter titled "The Concept of Justice in Polish Municipal Law in the 16th–18th Centuries" written by Maciej Mikuła of the Jagiellonian University in Kraków. He draws attention to the fact that the concept of justice was invoked in various types of legal sources in Polish cities of the 16th–18th centuries. In the collection of municipal law *Ius municipale Magdeburgense* [Municipal Magdeburg Law] one can find the view that only a regulation that conformed to natural law could be considered just. Justice thus acted as a precondition of law. Although practitioners of municipal law probably intuitively decoded the meaning of the concept of justice, the records of practitioners found allow us to confirm that it was the subject of reflection. They also reveal that the meaning of the term "equity" varied. In philosophical and legal writings, it went beyond the legal sphere (Sigismundus Lauxmin, *De iure et iustitia*, 1647/1648), while in texts of the legal practice it could simply mean "compliance with the law," and thus referred to the legal sphere analogously to the term "justice." An analysis of some one thousand records of city criminal courts makes it possible to show that almost every ninth one referred to the notions of "justice" and/or "holy justice." The concept of justice was mentioned, among other things, in several judgements that considered the legitimacy of not applying the written law. It was used both to legitimise not applying the written law in favour of unwritten customary law and, conversely, to emphasise that the application of written law is just, and that not applying it can be understood as judicial mercy.

The next chapter concerns a time much closer to the present day. The one written by Norbert Varga of the University of Szeged is "Good Morals as the

Yardstick of Cartels' Validity in Hungarian Private Law at the Turn of the 20th Century." The aim of this study is to present the legal practice on the assessment of cartels from the second half of the 19th century until the Hungarian Cartel Act of 1931. The author examines the practice of the Hungarian supreme court, the Curia, during that period. The primary sources were the relevant decisions of the Curia. In the absence of legislation, the courts judged cartel agreements on the basis of general principles of private law, in particular good morals. They examined the validity of cartel agreements and their potential immorality on a case-by-case basis. There was a reversal in the way the courts judged cartel agreements in the first half of the 20th century, i.e., they accepted them under certain circumstances in light of the changed economic and social circumstances. A detailed and systematic analysis of the practice of cartel law prior to the adoption of the statute of 1931 is a valuable contribution to the national and international literature.

The second part of the book considers tensions between law and equity. It begins with a paper by Adrian Schmidt-Recla of the Friedrich Schiller University Jena. His chapter, entitled "Legitimacy and Equity in the 11th century? Age-Old Messages from Susali," concerns the beginnings of medieval Saxon law. The author begins by saying that ever since people have been writing about conflicts and interests they have been using common methods and reasoning. Using the example of medieval Saxon law, he attempts to prove that the above assertion applies to legitimacy and equity as well as to law. In his *Chronicon*, the cleric and historiographer Thietmar, Bishop of Merseburg (975–1018), recorded information concerning an act of Count Friedrich I (960–1017) of Eilenburg, a county in the Saxon Susali district (in what is nowadays the north of the federal state of Saxony in Germany). This record is one of the first legal messages concerning Saxon law. Thietmar's report shines a light on the ideas and beliefs of the people involved and of a cleric writing as a contemporary. Those ideas included sovereignty, family relationships, inheritance, judiciousness, and gender, which are still present in political and ethical discourse. Thietmar tied these concepts together into a single word: legitimacy. He thus contributed to the eternal discussion concerning ethical and normative concepts. If the balance of interests is taken into account, one could prove whether the concept of equity was present at the dawn of law. Religion and the pursuit of power were definitely not.

The next chapter, written by Guido Rossi of the University of Edinburgh, presents a comparative study under the title "Visions of Equity." It looks at the development of the concept of equity as understood and applied by lawyers and jurists in the Middle Ages and the first early modern period, both in the so-called learned law and among merchants. The enquiry focuses on various times and places: England, 15th to 17th centuries; Italy, 12th to 13th centuries; and the Low Countries, 16th century. Rossi's work is based on both secondary and especially primary sources (manuscripts and early modern editions), seeking to understand and contextualise them, as well as comparing their approach and focus so as to better highlight the development of the concept of equity within different frameworks. The study emphasises the historical development of the subject of the book, the concept of equity. In terms of its contribution to the study, the paper provides a comparative approach to the development of the concept of equity which highlights the different paths chosen in various countries and within different legal traditions.

The seventh chapter is authored by Kamila Staudigl-Ciechowicz of the University of Vienna ("The Concept of Equity in Austrian Private Law. From the Origins of the Austrian General Civil Code (ABGB) to the Present Day"). Her article deals with the role of equity in the development of Austrian private law, focusing on the 19th and 20th centuries. It revolves around the question of the extent to which equity has been preserved in Austrian legal practice and legal culture even after the codification movement, which was hostile to the concept of equity, and which developments led to a greater consideration of equity aspects. As a longitudinal study, this article covers the main themes of the book – the relationship between law and equity and the extent to which equity can make law just. The fathers of the Austrian civil law codification rejected the concept of equity as general, single-case justice by a judge, but the idea of legally guided equity – through incorporation by special provisions – led to changes in the Austrian civil code (ABGB) and in particular private law statutes in the course of the 20th century. The concept of equity is therefore not only of historical significance as a common heritage, but also remains a current phenomenon. In her study, Staudigl-Ciechowicz makes use of contemporary works by legal scholars, modern literature on the subject, as well as parliamentary materials and contemporary judgements of the Austrian courts.

The third and last part of the book is entitled "Law and Equality" and consists of two chapters. Francisco J. Andrés Santos of the University of Valladolid contributed the paper "Liberty and Inequality in Cicero's *Oratio pro Sestio.*" It concerns relations between equality and freedom in the Roman Republic, particularly in its final period, when the idea of equality tried to make its way into the world of socio-political values in Rome, a traditionally stratified and strongly hierarchical society. There is a marked contrast with the axiological-political universe of classical Greece, in which the notion of equality acted in parallel with that of freedom to shape an ideal of justice. It is in this historical framework of the 1st century BCE that Cicero appears, representing Rome's greatest contribution to the history of political theory. Andrés Santos analyses the vicissitudes and arguments that took place on the occasion of a trial in 56 BCE, in which Cicero acted as defence counsel. Cicero took advantage of the occasion to expound on some of the political ideas based on the traditional republican model under the pre-eminence of the Senate (i.e., the oligarchy) in the face of pressure for greater popular participation in the interests of a true equalisation of political rights and a more equitable distribution of material resources. The chapter is intended as an instructive example of the general aims of this volume, aimed at studying the interrelations between freedom, equality and justice in a broad temporal framework, but under a similar cultural prism.

The last chapter is authored by Jan Halberda of the Jagiellonian University in Kraków and refers to the Anglo-American legal tradition ("Equity and Equality in Richard Francis's *Maxims of Equity*"). His paper presents various patterns of using the term "equity" in Richard Francis's book *Maxims of Equity* (London 1727) and its affinity with both law and equality. It examines a work of legal literature published during the period when the understanding of the concept of equity was being transformed: the shift from case-by-case adjudication towards the establishment of equity law as a mature legal system based on the emerging doctrine of precedent. The titular maxims of equity were, and are, the guiding principles of the legal order around which the interpretation of particular legal doctrines revolves. The chapter researches the links between the concepts of law, equity, justice, and equality. It seeks to discover the ways in which the notion of equity was used by Francis. There were, indeed, several patterns of how the term "equity" was used. On the one hand, it bore the hallmarks of Aristotle's *epieikeia*. On the other, it was used as an equivalent of "natural justice," or as a reference to a set of rules applied by the Court of Chancery. As the paper focuses on the maxim "Equality is equity," it shows that the problem of equal treatment of similarly positioned parties was a key concern of the Court of Chancery. In this respect, equity was understood as somehow similar to *aequitas* in Roman law.

The proposed collection of texts was born out of curiosity and, at the same time, anxiety about fundamental questions: what is justice, how to understand equity, and how does the principle of equality correspond to them?

Taking as a guide the Aristotelian term *phronesis*, the essence of which is the fulfillment of these values (Iwona Barwicka-Tylek), it was emphasised that the creator, addressee and depositary of practical wisdom is the individual. Although he or she is entangled in history, circumstances and various constraints, at the same time that person remains capable of shaping the grand narratives of reality (Tomáš Gábriš). It should be noted that great narratives do not come from nowhere. They are made up of tiny elements, just like the kaleidoscope mentioned at the beginning of this introduction. Certainly, it is worth keeping a close eye on these smaller gems. The adventures of individuals form the axis of the book's consideration of the meaning of "equity" and "justice" in the context of private law (Adrian Schmidt-Recla) and criminal law (Maciej Mikuła).

The decoding of the meaning of "justice" and "equity" has always taken place in specific conditions and contexts, as evidenced by late medieval and early modern merchant law and the reflection of legal scholars on the European *ius commune* (Guido Rossi). In legal practice, however, it was not uncommon for an intuitive understanding of these concepts to prevail. This was particularly the case where there was a lack of explicit reference points anchored in the law, for instance, in early medieval Saxony (Adrian Schmidt-Recla) where, at the beginning of the second millennium, the foundations of the future Saxon inheritance law were forged through the prism of the (not explicitly formalised) principle of equity. Also in the Kingdom of Poland conscious and explicit reflection on the nature of justice was not unknown to judges of its municipal criminal courts. Their judgements echoed the hesitation concerning whether justice was a feature of written law, however inadequate it might be in a given case, or whether, on the contrary, justice would have been achieved by departing from it in favour of unwritten customary law (Maciej Mikula). This was the very dilemma that the founding fathers of modern Austrian civil law wanted to spare judges from. The attempt to ensure just law by incorporating the principle of equity was a challenge for the code drafters during the 19th and 20th centuries (Kamila Staudigl-Ciechowicz). At the same time, in the absence of a law normalising the activity of cartels, it was equity, interpreted under general principles of civil law, which was the guide for judges of the Hungarian Supreme Court (Norbert Varga).

The principle of equity, verbalised in various ways and forms, not only allowed individual cases to be decided until specific rules were established, as Adrian Schmidt-Recla and Norbert Varga have written, but also assumed the function of a keystone of the legal system. In this case, it became a proxy for other principles. Jan Halberda has shown how in the Anglo-American legal tradition it was linked to other strongly axiological oriented principles, including equality. In a European legal culture based on ancient traditions such as the *Orationes* of Cicero (Francisco J. Andrés Santos), the conviction that equality is fair remained unacknowledged for centuries. Ultimately, however, it has led to a radical improvement in the lives of millions of people.

And that is undoubtedly one of the aims of practical wisdom.

References

Bloch, Marc. *The Historian's Craft*. Translated by P. Putnam. New York: Vintage Books, 1964.

Gángó, Gábor, and Knud Haakonssen. "Preface." In *Early-Modern Natural Law in East-Central Europe*, edited by Gábor Gángó, VII. Leiden and Boston: Brill, 2023.

Maitland, Frederic W. *The Collected Papers of Frederic William Maitland*, vol. 3. Edited by Herbert A. L. Fisher. Cambridge: Cambridge University Press, 1911.

Sandberg, Russell. *Subversive Legal History: A Manifesto for the Future of Legal Education*. London and New York: Routledge, 2021.

1 The Historian's Craft and Ethical Values. A Lesson from Aristotle

Iwona Barwicka-Tylek

Open Access of this chapter was financed by the ID.UJ Program at Faculty of Law and Administration of Jagiellonian University.

1.1 Introduction

At first sight, it seems like historians and lawyers have much in common, and so legal history should be a welcome discipline at law schools. Marc Bloch, a French historian from the *Annales* school, observed that, even though the paths of a historian and a judge divide at some point of their intellectual journey, initially they proceed in a similar manner. Both must do their best to stay impartial and focus on the facts.[1] The method of historical inquiry "is basically a method of investigation, and secondarily a method of describing and interpreting the results of investigation"; therefore, "training in historical research has a peculiar value as pre-professional training for the law student."[2] What is more, since "[t]he law is notoriously a learned profession," historians can provide lawyers with "an appropriate erudition" and "legal history, when seriously considered, has been considered an alchemy for distilling legal principles."[3] Finally, as observed by Richard Posner: "Law is the most historically oriented [...] of the professions,"[4] which is at least partly due to its aspiration to become an autonomous discipline: "[t]o the extent that a field, whether it be music, mathematics, or law, is autonomous, developing in accordance with its internal laws, its current state will bear an organic relation to its previous states."[5]

By reading such quotes, legal historians might feel reassured that the law needs them. Every historian knows, however, that selectively chosen facts (in this case: sentences from different academic texts) reveal no truth on how things really are, unless they are presented against the whole background of other facts which coexist with them. It is enough to peruse the two articles I

1 Marc Bloch, *The Historian's Craft*, trans. P. Putnam (New York: Vintage Books, 1964), 139.

2 Laurence L. Howe, "Historical Method and Legal Education," *Bulletin of the American Association of University Professors* 36, no. 2 (1950): 349.

3 Daniel J. Boorstin, "Tradition and Method in Legal History," *Harvard Law Review* 54, no. 3 (1941): 424.

4 Richard A. Posner, "Past-Dependency, Pragmatism, and Critique of History in Adjudication and Legal Scholarship," *University of Chicago Law Review* 67, no. 3 (2000): 573.

5 Posner, "Past-Dependency, Pragmatism, and Critique of History," 586.

DOI: 10.4324/9781003654131-2

have just quoted to see how the picture changes. In each of these texts, there is a large dose of criticism of the usefulness of history – the ways it is being taught in law school, used in the education of lawyers, and, last and not least, used by legal professionals. For Posner, whose criticism of history is perhaps the most straightforward, the past-dependency of law makes the latter "suspicious of innovation, discontinuities, 'paradigm shifts,' and the energy and brashness of youth. These ingrained attitudes are obstacles to anyone who wants to reorient law in a more pragmatic direction."[6]

The important changes in epistemology of social sciences, which were initiated in the 20th century, have rejuvenated legal science and in a way pushed it in the direction expected by Posner. Legal philosophers and theorists seem to appreciate once again what he would perhaps categorise as "the brashness of youth": engagement, creativity, courage in seeking solutions to contemporary problems, and readiness to justify such solutions on ethical rather than merely utilitarian grounds. The question thus arises whether, under circumstances such as these, the distance between history and law is growing, justifying pushing legal history to the margins of jurisprudence and legal education, or perhaps some new grounds for their mutual affinity can be established.

I believe that the answer to the above question is yes: history still deserves to be treated seriously at law faculties. In this chapter, I refer to Aristotle's concept of human "political" nature (*politikon zoon*) and his concept of *phronesis* (*prudentia* in Latin – prudence, practical wisdom) to construct a perspective in which such an answer may be justified. I argue that history, although perhaps it is no longer a *magistra vitae*, deserves at least the name of *magistra prudentiae*.

1.2 Three Ways of Life

In the *Nicomachean Ethics*, Aristotle[7] identified three kinds of life: the contemplative, the political, and "the life of indulgence" that is focused on increasing pleasure.[8] Each of these kinds of life, he argued, requires having a specific kind of knowledge, and each of these kinds of knowledge has a distinct attitude towards time. In the case of the most perfect contemplative life, one needs knowledge of the universals, which are immutable. A contemplative philosopher (Plato was the most illustrative example) employs reason to attain the eternal metaphysical truth, which resides outside human history, as the latter is

6 Posner, "Past-Dependency, Pragmatism, and Critique of History," 573.

7 The literature on Aristotle is vast, and the interpretations of the concepts which are of primary interest here vary, often significantly. That is why I refer directly to Aristotle's works. A reader who is interested in a different and much more extensive interpretation may consult: C.D.C. Reeve, *Practices of Reason: Aristotle's Nicomachean Ethics* (New York: Oxford University Press, 1992).

8 Aristotle, *Nicomachean Ethics*, trans. C.D.C. Reeve (Indianapolis: Hackett Publishing, 2014), 5.

happening in the constantly changing material world, which consists of diverse particulars that often seem to contradict one another and tend to deteriorate with time, being replaced with new ones. It does not mean, however, that time is merely an obstacle to living a philosophical life. On the contrary, since every philosopher occupies a specific position in historical time (which for him is the present), seeking the truth naturally encourages him to look into the past, as there the origins of the truth are concealed. To reach the truth, one should, in fact, think backwards, as relying on the past it is easier to differentiate between the knowledge that is eternally valid and will remain true forever, and the knowledge whose validity is temporally and spatially limited. This way, living as the universal truth suggests, the philosopher becomes almost as self-sufficient as the gods, but the cost is separation from the present world of human affairs, in which his reason could accidentally be blinded by sensations and desires coming from his body.

Two other kinds of life are more challenging to differentiate. Both are active lives in the sense that they both require doing something in (and with) the world that consists of many things which "can be otherwise" and so they are "practical" things (*ta prakta* – things to be done)."[9] The shape and content of such things can be chosen to some extent, which makes the world of human affairs (human *praxis*) dynamic, changeable, and full of diversity. And since it is impossible to discuss any change without reference to time, it makes the human world sensitive to the multiple relationships between the past, the present, and the future, as without them it would be impossible to understand any change, let alone to introduce it deliberately.

The life of indulgence is the least developed, as it is in fact the animal life form, perception dependent, in which one's reason becomes the means to increase pleasure and to avoid pain. Since perception requires the presence of some object, such life's focus is first of all on the present and the knowledge that serves it best is productive knowledge (*poiesis*), focused on making things that help to satisfy particular needs (animals also have it: they make nests or dens, for example). Productive knowledge, explained Aristotle, is concerned "with crafting things and getting a theoretical grasp on how something may come to be that admits of being and of not being and whose starting point is in the producer and not in the product."[10] Although present-oriented, productive knowledge does not ignore the past as it draws on the already gathered experience that makes the whole process of production more efficient.

Both forms of life described so far are not in fact *human* in the full sense. Aristotle was known for his taste for moderation, and so it is no wonder that neither the god-like nor the animal-like extremes could satisfy him. In his view, the most *human* was the third kind of life, the political life, in which both the god-like and the animal-like capacities would be combined in such a manner

9 Aristotle, *Nicomachean Ethics*, 101–102.
10 Aristotle, *Nicomachean Ethics*, 101.

as to result in a qualitatively distinct and specific human nature. According to the famous Aristotelian definition of man, we are *zoa politika*, that is, animals "among whom some one work common to all is produced."[11] For the philosopher, it was the natural and universal aspect of individual human development to establish relationships with others at multiple levels, which results in creating many political[12] communities, the most important of which is a state. Once established, the state is prior to its parts (individual citizens),[13] but only insofar as it is a good state, a state in which our humanity, complex as it is because of its animal- and god-like elements, may flourish. The task of the state is to facilitate living together, but above of all the possibility of living well.[14] That is what makes ethical language (with concepts like justice and equality) an important part of political science.[15]

The state is, to a significant extent, an artificial product of *poiesis*. Because we possess reason, human productive capacity is greater than that of any other animal. We are capable not only of understanding nature, but also of imitating it in order to create new things, which are at least partly the products of the will of their producers. Acting collectively, we gain access to the experience of former generations and because of that our "theoretical grasp" improves with time, leading also to the professionalisation of productive activity. In the 21st century, we see much more clearly than Aristotle did how the present condition of the human world depends on past discoveries and inventions, including those which are now outdated and no longer in use. Observing these historical changes, the words "development" and "progress" come to mind almost automatically, and perhaps, as suggested, for instance, by Steven Pinker,[16] one should not avoid looking at human history from such an angle. Aristotle would have also agreed that human *praxis* – since it is "practical" (variable, full of new possibilities) – should improve rather than deteriorate. Yet, he would have advised caution in equating development or progress with our *poietical* achievements. This is because things produced (as diverse as computers, sushi, films, or laws) are merely the means to satisfy particular and present needs, so judging them we are inclined to take into account their short-term utility. Such judgements lack the deliberation and imagination necessary to make them ethical, long-term, and future-oriented judgements – to consider whether and how they could really contribute to the development of the most human ways of life.

There is also another, strictly political problem with the things produced. They have the potential to trigger emotions and desires of both those who

11 Aristotle, *Generation of Animals & History of Animals I, Parts of Animals I*, trans. C.D.C. Reeve (Indianapolis–Cambridge: Hackett Publishing, 2019), 5.

12 In the broad sense of producing, having something in common.

13 Aristotle, *Politics*, trans. C.D.C. Reeve (Indianapolis: Hackett Publishing, 1998), 4.

14 Aristotle, *Politics*, 81.

15 Aristotle, *Nicomachean Ethics*, 3.

16 Steve Pinker, *Enlightenment Now* (London: Penguin Books Ltd., 2019).

have them and those who don't have them. Their lack is painful, and so it triggers greed, which distorts the individual sense of justice.[17] Having something in abundance is no better. It encourages a life of indulgence and the pursuit of one's own private interests and new pleasures, instead of caring about the political community to remain "some one work common to all." The negative consequences include various conflicts and, finally, the weakening of communal bonds. Aristotle's master, Plato, also understood this basic problem, as both observed the worsening condition of Athenian democracy. Paradoxically, the more developed the communal political life (as is the case of democracy in which all citizens are expected to live as *zoa politika*), the more prone it seems to be to deterioration and corruption. If such processes are left unchecked, instead of bringing citizens closer together to facilitate *human* cooperation at multiple levels, they drive them further apart over time. This is detrimental not only for the whole community, but also for individual citizens, for whom it becomes more and more difficult to trust other people's actions and to respond in a trustworthy manner by acting towards the common good and respecting the ethical requirements of justice.

Plato's solution to the problem required reducing the influence of the "animal" properties of human nature upon the political community. He advocated limiting the free activity of individual citizens to performing assigned social functions, determined either by perfect contemplative philosophers (*The Republic*) or meticulous laws (*The Laws*). For Aristotle, this solution was unacceptable as any political unity thus achieved would be a miserable imitation of political cooperation[18] undeserving of the name. It is not the responsibility of a state to transform people into a kind of domesticated animals that merely behave as *zoa politika* because of some external motivations provided by the state. Ideally, they should really become individuals who are engaged in public actions and contribute consciously to the producing of "some one work common to all" since it would simply be a natural aspect of their own personal growth. The goal of such personal growth is to finally become a mature, and to a large extent unique, representative of humankind, and not merely a standardised product of a particular state.

To understand Aristotle's solution to the problem (in short: how to encourage individual citizens to become more human and to choose political life rather than a life of indulgence in spite of the fact that every state is focused on triggering first of all our productive capacities), it is necessary to underline his naturalist position. "Nature makes nothing pointlessly," he claimed, and since it endowed every human being not only with reason and speech, but also a "perception of good and bad, just and unjust, and the rest,"[19] each of us is at least potentially capable of making ethical judgements. This way an individual

17 Aristotle, *Nicomachean Ethics*, 78.
18 Aristotle, *Politics*, 27.
19 Aristotle, *Politics*, 4.

may consciously choose actions which are not only efficient according to productive standards, but also have a chance to be noticed and recognised as good with respect to the desired and universal ideal of truly human life. To achieve this, however, another kind of knowledge is necessary. Aristotle calls it *phronesis* (other historical names: *prudentia*, prudence, practical wisdom, practical reason).[20]

Unlike *poiesis*, which helps to make things which are "producible," *phronesis* refines the things "doable in action."[21] Introducing this differentiation, Aristotle seems to refer to a rather simple observation that there are "things" which appear only in action: they are inseparable from the acting individual. Courage, for instance, is not a producible thing. Admittedly, we may try to define what courage is in general,[22] but to demonstrate it (and thus to make it "a thing" that influences the world of *praxis*), there needs to be someone acting courageously. The same is true for justice[23] and many other "things," which are for Aristotle the virtues of character. It is important to emphasise that things "doable in action," just as "producible" things, are practical, which means that they "admit of being otherwise,"[24] and so they allow diversity and change of their particular manifestations.

Phronesis is itself wisdom doable in action: it is performed by individuals and can be observed in their actions only. For Aristotle, "action" is a very broad term that covers "everything that expresses the mental life, that reveals a rational personality."[25] Action is the outward manifestation of one's character in the presence of others, with the awareness that both the doer and the action are subject to evaluation. Therefore, it is important that the action be justifiable under particular circumstances as only then can it be approved as good. Consequently, Aristotle reaches the following conclusion: "It seems, then, to be characteristic of a practically wise person (*phronimos*) to be able to deliberate correctly about what is good and advantageous for himself, not partially (for example, about what sorts of things further health or further strength) but about what sorts of things further living well as a whole."[26]

20 The interpretation of *phronesis* offered here is derived directly from Aristotle's works. It goes without saying that the account of *phronesis* offered here is only one of many possible interpretations. This is due to the fact that Aristotle was deliberately vague (see: Aristotle, *Nicomachean Ethics*, 3) in presenting the concepts belonging to his practical philosophy, which is no wonder since his aim was to provide knowledge which would remain "practical" itself, inspire independent thinking and promote diversity. Readers interested in learning more about the concept of *phronesis* may start with: Robert Hariman, ed., *Prudence: Classical Virtue, Postmodern Practice* (University Park: Penn State University Press, 2003).

21 Aristotle, *Nicomachean Ethics*, 101.

22 Aristotle, *Nicomachean Ethics*, 29.

23 Aristotle, *Nicomachean Ethics*, 21.

24 Aristotle, *Nicomachean Ethics*, 101.

25 Samuel H. Butcher, *Aristotle's Theory of Poetry and Fine Art* (London: MacMillan and Co., 1932), 123.

26 Aristotle, *Nicomachean Ethics*, 101.

When attempting to conceptualise *phronesis*, it is important to keep in mind that, because of its direct relation to action, it encompasses the whole time spectrum: the past, the present, and the future. Every action occurs in the present, yet the external conditions under which it is undertaken are determined by the past. And so practical wisdom must be informed by past experience. Also, it must guide the mind towards the future as there is no point in deliberating upon things which have already happened.[27]

In fact, in the concept of *phronesis* there are two overlapping, hidden dimensions of time, and, moreover, they are supplemented with something that is timeless and universal. A good way to understand this may be to look at two allegorical representations of *phronesis-prudence*. The first one is Titian's painting known as *The Allegory of Prudence*,[28] in which one can see three male heads: a young one on the left side of the viewer, a mature one in the middle, and an old one on the right. Depending on whether one looks at the faces from left to right or right to left, the painting becomes a representation of history (the old past – the mature present – the young future), or the representation of individual human life (first youth, then maturity, then old age). One seldom thinks about it, but these two dimensions of time run in opposite directions. The historical future is forever young and full of many possibilities (it is "practical" according to Aristotle's standard), while the future of every individual is to become old. Consequently, we have a preference for tried-and-true routines and habits whose validity and efficiency have already been proved. Adapting and conforming to them, individuals become more and more skilful producers of their own private happiness. Yet, this success, if viewed from a wider, historical perspective, may be seen as disadvantageous. It slows down changes which are sometimes necessary for the historical future to be wiser, and to eliminate the errors inherited from the past. The concept of practical wisdom, if examined against the background of Titian's painting, also suggests that individuals may benefit from diverting their eyes from their private future (which is slowly becoming the historical past), and courageously imagining and acting on behalf of a good future for all of humanity. Doing that, they save their own youth, so to speak, as they constantly exercise capacities and features naturally associated with it: imagination, engagement, courage to act, the need for novelty and change, and the ethical sensitivity that makes them expect justice, freedom, and equality to be present in the world of human affairs.

The second image that reveals some essential aspects of *phronesis* can be found in Cesare Ripa's *Iconologia*, where Prudenza was shown as a woman

27 Aristotle, *Nicomachean Ethics*, 99–100.

28 The painting can be seen in the National Gallery in London; reproduction is available online. Accessed June 23, 2025. See: https://commons.wikimedia.org/wiki/Category:Allegory_of_Prudence_by_Titian.

with two faces (old and young),[29] which also suggests a kind of an exchange between the past and the future. Among the many attributes of prudence whose allegorical meanings are referenced by Ripa, there is a mirror, in which the young face looks (which is evidenced by the reflection on its surface). As Ripa explained, the mirror signifies that practical wisdom does not guide the actions of those who are unaware of and thus unable to correct their defects.[30] This confirms that prudence requires education that includes much more than providing expertise in this or that area (Aristotelian "theoretical grasps") and supplementing it with some trained routines and procedures (*techne*), which are crucial elements of *poiesis*. Such education should take into account human development and should also have formative value.

1.3 Crafts and *Phronimoi*

While eating chocolate may increase pleasure, eating too much sugar is not beneficial to humans in the long term. It is possible that a candy maker who discovers a cheaper way to make tasty chocolate will be praised as useful, and so will his productive knowledge. Nevertheless, such a producer lacks *phronesis*, and eventually this deficiency may result in a number of unexpected problems (medical, economic, psychological, etc.) in the wider society. To circumvent this, it is possible to implement legislation that reduces the risk by prohibiting certain actions (such as the use of harmful flavour enhancers). However, this is often done retrospectively, when the harm is already done and the negative consequences of certain practices become apparent. Furthermore, this approach to externally guide actions restricts the human components of *praxis* by limiting our freedom, imagination, and creativity, which are essential for deliberation and innovation.

The concept of *phronesis* introduces a novel perspective on the limitations of human activity. In this case, the limitation is not external but internal, as it depends on the natural human development process, in which it is the task of an individual to become a mature human being. The term "mature" in this context refers to an individual whose actions are adjusted to specific circumstances (which increases, but does not guarantee, their productive success). However, these actions also reveal a personality that seems to be the reliable embodiment of universal human nature. *Phronimoi* use all the capacities that make us human in a humane way, and thus in their actions it is possible to grasp the important "doable things" that we all have in common: human values, performed as virtues. This way they encourage others to cooperate rather than compete. The presence of *phronimoi* in society is invaluable, especially in areas where (and at times when) "things" produced tend to get too practical

29 Cesare Ripa, *Iconologia, ouero Descrittione d'imagini delle virtu', vitij, affetti, passioni humane, corpi celesti, mondo e sue parti* (Padova: Per Pietro Paolo Tozzi, 1611), 442.

30 Cesare Ripa, *Iconologia*, 441.

(variable), and the diversity of opinions as to what to produce and how grows, setting individuals and groups apart. "We also speak of people as practically wise in some area," adds Aristotle, "when they rationally calculate well about what furthers some excellent end, concerning which no craft exists."[31]

There are crafts in which the development of both *poiesis* and *phronesis* should matter. These are the crafts whose products have a direct impact on interpersonal relationships. Aristotle identified politics as the most significant of these crafts. Politics is first and foremost the exercise of power in a poietic manner, with the intention of producing a specific effect determined in advance. Nevertheless, those engaged in politics need more than poietic political *techne*. In order for good politics to be achieved, both citizens and politicians must possess a certain degree of practical knowledge. In the democracy known to Aristotle, citizens should perform their *phronesis* mainly through legislative activity.[32] With regard to politicians, the most exemplary democratic *phronimos* was Pericles.[33] As Aristotle makes clear,[34] it was largely due to Pericles that Athenian democracy was for a period of time a good democracy.[35]

The language of *phronesis* is also pertinent to the field of law. We do not expect a carpenter to produce chairs prudently and with an overt interest in the eventual prudence (or lack thereof) of his clients. This does not imply that chairs cannot be employed in public (political) action, or that such action cannot be judged ethically. In ancient Rome, for example, the curule seats (*sealle curules*) constituted an important element of the authority of the magistrates. At times, there were those who advocated the destruction of chairs when they perceived that this authority had been misused.[36] Nevertheless, regardless of the specific manner in which the chairs may be used in the realm of human *praxis*, a carpenter should not be accused of being an accomplice in doing injustice of any kind. The case of lawyers is different, though. Their productive activity cannot be separated from everyday practical life. The legal profession, being generally a craft, should facilitate human life, with its political and ethical dimensions.

It is, perhaps, no accident that many contemporary legal theorists prefer the term "jurisprudence" to legal science, and the often posed question is "whether legal theory represents a *prudentia* which engages in practical

31 Aristotle, *Nicomachean Ethics*, 101.
32 Aristotle, *Nicomachean Ethics*, 105.
33 Aristotle, *Nicomachean Ethics*, 102.
34 See: Aristotle, "Constitution of Athens," in *Aristotle's Politics. Writings from the Complete Works: Politics – Economics – Constitution of Athens*, ed. Jonathan Barnes, trans. F.G. Kenyon (Princeton–Oxford: Princeton University Press, 2016), 286.
35 See: Iwona Barwicka-Tylek, "Intricacies of Practical Wisdom: Or Why Would Aristotle Vote for Pericles Rather Than Lenin?," *Krakowskie Studia z Historii Państwa i Prawa* 11, no. 3 (2018): 324.
36 See: Cassius Dio, *Roman History, Volume III: Books 36–40*, trans. E. Cary and H.B. Foster (Cambridge, Mass.: Harvard University Press, 1914), 69.

accounts of law, or a *scientia* that studies objective facts about it."[37] The theoretical impulses to merely "observe the truth" (such is the original meaning of the Greek *theoreia*) are replaced by efforts to empathically support the world of *praxis*, also by elaborating on the common criteria of passing ethical and political judgements on the individual and collective actions undertaken. Diversity is viewed as natural and the unpredictability of human affairs is acknowledged. The initial fear that admitting that would result in extreme relativism and constructivism is at least partly assuaged, and a very Aristotelian taste for moderation seems to be spreading. Some researchers overtly admit that it is time for Aristotelian social science,[38] in which concepts like practical wisdom, *phronesis*, and prudence play an important role.[39]

In recent decades, some experts, including in the field of law, have argued[40] that lawyers need knowledge that is more than just productive and a language in which it could be expressed so it could be taught. In this language, ethical concepts (freedom, equality, justice, dignity, etc.) become the guiding principles for practical reasoning. The language must supplement the language of legal routines, as following such routines in an imprudent manner risks the debasement of community practices over time. Human *praxis* is in a state of constant change, and thus lawyers' activity should be time-sensitive in order to account for such changes and to respond to them in an active manner. This implies responding not merely as craftsmen, but as *zoa politika* who strive to contribute to a better (more human) future for all of us. As succinctly stated by Roscoe Pound, "[l]aw must be stable, and yet it cannot stand still."[41]

In contrast to the two other forms of knowledge, the nature of *phronesis* is not readily explicable. That is true of all of the Aristotelian middle terms, which are for him the most crucial. As a middle term, *phronesis* extends in both directions. It reaches particulars, just as *poiesis* does (it draws on – and manipulates – all that is perceptible, experiential, time-dependant). However, it also reaches universals, just as theoretical knowledge does. Consequently, *phronetic* action is a particular, individual conclusion[42] of practical reasoning that aims to overcome, or at least soothe, dialectical tensions between particularity and universality. It takes a lot of effort to reach and also to carry out such

37 Sean Coyle and George Pavlakos, *Jurisprudence or Legal Science?: A Debate about the Nature of Legal Theory* (Oxford: Hart Publishing, 2005), 2.

38 Stephen G. Salkever, "Aristotle's Social Science," *Political Theory* 9, no. 4 (1981): 479–508.

39 See: R. Andrew Sayer, *Why Things Matter to People: Social Science, Values and Ethical Life* (Cambridge–New York: Cambridge University Press, 2011); Bent Flyvbjerg, Todd Landman, and Sanford F. Schram, *Real Social Science: Applied Phronesis* (Cambridge–New York: Cambridge University Press, 2012).

40 See: Anthony Kronman, *The Lost Lawyer: Failing Ideals of the Legal Profession* (Cambridge, Mass.: Harvard University Press, 1993).

41 Roscoe Pound, *Interpretations of Legal History* (New York: Macmillan Co., 1923), 1.

42 Donald Davidson, *Truth, Language and History* (Oxford–New York: Oxford University Press/Clarendon Press, 2005), 280.

an original conclusion. No wonder that to become practically wise, individuals need to develop all the "equipment" they have as humans: perception, volition, engagement, imagination, virtue, reason, etc.

That is not all. *Phronimoi* provide examples of actions that fulfil the normative standard of being human. Any action of this kind is, and remains, risky and may thus be deemed imprudent. This is especially true since, according to Aristotle, "noble things and just things," as well as "good things," "admit so much difference and variability that they seem to exist by conventional law alone and not by nature."[43] That is why *phronimoi* must participate in the political and ethical dialogue on what is good. First, not only to enrich this dialogue with their own expertise, but also to gain better insight into the prevailing opinions to be able to choose an action that would probably be widely accepted as serving the common good under particular circumstances. There is one crucial inconvenience here. Increasing probability cannot be equated with certainty. Practically wise persons realise that errors are part and parcel of their *phronesis*. There may be multiple errors: in deliberation, in perception of a given situation, in adjusting the means to the ends, in specifying the right time – *kairos* – to take up the action, and others. Most of such errors are simply entangled in the inevitable particularity of acting. That is why each *phronimos* needs far-reaching ideals (some universals conceived as values) to orient oneself in life, and not to give up acting humanly when (productive) successes do not come right away.

Unfortunately, when there arises a discrepancy between an artificially produced world of human affairs and the requirements of human nature that is too great, success may never come. Under such circumstances any prudent action may pass unnoticed, judged as violating all too well-known routines or be rejected as not productive enough. Paradoxically, that is exactly the time when the lack of *phronesis* becomes not only an ethical, but also a political issue: the time when the sense of justice in society and trust in institutionalised communal practices diminishes.

1.4 "Triviality" of History?

The problem with providing a comprehensive account of *phronesis* is evident in Aristotle's practical philosophy. This is further compounded by the challenge of educating professionals from diverse fields in this rather unique competence. In fact, such an endeavour is arguably unfeasible, given that practical wisdom is more of an individual endeavour than the result of a specific training programme that would include some content-based knowledge and know-how.[44] Nevertheless, *phronesis* appears to be of significant importance

43 Aristotle, *Nicomachean Ethics*, 4.

44 A good example of this can be found in the second book of *Politics*, where Aristotle discusses a problem that is quite *phronetic*: whether and when to change the laws. After having examined

to Aristotle, related directly to the perspectives for the changes that would deserve to be classified as development, progress, and improvement. In a political community where there is room and encouragement for individuals to act as *phronimoi* (and not merely to fulfil their professional duties), it is easier for others to retain the ideal of humanity. This ideal, if treated *phronetically*, is not something that could ever be produced in a specified manner (*poietically*). It is a distant ideal that always lies in the future and should motivate individuals to grow personally as humans, thus also improving interpersonal relationships.

The lack of clarity surrounding the concept of *phronesis* should not be a reason to avoid discussing it or advocating it whenever the well-being of the existing political communities is at stake. Aristotle himself exemplified this approach, becoming a practical philosopher rather than merely a contemplative one. He felt compelled to present his opinions on politics and ethics, despite the fact that they would not be as indisputable as the theoretical (objective) truth. Furthermore, he acknowledged alternative, non-philosophical, approaches to becoming familiar with *phronesis.*

Since *phronesis* is action, to comprehend it, and thus become more familiarised with it, crafts and arts (both are poietic activities, as they offer specific products) which focus directly on presenting human actions could also help. History and poetry were two suitable candidates for this function. Cicero, an admirer of the Aristotelian concept, thanks to whom *phronesis* became *prudentia* in Latin, suggested that it was history one should trust, as it was, according to him, the "teacher of our lives" (*magistra vitae*)[45] precisely because it presented past actions and allowed for the analysis of all their aspects, both particular (time and space dependent) and universal (related to universal political and ethical ideals). Aristotle, however, held a different view. For him, poetry was the most appropriate medium for achieving this purpose.

Aristotle mentioned history only briefly and with a clear intention to praise poetry at its expense. Both history and poetry, he admitted, were interested in human affairs and performed actions. Yet, a historian speaks of things "that have happened." while a poet speaks "of the sort of things that might happen and possibilities that come from what is likely or necessary."[46] History, according to Aristotle, deals "with singular events yoked together merely by the time

several arguments in favour of and against legal innovations, Aristotle concludes: "therefore, we had better reserve the discussion of them to a more suitable occasion." The occasion did not come. Aristotle seems to understand that, although deliberation on problems like that is necessary, it is impossible even for a practical philosopher to provide an algorithmic, productive answer. The answer must be action, always undertaken by a particular doer, under conditions of uncertainty.

45 Marcus T. Cicero, *On the Ideal Orator*, trans. James M. May and Jakob Wisse (New York–Oxford: Oxford University Press, 2001), 133.

46 Aristotle, *Poetics*, trans. Joe Sachs (Newburyport: Focus Publishing/R. Pullins Co., 2011), 32.

of their occurrence,"[47] notices Thomas C. Powell. For this reason, historical knowledge is hardly *knowledge*. In accordance with the standard introduced by Aristotle, *knowledge* must be universal enough to be used to achieve some good, to allow living well.[48] The particularity of history precludes any possibility of universalisation. Consequently, the historian is a craftsman whose works are of use to an erudite person at best, one who enjoys entertaining others by citing curiosities found in the past. Such works do not contain anything that could enrich our cognizance of human affairs as they are and should be practiced.

Poetry is also a craft. The work of a poet is a product of his own making. But art, according to Aristotle, imitates nature. A poet who understands his craft properly is able to present his subjective narrative as a plot in which *human* action comes to the fore. Aristotle explained:

> A story is one, not, as some people suppose, if it is about one person, for many – countlessly many – things are incidental attributes of one person, with no unity taking in some of them. [...] But Homer, just as he excelled in other respects, also seems to have recognized this beautifully, whether by art or by nature. For in making an *Odyssey*, he did not make it out of all the things that happened to the man [...], things of which none was necessary or likely to happen because of another thing that happened, but the *Odyssey* is organized around one action of the sort we are speaking of.[49]

That is what makes poetry serious. Poetic narrative, though fictious, draws on human nature and so it is aimed at revealing some truth about human action as such. "It is what is universal, the sorts of things that a certain sort of person turns out to say or do as a result of what is likely or necessary, that poetry aims at, even though it puts names on people," stated Aristotle.[50] Offering *some* truth about human action, poetry encourages deliberation on human affairs and contributes to the improving of human *praxis*. What is of great significance, moving the imagination of the audience, poetry allows for a complete though passive experience, with its crucial emotional component, but without risk entailed in actually performing actions in reality, where painful mistakes cannot be undone. The aesthetic experience is *experience*, and according to Aristotle only an experienced person can hope to become practically wise.[51] It is impossible to gain enough experience only by acting by oneself. Not

47 Thomas C. Powell, "Why Aristotle Has No Philosophy of History," *History of Philosophy Quarterly* 4, no. 3 (1987): 346.
48 Aristotle, *Nicomachean Ethics*, 5.
49 Aristotle, *Poetics*, 31.
50 Aristotle, *Poetics*, 32.
51 Aristotle, *Nicomachean Ethics*, 105.

only would such experience be too modest, but also much too risky. Poetry, especially tragedies in the times of Aristotle, inspired thinking about what was possible and what was necessary without any personal risk. Following the plot, the audience observed the doer in an environment that was beyond his control and by observing him they got a chance to understand better what it meant to act and how different actions were received and judged. Aristotle insisted that narratives of this kind, though fictional, improve ethical and political judgement with the help of imagination. Not without significance is the sensual (emotional) element of the aesthetic experience, as cultivating appropriate emotions (including by "bleeding" them at the moment of *katharsis*) is important in the process of forming a mature (virtuous) character.

There are numerous parallels between Aristotle's account of history and the program of scientific history, which was developed by prominent German historians Barthold D. Niebuhr and Leopold von Ranke.[52] This program also shaped the emergence of legal history as an autonomous scientific discipline.[53] In the 19th century, the approach that Aristotle had previously criticised the particularity of history – was embraced as a virtue. The sciences of that time rejected the metaphysical assumption that the immutable truth to be observed (*theoreia*) resides outside the material world. Instead of rational contemplation (Plato) and dialogical deliberation on what to choose from many possibilities (Aristotle's practical reasoning), an empirical investigation was advanced, and so history could become science easily – an idiographic science, but still a science. However, this scientific image of history is accused of being much too modest, or even misleading, in the present day. One of the most compelling arguments against this approach is directly Aristotelian in nature. When it comes to knowledge, history (and legal history) is deemed to be useless and impractical. The only thing it can teach us would be something akin to the following: "The past is a foreign country; they do things differently there."[54] Unless historians become poets, which is, again, an idea present in *Poetics*.[55]

There are historians who advocate joining the poetry side to make the past experience more serious and relevant for contemporary societies, and such trends have grown in importance ever since Hayden White overtly admitted that a historical narrative is close to literature: "stories in turn are made out of chronicles by [...] 'emplotment.'"[56] The problem is, however, that poetry is no longer serious according to Aristotle's criteria. It does not provide any knowledge as it is not obliged to reach anything universal enough to anchor

52 Chris Lorenz, "Scientific Historiography," in *A Companion to the Philosophy of History and Historiography*, ed. Aviezer Tucker (Oxford: Blackwell Publishing 2009), 393.

53 Thomas Gil, "Leopold Ranke," in *A Companion to the Philosophy of History and Historiography*, ed. Aviezer Tucker (Oxford: Blackwell Publishing 2009), 386.

54 Leslie P. Hartley, *The Go-Between* (New York: Alfred A. Knopf, 1953), n.p.

55 Aristotle, *Poetics*, 33.

56 In: Robert H. Canary, Kieran Egan, and Henry Kozicki, eds., *The Writing of History: Literary Form and Historical Understanding* (Madison: University of Wisconsin Press, 1978), 46.

particular narratives in some common ground of human (ethical) nature. And so, this new attitude often leads to attempts to satisfy the tastes of a particular audience.

The tendency to make the past useful in (and for) the present allows different individuals and groups to act backwards on history, with a clear intent to "consume" [57] it rather than learn from it. Such "consumption" of the freely chosen elements of the past results in "pluralising pasts,"[58] which often divides particular consumers of history, turning them into political competitors in the present. Each of such "pasts" is produced to satisfy the particular needs of the present "doers."

In the field of law, the poetisation (or rather "poietisation") of history is also possible. In his critique of the historical argument employed in the *Texas v Johnson* case (the "flag burning case"),[59] Calvin R. Massey demonstrates that it is not based on facts but becomes an "emotion-laden poetic fantasy" that "debases historical coin," as well as "cheapens the process of constitutional adjudication."[60] The same reasons for the criticism are tangible also in the words of Richard Posner: "the legal profession's use of history is a disguise that allows the profession to innovate without breaching judicial etiquette, which deplores both novelty and a frank acknowledgement of judicial discretion and likes to pretend that decisions by nonelected judges can be legitimated by being shown to have democratic roots in some past legislative or constitutional enactment. Since the most convincing deceptions are those rooted in self-deception (because then the deceiver is not in danger of giving himself away), one is not surprised that many lawyers and judges think of law as the application to the present of the lessons of the past."[61] As Posner suggests, when lawyers draw on history, they are, in fact, producing fictions. These are not at all serious fictions, and, although such fictions may be beneficial tools in judicial activity, there are more effective alternatives available for contemporary judges. Consequently, Posner recommends that the legal profession should adopt a more pragmatic approach. This entails favouring a pragmatic judge who "wants to decide cases in the way that will best promote, within the constraints of the judicial role, the goals of society."[62]

No matter how convincing his criticism of history is, Posner's pragmatic approach, when viewed through the lens of Aristotle's practical philosophy, may be equally self-deceiving. Focusing upon the present, it tends to equate

57 Jerome De Groot, *Consuming History: Historians and Heritage in Contemporary Popular Culture* (London: Routledge 2009).

58 See: Gregory J. Ashworth, Brian J. Graham, and John E. Tunbridge, *Pluralising Pasts: Heritage, Identity and Place in Multicultural Societies* (London: Pluto Press, 2007).

59 *Texas v Johnson*, 491 U.S. 397 (1989).

60 Calvin R. Massey, "The Jurisprudence of Poetic License," *Duke Law Journal* 38, no. 4 (1989): 1052.

61 Posner, "Past-Dependency, Pragmatism, and Critique of History," 581.

62 Posner, "Past-Dependency, Pragmatism, and Critique of History," 593.

practical knowledge with productive knowledge. If the role of lawyers is merely to advance the goals of society and resolve perceived problems, without engaging their expertise in the wider discourse on the relationship between these goals and human life as such, then their ethical and political responsibility is no greater than that of a carpenter. Lawyers end up being craftsmen, which was the function assigned to them at the beginning of the modern era. Admittedly, there have been many innovations in the performance of this craft. First of all, it is no longer possible for legal professionals to claim that their activity relies merely on a "theoretical grasp" of the nature of law. However, assisting society in "coping with the present" does not imply judging the goals aimed at by particular groups in such a manner that the future will have a chance to be our common, *human* future.

1.5 Conclusion: In Defence of the Seriousness of History

The word "development," if applied to the world of human affairs, raises doubts nowadays, as it brings to mind the modern progressivist dreams of reaching the final stage of history with the help of science. One of such possible "ends of history" was expected to come as the result of universalisation of liberal democracy. If successful, such universalisation of politics of a certain kind, justified in ethical terms as meeting the requirements of freedom and equality, would justify equivocating productive with *phronetic* knowledge. This is because then many "things" which were practical for Aristotle and required constant and active personal care would have simply become universally approved without further deliberation and innovation. Thus, the importance of *human* action (the individual action in which the knowledge on how to live together well is displayed) would be diminished. Although this particular attempt to finish with history by universalising the political part of human *praxis* failed, the feeling that history is coming to an end is still present. The still often used prefix "post-" (post-modernism, post-history, post-democracy) reflects the sense of the present being the product of the past with no future – a present in which the most practical human choice should be to delve into interpersonal and intergroup differences to allow particularities to speak and to act for themselves so they can at least enjoy public recognition.

In certain respects, Aristotle's perspective is arguably more radical. In seeking the most universal point of reference, which would enable the differentiation between *poiesis* and *phronesis*, he pointed to the individual human being. This is not an obvious choice. If we think about the world of human affairs, individuals are its most particular and the weakest elements, seemingly lacking knowledge and power to alter what has already been done and produced. Confronting the "things" present in our practices, we take them for something solid enough not to be consciously and deliberately practiced but simply used. For Aristotle, however, things were different. Quite convincingly, he argued that an individual is neither the most particular nor the weakest element of *praxis*. Aristotle's naturalist position suggests that each of us has direct access to the most universal aspect of humanity, namely, human nature. Not only are human beings capable of producing various things (*mimesis* is the key to any craft), but they can also manifest human nature via *phronetic* actions.

Phronimoi, apart from exercising their professional capacities, perform the universal normative standard of living together and living well in their own, very particular way. They are able to recognise this standard in themselves. They use their imagination and reason not only to find an efficient solution to some imposing problem, but also to judge all possible solutions and to opt for the one that can be justified as not only efficient but also good and just. Perceiving the tension between what is and what should be, they try to bridge it while acting. The greater the discrepancy, not only the more distinguishable their actions against the background of many other productive ones, but also the greater the risk that eventually such actions could be rejected rather than followed. Therefore, *phronimoi* must keep the balance between the short-term and the present-focused perspective of *poiesis* and the long-term, future-oriented perspective of *phronesis* to increase the possibility that their activity will gain wider recognition as something good.

Attempts to identify a third kind of knowledge, which would simultaneously be more practical and more human (with the direct political and ethical overtones this adjective implies), extend far beyond Aristotle's works. Furthermore, since his metaphysical account of nature lost its initial persuasiveness, then perhaps also his criticism of history as impractical can be questioned. In my opinion – and it is simply an opinion (*doxa*) – the wide interest in *phronesis* provides an opportunity for traditional legal historians to show that they can also contribute to the identification of a crucial but vague line that separates productive from phronetic knowledge. Blurring this line might be inadvisable, including in the field of law, as it encourages to judge some things as good only because they are already produced or producible.

As Marc Bloch insightfully observed, history is not so much the science of the past as it is the science of men in time, and a historian knows that "wherever he catches the scent of human flesh, there his quarry lies."[63] This quotation makes it clear that historians cannot ignore human actions, even if they refrain from seeking any universality in them.

The study of the past prescribes caution in the use of the criterion of effectiveness in evaluating human action. Increasing the effectiveness of an action requires reducing the temporal perspective to the minimum, thereby enabling the doer to exercise full control over the situation and to rely on cause-and-effect relationships that guarantee success. The short-term goals of productive activities are not *practical* in the Aristotelian sense, even if they refer directly to the language of ethics and concepts like justice or freedom. They are at best means to an end, which for every human being should be living well with others. Adolf Hitler and Joseph Stalin were highly effective in their political

63 Marc Bloch, *The Historian's Craft*, 22–27.

actions. According to Isaiah Berlin, they possessed a keen "sense of reality,"[64] enabling them to exploit the specific circumstances of a given time and place in order to seize power. They employed this power to govern effectively for some time. Nonetheless, their impact on human *praxis* proved to be profoundly destructive over time, including for their own societies. *Phronesis* requires much more than a sense of reality. It also requires a sense of the possible and a sense of the good.

The example of Hitler and Stalin also highlights an additional problem related to the presence of ethical values in the human world. They are things to be done and not the things to be produced. Yet, history shows that in the world of human affairs it is surprisingly easy to poeticise them and even to use them as tools. In the hands of skilful craftsmen, concepts like freedom and justice may serve not to facilitate cooperation between human beings but to deepen mutual hostility, as evidenced, for instance, in the cruelty of the Jacobins or Bolsheviks. Again, history suggests caution whenever the language of ethics is used, not only in politics, but also in social science. In this respect, historical observations are extremely serious, and so should they be treated also by practical philosophers and social researchers. As much as history helps to demonstrate that productive knowledge may mask itself as *phronesis*, it can also help to demonstrate that *phronesis* often desires to become productive knowledge, which is equally unwise.

For a historian, all ethical ideals remain out of reach. Their factuality is limited mainly to their presence in language. They seem to exist out of historical time. To use Aristotelian vocabulary, they are metaphysical final causes (not efficient causes), and so they remain in the future forever. The conclusion that they are fictions comes naturally, but denying the seriousness of such fictions would be contrary to past experience. Terms like "justice," "freedom," and "equality" have always had undeniable motivational value, and this value was not rhetorical, but real and practical. It was real and practical because actions which were justice-oriented or freedom-oriented were not simple implementations of some projects based on a "theoretical grasp" of what justice or freedom was (how it was defined here or there). They were born out of very concrete experiences – the facts – of injustice and enslavement. To recognise them as such, it suffices merely to be human. One may deeply disagree with the idea of justice suggested by Karl Marx but still convincingly criticise the capitalist reality of the 19th century for doing injustice to workers.

Experiences of injustice and enslavement vary with respect to time and space, and so the imagined conditions for justice or freedom also vary, depending on the world existing at a given place and time (a particular historical context). That is why examining history we find many different, particular *concepts* of justice and freedom. That does not necessarily justify, however, the conclusion

64 Isaiah Berlin, *The Sense of Reality: Studies in Ideas and Their History*, ed. Henry Hardy (Princeton, N.J.: Princeton University Press, 2019).

that there is nothing universal in them. From the *phronetic* perspective, what gets particularised are not values as such (as they are still universal human values), but our opinions (*doxai*) on them. It is possible to judge such opinions, taking into account whether practicing them led to any changes, which – when related to their historical context – made some things better. History, with its comparative methods, allows some generalisations here. It is a peculiar feature of truly *phronetic* opinions that they can be contextualised or universalised with similar ease. It is no accident that when reading historical records (if one happens not to be a historian) it is so easy to become anachronistic and to perceive the past as being close at hand and ready to be used.

History contributes to the search for practical knowledge rather indirectly, but it is not a small contribution. Historians do their best to deal with *res factae*, but doing this they often approach the line (or rather a vast border area) behind which the realm of action lies. They are able to elucidate this realm and to gather evidence which shows that, quite often, human actions determine our common future. Having enough experience as craftsmen in the field of history, they can also venture to become its *phronimoi*. Not necessarily becoming full-fledged poets, they may use historical experience to improve our taste for actions which are value-oriented.

A legal historian does not have to become a philosopher or a theoretician to engage in a dialogue on the specificity of human activity and terms like "justice," "freedom," and "equality" in areas such as law. Perhaps he even should not. In his youth, Frederic Maitland wrote a thesis with a long title: *A Historical Sketch of Liberty and Equality as Ideals of English Political Philosophy from the Time of Hobbes to the Time of Coleridge*, with which he hoped to win the Fellowship of Philosophy in Cambridge at the age of 25. It was not a fortunate work, and the author himself admitted that it "should have been 'wiped up' like the products of the infant Grotius."[65] Maitland ended up becoming a legal historian who himself did much to make history matter for lawyers, and – if one can trust his opinions and the opinions of his biographers – in a quite *phronetic* manner. On the one hand, he deplored the tendency to aim for "wider and wider generalisations"[66]; yet, "he combined the philosopher's power of analysis with the faculty of seeing everything in the concrete"[67] and moved "from the general to the particular and vice-versa with astonishing ease."[68] To him "the history of law was the history, not of forms, but of

65 In: Cecil H.S. Fifoot, *Frederic William Maitland. A Life* (Cambridge, Mass.: Harvard University Press, 1971), 49.

66 Frederic W. Maitland, *A Historical Sketch of Liberty and Equality: As Ideals of English Political Philosophy from the Time of Hobbes to the Time of Coleridge* (Indianapolis: Liberty Fund, 2000), 200.

67 Charles H. Haskins, "Frederic William Maitland (1850–1906)," in: *A Historical Sketch of Liberty and Equality*, Frederic W. Maitland (Indianapolis: Liberty Fund, 2000), 3.

68 The words of James Holt, in: Jonathan Rose, "Studying the Past: the Nature and Development of Legal History as an Academic Discipline," *The Journal of Legal History* 31, no. 2 (2010): 115.

ideas."[69] At the beginning of the 20th century, Maitland wrote: "It may be noted, too, that strenuous endeavours to improve the law were not impeded, but forwarded by a zealous study of legal history. [...] Nowadays we may see the office of historical research as that of explaining, and therefore lightening, the pressure that the past must exercise upon the present, and the present upon the future. Today we study the day before yesterday, in order that yesterday may not paralyze today, and today may not paralyze tomorrow."[70] In the end, it may be interesting to compare Maitland's words with the motto of Titian's *Allegory of Prudence:* "from the experience of the past, the present acts prudently, lest it spoil future actions."

References

Primary sources

Old prints and incunabula

Ripa, Cesare. *Iconologia, ouero Descrittione d'imagini delle virtu', vitij, affetti, passioni humane, corpi celesti, mondo e sue parti.* Padoua: Per Pietro Paolo Tozzi, 1611.

Edited sources

Aristotle. "Constitution of Athens." In *Aristotle's Politics. Writings from the Complete Works: Politics – Economics – Constitution of Athens*, edited by Jonathan Barnes and translated by F. G. Kenyon, 260–326. Princeton and Oxford: Princeton University Press, 2016.

Aristotle. *Generation of Animals & History of Animals I, Parts of Animals I.* Translated by C. D. C. Reeve. Indianapolis and Cambridge: Hackett Publishing, 2019.

Aristotle. *Nicomachean Ethics.* Translated by C. D. C. Reeve. Indianapolis: Hackett Publishing, 2014.

Aristotle. *Politics.* Translated by C. D. C. Reeve. Indianapolis: Hackett Publishing, 1998.

Aristotle. *Poetics.* Translated by Joe Sachs. Newburyport: Focus Publishing/R. Pullins Co., 2011.

Cicero, Marcus T. *On the Ideal Orator.* Translated by James M. May and Jakob Wisse. New York and Oxford: Oxford University Press, 2001.

Dio, Cassius. *Roman History, Volume III: Books 36–40.* Translated by Earnest Cary and Herbert B. Foster. Cambridge, Mass.: Harvard University Press, 1914.

69 Haskins, "Frederic William Maitland (1850–1906)," 3.

70 Frederic W. Maitland, *The Collected Papers of Frederic William Maitland*, vol. 3, ed. Herbert A.L. Fisher (Cambridge: Cambridge University Press, 1911). Accessed June 23, 2025. https://oll.libertyfund.org/titles/fisher-the-collected-papers-of-frederic-william-maitland-vol-3.

Secondary studies

Ashworth, Gregory J., Brian J. Graham, and John E. Tunbridge. *Pluralising Pasts: Heritage, Identity and Place in Multicultural Societies.* London Ann Arbor: Pluto Press, 2007.

Barwicka-Tylek, Iwona. "Intricacies of Practical Wisdom: Or Why Would Aristotle Vote for Pericles Rather Than Lenin?" *Krakowskie Studia z Historii Państwa i Prawa* 11, no 3. (2018): 321–41. https://doi.org/10.4467/20844131KS.18.022.9048.

Berlin, Isaiah. *The Sense of Reality: Studies in Ideas and Their History.* Edited by Henry Hardy. Princeton, NJ: Princeton University Press, 2019.

Bloch, Marc. *The Historian's Craft.* Translated by P. Putnam. New York: Vintage Books, 1964.

Boorstin, Daniel J. "Tradition and Method in Legal History." *Harvard Law Review* 54, no. 3 (1941): 424–36.

Butcher, Samuel H. *Aristotle's Theory of Poetry and Fine Art.* London: MacMillan and Co., 1932.

Canary, Robert H., Kieran Egan, and Henry Kozicki, eds. *The Writing of History: Literary Form and Historical Understanding.* Madison, WIisc.: University of Wisconsin Press, 1978.

Coyle, Sean, and George Pavlakos. *Jurisprudence or Legal Science?: A Debate about the Nature of Legal Theory.* Oxford: Hart Pub., 2005.

Davidson, Donald. *Truth, Language and History.* Oxford and New York: Oxford University Press and Clarendon Press, 2005.

De Groot, Jerome. *Consuming History: Historians and Heritage in Contemporary Popular Culture.* London: Routledge, 2009.

Fifoot, Cecil H. S. *Frederic William Maitland: A Life.* Cambridge, Mass.: Harvard University Press, 1971.

Flyvbjerg, Bent. *Making Social Science Matter: Why Social Inquiry Fails and How It Can Succeed Again.* Oxford and New York: Cambridge University Press, 2001.

Flyvbjerg, Bent, Todd Landman, and Sanford F. Schram. *Real Social Science: Applied Phronesis.* Cambridge and New York: Cambridge University Press, 2012.

Gil, Thomas. "Leopold Ranke." In *A Companion to the Philosophy of History and Historiography*, edited by Aviezer Tucker, 383–92. Oxford: Blackwell Publishing, 2009.

Hariman, Robert, ed. *Prudence: Classical Virtue, Postmodern Practice.* University Park: Penn State University Press, 2003.

Hartley, Leslie P. *The Go-Between.* New York: Alfred A. Knopf, 1953.

Haskins, Charles H. "Frederic William Maitland (1850–1906)." In *A Historical Sketch of Liberty and Equality*, edited by Frederic W. Maitland. Indianapolis: Liberty Fund, 2000.

Howe, Laurence L. "Historical Method and Legal Education." *Bulletin of the American Association of University Professors* 36, no. 2 (1950): 246–356.

Kronman, Anthony. *The Lost Lawyer: Failing Ideals of the Legal Profession.* Cambridge: Harvard University Press, 1993.

Lorenz, Chris. "Scientific Historiography." In *A Companion to the Philosophy of History and Historiography*, edited by Aviezer Tucker, 393–403. Oxford: Blackwell Publishing, 2009.

Maitland, Frederic W. *The Collected Papers of Frederic William Maitland,* vol. 3. Edited by Herbert A. L. Fisher. Cambridge: Cambridge University Press, 1911. https://

oll.libertyfund.org/titles/fisher-the-collected-papers-of-frederic-william-maitland-vol-3 (accessed on 23 June 2025).

Maitland, Frederic W. *A Historical Sketch of Liberty and Equality: As Ideals of English Political Philosophy from the Time of Hobbes to the Time of Coleridge.* Indianapolis: Liberty Fund, 2000.

Massey, Calvin R. "The Jurisprudence of Poetic License." *Duke Law Journal* 38, no. 4 (1989): 1047–52.

Pinker, Steve. *Enlightenment Now.* London: Penguin Books Ltd., 2019.

Posner, Richard A. "Past-Dependency, Pragmatism, and Critique of History in Adjudication and Legal Scholarship." *The University of Chicago Law Review* 67, no. 3 (2000): 573–606.

Pound, Roscoe. *Interpretations of Legal History.* New York: Macmillan Co., 1923.

Powell, Thomas C. "Why Aristotle Has No Philosophy of History." *History of Philosophy Quarterly* 4, no. 3 (1987): 343–57.

Reeve, C. D. C. *Practices of Reason: Aristotle's Nicomachean Ethics.* New York: Oxford University Press, 1992.

Rose, Jonathan. "Studying the Past: The Nature and Development of Legal History as an Academic Discipline." *The Journal of Legal History* 31, no. 2 (August 2010): 101–28.

Salkever, Stephen G. "Aristotle's Social Science." *Political Theory* 9, no. 4 (1981): 479–508.

Sayer, R. Andrew. *Why Things Matter to People: Social Science, Values and Ethical Life.* Cambridge and New York: Cambridge University Press, 2011.

2 Justice as an *Empty Principle* in Post-Structuralist Legal Thought. Towards Neohistorical Jurisprudence?[1]

Tomáš Gábriš

2.1 Introduction

Systemic models of legal scholarship throughout history have sought to create or discover an all-encompassing system of law, where any and all elements could be derived from one another in a sort of a structure, possibly in logically clear and formalistic steps. However, at least since Immanuel Kant, this idea has been challenged by the claim that if justice is considered as the supreme principle on top of a legal pyramid, this undertaking must fail since it is not possible to grasp justice in legal terms.[2] Legal positivism, especially in its exclusivist version, was hence rather focused on written laws and rules, with justice considered equal to legality and perceived as formal justice solely.[3] This, however, proved to be untenable[4] in régimes which were themselves undemocratic and had their very own perception of justice – be it Nazi or fascist regimes, or the communist party regimes after World War II. The inner structure of legality (legal justice) within the legal system failed when confronted with the outer perception (and revolutionary changes) of material justice.

In light of the above, structuralist thought of the 20th century correctly identified structural ties within not only the legal system itself, but also pointed to the natural ties between man-made systems and their social backgrounds.[5] This was the idea that both structuralism and Marxist-Leninist

1 This research has been supported by the Slovak Research and Development Agency (project title "Transformations of Jurisprudence – Historical and Current Forms of Law and of the Science of Law," APVV-22-0079).

2 Matthias Reimann, "Nineteenth Century German Legal Science," *Boston College Law Review* 31 (1990): 842–843. Accessed March 31, 2024. http://lawdigitalcommons.bc.edu/bclr/vol31/iss4/2.

3 Tom D. Campbell, "Rights without Justice," *Mind* 83, no. 331 (July 1974): 445–448.

4 See Gustav Radbruch, *Rechtsphilosophie III*. Vol. 3 of the *Gustav Radbruch Gesamtausgabe*, ed. A Kaufmann (Heidelberg: C.F. Müller, 1990), 89.

5 See Sotirios A. Barber and James E. Fleming, *Constitutional Interpretation: The Basic Questions* (Oxford–New York: Oxford University Press, 2007), 117–134.

DOI: 10.4324/9781003654131-3

theory advocated.[6] In this perspective, justice becomes an element of a larger system (structure) where the ideas, contents, and shapes of justice are formed outside of the legal system and become interconnected with or involved in the legal system by special tools. These outside elements were called by some structuralists "empty places."[7] Lawyers call similar elements "vague notions" or "indeterminate concepts," such as good morals, rightful interests, etc.[8] Marxist-Leninist theory similarly saw a clear link between the legal system and the outer idea of justice – class justice favouring those classes that were formerly oppressed. However, both structuralist as well as Marxist-Leninist ideas were subsequently abandoned in Europe due to their rigidity and determinism, which failed to explain the claimed scientifically uncovered and structurally determined collective idea of justice and its conflict with the individual perceptions of justice.

These theories, therefore, needed some sort of updating, which took place in the later post-structuralist thought, which voiced distrust of the immutable structural ties[9] and methodological collectivism[10] of both structuralism and Marxism-Leninism. Instead, methodological individualism[11] and its combination with collectivism in the form of methodological pluralism was called for even in legal scholarship, manifested in current legal post-positivism and its emphasis on principles, values, human rights, and the ideals of justice, which are a precondition for the actual fulfilment of the idea of justice in individual cases.[12] Justice in individual cases is not believed to be ensured by general (collectivist) rules of either structuralist or Marxist-Leninist invention. The determinism of both schools apparently hampered the actual idea of reaching individual justice as a proper solution for specific situations and specific

6 Elaborated in detail in Steven Spitzer, "Marxist Perspectives in the Sociology of Law," *Annual Review of Sociology* 9 (1983): 103–124.

7 Gilles Deleuze, "How Do We Recognize Structuralism?" in *Desert Islands and Other Texts*, trans. Melissa McMahon and Charles J. Stivale, ed. David Lapoujade (New York–Cambridge: Semiotexte/MIT Press, 2004), 170ff.

8 Andrei Marmor, *The Language of Law* (Oxford: Oxford University Press, 2014), 85–106.

9 Nigel Pleasants, "Free Will, Determinism and the 'Problem' of Structure and Agency in the Social Sciences," *Philosophy of the Social Sciences* 49, no. 1 (2019): 3–30.

10 Also known as methodological holism. It argued that social forces and facts are the moving agents of history and society instead of individual choices. See Julie Zahle, "Methodological Holism in the Social Sciences," in *Stanford Encyclopedia of Philosophy* (Winter 2023 edition), eds. Edward N. Zalta and Uri Nodelman. Accessed March 31, 2024. https://plato.stanford.edu/entries/holism-social/.

11 Amounting to the claim that social phenomena must be explained by showing how they result from individual actions, which, in turn, must be explained through reference to the intentional states that motivate the individual actors. See Joseph Heath, "Methodological Individualism," in *Stanford Encyclopedia of Philosophy* (Summer 2020 edition), ed. Edward N. Zalta. Accessed March 31, 2024. https://plato.stanford.edu/entries/methodological-individualism/.

12 On the importance of constitutional values in interpretation and application of law, see Jan Wintr and Patrik Koželuha, "Teleological Interpretation in Czech Case Law," *The Lawyer Quarterly* 2 (2015): 149.

cases. This can be done only when doing away with collectivism, or at least when improving it by adding individualism to it. Thus, there is a search for a dialectical combination of the two opposing approaches. The same applies to both the current methodology of law and attempts to reflect upon the ideas of justice. The interplay between individualist and collectivist perceptions of justice and their evolution comes into play, hand in hand with attempts to dialectically unify structural legal positivism with the ideas of seeking justice even where positive law is deficient.

This approach thus also represents a revived chance for legal history as a discipline, which was neglected by positivist legal scholars and abused by the Marxist-Leninist philosophy of history. After the decline of those ideologies, it is, in fact, legal history and other methodologically pluralistic disciplines that can contribute to a better understanding of the constant evolution of law and society and the shifting ideas of justice that is noticeable nowadays as manifested in the return to formerly forgotten non-positivistic elements such as principles, values, human rights, and the ideals of justice, which can be grasped mostly by non-dogmatic legal disciplines.

2.2 Law as a System, Law as a Structure, and a Post-Structuralist Idea of Justice in Law

With its roots in medieval universities and with its heyday in 19th-century German legal scholarship, law was traditionally perceived as a system or a structure. In its boldest normativistic statements, it was even considered to be a pyramid.[13] This reflects very much the ideals of legal positivism and normativism as movements of the turn of the 19th and 20th centuries (František Weyr, Hans Kelsen, Adolf Merkl) which combined nicely with the early-20th-century ideas of structuralism claiming that the whole of reality is a structure with mutual interconnectedness and fixed ties. It was argued that the phenomena of human life are intelligible only through their interrelations.[14] In the early 20th century, this was emphasised by thinkers in France, Russia, and Czechoslovakia, mostly having to do with linguistics and literary studies (for example, Ferdinand de Saussure, Nikolai Sergeevich Trubetzkoy, Roman Jakobson, and Jan Mukařovský).

Still, there was a distinction between understanding law as a system and understanding reality as a structure; namely, while positivist legal scholarship was traditionally interested in law as an inner system,[15] or as an autonomous (semi-autonomous) structure, structuralists in other disciplines (foremost in

13 Nadia Elizabeth Nedzel, "Fuller, Dworkin, Scientism, and Liberty: The Dichotomy between Continental and Common Law Traditions and Their Consequences," *Laws* 12, no. 3 (2023): 1–47.

14 Simon Blackburn, "Structuralism," in *Oxford Dictionary of Philosophy*, 2nd rev. ed., ed. Simon Blackburn (Oxford: Oxford University Press, 2008), 353.

15 Alani Golanski, "Structuralist Concept of the Rule of Law," *British Journal of American Legal Studies* 10, no. 1 (2021): 121–153

linguistics), in contrast, distinguished between inner and outer structure, or, in other terms, between a synchronic and diachronic approach.[16] In contrast to the inner structure, it was claimed there is also a different type of structural relationship with outer elements, helping to give dynamics to the evolution of the structure in its diachronic movement. This idea was embraced also by structuralist legal theory,[17] while – in contrast – the normativist theory of law claimed that these aspects should be reserved for other disciplines outside of law and legal scholarship, claiming they do not belong to the inner system/structure of law and legal scholarship proper.

However, with the passing of time, both the ideas of normativism or positivism in legal scholarship and the ideas of structuralism in other disciplines were gradually challenged more and more from the middle of the 20th century.[18] They were heavily criticised mostly for being positivistic, meaning they were accused of being formalistic and deterministic, and finally ended up being rejected in both Eastern and Western Europe – albeit based on slightly different argumentation. While the West shifted towards post-structuralism, denying the formalism and determinism of structuralism, in the East, Marxism-Leninism was embraced, which claimed to better explain the actual interrelationship between the material base and superstructure, meaning, in fact, materialistic explanations of the evolution of society combined with the ideas of dialectical overcoming of contradictions.

Many Western legal scholars refused to accept the idea of formal legality being equal to formal justice,[19] as suggested (but not guaranteed in practice) by legal positivism. In Germany, facing the terrors of World War II, this led to the emergence of the "jurisprudence of values" (*Wertungsjurisprudenz*) instead, giving rise to embracing new non-positivist elements in law and legal scholarship.[20] In general thought and in other disciplines, this shift can be linked to the emergence of post-structuralism, which was gradually introduced in place of structuralism, foremost in France, challenging the dogmas of structuralism.[21]

16 David W. Kennedy, "Critical Theory, Structuralism and Contemporary Legal Scholarship," *New England Law Review* 21 (1986): 259.

17 Donald H.J. Hermann, "Phenomenology, Structuralism, Hermeneutics, and Legal Study: Applications of Contemporary Continental Thought to Legal Phenomena," *University of Miami Law Review* 36, no. 3 (1982): 398.

18 Étienne Balibar, "Structuralism: A Destitution of the Subject?" *differences* 14, no. 1 (2003): 1–21.

19 See, e.g., Hans-Peter Haferkamp, "Legal Formalism and its Critics," in *The Oxford Handbook of European Legal History*, eds. Heikki Pihlajamäki, Markus D. Dubber, and Mark Godfrey (Oxford: Oxford University Press, 2018), 929–945.

20 E.g., in the works of Robert Alexy, who was an important critic of legal positivism in continental Europe. See George Pavlakos, ed., *Law, Rights and Discourse: The Legal Philosophy of Robert Alexy* (Oxford: Hart Publishing, 2007).

21 James Williams, *Understanding Poststructuralism (Understanding Movements in Modern Thought)* (London: Routledge, 2005).

The new line of thought in Eastern Europe, on the other hand, challenged not only the existing structural links within the legal system itself, but also the links between legal systems and their social (or rather material) background. From this perspective, under the socialist (Marxist-Leninist) legal theory introduced in the East, justice became an element of a larger system (structure), where the idea of justice was formed based on the materialist and dialectical rules that were "discovered" by the classics of Marxism-Leninism. However, these rules, or "laws of evolution," were again too deterministic, revealing the same deficiencies as the preceding theory of structuralism itself. They did not allow for any exceptions or exemptions from the predetermined structures and evolutions, working with collectivist entities such as party, state, nation, or class (proletariat).[22] That is probably also the reason why after the fall of communist regimes in the East, post-structuralists were widely read also in the East[23] to compensate for the lack of a theory to replace the determinism of Marxist-Leninist teachings.

Instead of determinism and collectivism, individualism and its combination with collectivism in the form of methodological pluralism was longed for, which manifests itself precisely in contemporary post-structuralist and post-modern thought, and so-called post-positivism in various branches of scholarship. In legal scholarship, this trend is nowadays known under the label of legal post-positivism (the classics being works by Norberto Bobbio, Ronald Dworkin, Robert Alexy, Ota Weinberger, Neil MacCormick, and Manuel Atienza), which manifests itself in the emphasis on principles, values, human rights, and the ideals of justice to be applied and sought for in individual cases. It means, in fact, the actual overcoming of established collectivist dogmas by drawing attention to the unique nature of situations and cases which require overcoming or abandoning the formalistic and collectivistic approach.

Via these new "empty principles" (to borrow the term from structuralism to denote here the broader category of non-positivist figures), meaning in fact elements to be filled in by society, the inner and outer structures are again mutually interconnected, just like structuralism predicted, but this time without any methodologically collectivist general rules. The actual contents of the principles, values, human rights, and ideals of justice depart from collectivism. Instead, methodological individualism, or, in fact, methodological pluralism, should be advocated in order to better understand the role of individuals and individual cases and to guarantee the actual fulfilment of the idea of justice for each individual case.

Apparently, neither positivist, structuralist, nor Marxist-Leninist collectivist approaches ultimately proved capable of ensuring that justice was achieved in

22 Ervin Laszlo, *Individualism, Collectivism, and Political Power. A Relational Analysis of Ideological Conflict* (Dordrecht: Springer, 1963).

23 Marcel Cornis-Pope, "Introduction: Critical Theory and the Sociocultural Opening in Eastern Europe," *College Literature* 21, no. 1 (1994): 81–88.

those societies. Thus, both of the approaches – the first recognising law as the goal and guarantee of justice (under positivism) and the second recognising law as only a tool to meet the goals adopted by the collective society (structuralism and Marxism-Leninism) – failed. Justice could not be attained in those societies where the individual and his/her hopes and dreams were and still are an important factor. A compromise between the extremes of individualism and collectivism is, therefore, nowadays accepted in such a way that justice and respect for the individual (as a part of human rights and constitutional values) are considered as a legal goal to be achieved.[24] Europe turned first from a formalist rule of law to a material rule of law and then to post-positivism focusing on principles, values, human rights, and the ideals of justice, thereby abandoning any fixed collectivist ideas of justice.

Nevertheless, today there are still some places experimenting with collectivism – not surprisingly in the collectivist societies of the Far East,[25] where law is still perceived as a tool to achieve collective interests. This can be witnessed in the recent legal experiments with artificial intelligence (AI) taking place in China.[26] In contrast, methodological individualism is the reason why Western lawyers sceptically regard experimenting with AI for the purposes of judicial dispute resolution. It is thus the human judge who is believed to be able to avoid the application of rules that would cause the worst injustice if taken literally and formalistically. Already Aristotle and Cicero, as well as Thomas Aquinas, claimed that legal rules may fail in circumstances that were not taken into account when drafting the general rule. Therefore, human intervention is now necessary, paying attention rather to principles and common sense where a strict rule leads to unacceptable conclusions. To what extent this can be guaranteed by AI judges remains unknown.

On the other hand, certainly, human judges are often criticised for failing to meet their obligations and the expectations of justice as well.[27] Their personal traits may influence their decision-making both in positive terms by developing an "intuition for justice" as well as in negative terms by forming prejudices and biases. In this regard, any personal failures should be controlled and remedied by a compromise between methodological individualism and

24 Cf. Yota Negishi, "The *Pro Homine* Principle's Role in Regulating the Relationship between Conventionality Control and Constitutionality Control," *European Journal of International Law* 28, no. 2 (2017): 473.

25 See, e.g., Adam Cohen, Michael Shengtao Wu, and Jacob Miller, "Religion and Culture: Individualism and Collectivism in the East and West," *Journal of Cross-Cultural Psychology* 47, no. 9 (2016): 1236–1249.

26 Simon Chesterman, *We, the Robots? Regulating Artificial Intelligence and the Limits of the Law (Introduction)* (Cambridge: Cambridge University Press, 2021), 10. Accessed March 31, 2024. https://papers.ssrn.com/sol3/papers.cfm?abstract_id=4231363.

27 See, e.g., Daniel L. Chen, "This Morning's Breakfast, Last Night's Game: Detecting Extraneous Factors in Judging," *Pepperdine Law Review* 2016, no. 1(2): 341–355; Willem H. Gravett, "The Myth of Rationality: Cognitive Biases and Heuristics in Judicial Decision-Making," *South African Law Journal* 134 (2017): 53–79.

collectivism – searching for intersubjectively acceptable perceptions of justice and fairness, which are, in fact, proof of working methodological pluralism.[28]

The post-positivist shift in the Western legal paradigm has meant that, recently, law is becoming less and less identified with rules (norms) as originally suggested by legal positivists such as Weyr and Kelsen. In Europe, this had led to the actual practice of seeking justice becoming a sort of a return to the Aristotelian concept of *praxis* – seeing jurisprudence and law rather as a dialectical act of searching for the most acceptable solution in an individual case rather than applying a mechanism of formal legal syllogism based on predetermined prototypical solutions expressed in legal norms. These approaches are closer to perceiving law as an act of jurisprudence[29] (in an older tradition labelled as *Rechtsakt*,[30] or in much older Aristotelian terms *praxis*) rather than a simple fact (judicial award) or a norm (legal text). Clearly, this means at the same time also a shift from the dominance of legislation back to emphasising the role of judges. Current Italian legal theorist and philosopher Mauro Barberis speaks in this context about the "crisis of legislation," whereby he explains this evolution historically: laws perceived as a sole source of law started prevailing in continental Europe only because they were applied by courts and judges who embodied the authority of law. The courts thus lent their own authority to the laws by enforcing them. Currently, however, courts are taking back their authority from laws and legislators, which can be explained also by the more widely visible failure of legislation in attaining actual justice.[31]

According to Barberis, the second reason why legislation dominated in the 20th century was the popularity of codification projects, which were considered specifically useful in times of problematic data processing of a large body of law dispersed in numerous laws and case law. However, this problem can be overcome nowadays with the use of modern digital technologies. Finally, the third reason for the popularity of legislation starting from the end of the 19th century was that laws were enacted by parliaments representing democratic voters who thus themselves indirectly became the legislators. Democratic ideology thus legitimised the authority of law and legal norms in comparison with the non-democratic system of appointment of judges.[32] However, now that the actual functioning of legislation created by parliaments is hindered by flaws and failures, and judges have become much closer to the everyday life of the

28 Hoping to be able to reconcile individualism with pluralism.

29 Already advocated by Arthur Kaufmann, "The Ontological Structure of Law," *Natural Law Forum* 95 (1963): 79–96. Accessed March 31, 2024. http://scholarship.law.nd.edu/nd_naturallaw_forum/95.

30 Fritz Schreier, *Grundbegriffe und Grundformen des Rechts: Entwurf einer phänomenologisch begründeten formalen Rechts- und Staatslehre* (Berlin: Deuticke, 1924).

31 Mauro Barberis, "For a Truly Realistic Theory of Law," *Revus 29* (2016): 7–14.

32 Barberis, "For a Truly Realistic Theory of Law," 7–14.

broad masses of society, the usefulness of the priority of legislation is starting to be questioned.[33]

Finally, Barberis also observes an internal, structural transformation in the functioning of legislation in continental European legal systems where legislation is recently being perceived only as the application of a constitution and its values, similar to what judges do when applying laws. Legislators are thus only searching for the best ways to achieve the principles, values, human rights, and ideals of justice enshrined in the constitution and international law instruments guaranteeing basic human rights and freedoms. When legislators fail, judges can and should intervene. One often speaks in this regard of so-called neoconstitutionalism,[34] where the main sources of law are the principles, values, human rights, and ideals of justice enshrined in the constitution, which is to be interpreted and carefully applied by judges and courts (primarily constitutional courts).

This has resulted in renewed legal realist thought becoming popular due to its argument that legislatures offer only general instructions (normative dispositions), which in the end need to be given content and meaning by the authorities on the application of law, specifically the courts and judges.[35] They are at the same time necessarily influenced by current social discourse on justice and also institutional discourse, ultimately leading to methodological pluralism in the search for justice. Therefore, this is not a simple return to voluntaristic legal realism as called for by American legal realists.[36]

This line of thought, hence, questions the exclusive position of positive law (legal texts and legal norms) as the sole source or embodiment of law. Based on their regained position, new sources of law are being reconsidered and reintroduced – besides sources of legal order (legal texts), there are renewed attempts to revive the idea of customary law or judicial case law in continental European legal systems, or even legal doctrine as a source of law (*Juristenrecht*), which were all abandoned earlier in continental Europe mostly in connection with 19th-century ideas of legal positivism. Still, they are again starting to play an extremely important role in today's legal systems.[37]

Thus, to sum up, while developments in the 19th and 20th centuries led to the conclusion that law was starting to be identified solely with legal regulations, primarily with written laws, and with the crisis of ensuring justice through legislation, at the beginning of the 21st century this development needs to be reassessed. The newly emerging post-positivist views are expanding above and beyond the "written law" (legislation) as if they were returning

33 Barberis, "For a Truly Realistic Theory of Law," 7–14.

34 Miguel Carbonell, *Teoría del neoconstitucionalismo: Ensayos escogidos* (Madrid: Trotta-UNAM, Instituto de Investigaciones Jurídicas, 2007), 334ff.

35 Riccardo Guastini, "A Realistic View on Law and Legal Cognition," *Revus* 27 (2015): 45–54.

36 See, e.g., Jerome Frank, *Law and the Modern Mind*, 6th ed. (Garden City, NJ: Anchor Books, 1963).

37 Barberis, "For a Truly Realistic Theory of Law," 7–14.

to the pre-positivist period. However, instead of emphasising pre-modern societal, pan-human, or religious values or finally principles of rational natural law (*Vernunftsrecht*), the legal thought of today reveals an obvious dominance of legal principles, values, human rights, and ideals of justice to be applied in the effort to attain justice – a task that is difficult to entrust to algorithms embodying the positivistic approach to law in contrast to post-positivism.

2.3 Challenges and Opportunities for Legal History in the Post-Structuralist Search for Justice

The current post-positivist shift in the legal paradigm obviously reflects the general post-positivistic paradigmatic shift present also in the general philosophy of science. This shift in the legal paradigm thereby necessarily poses the question of the necessity of a shift in legal historiography and its own paradigm as well. Is there a new methodology necessary for legal historiography? And should the new approach be structuralist or post-structuralist?

Today, for example, the American legal historian Justin Desautels-Stein seeks a new approach to legal historiography,[38] pointing to the need for a limited confrontation of the history of legal regulations solely with the history of legal doctrine.[39] He proposes that research on the interconnectedness between legal regulations (norms) and changes in legal doctrine become the backbone of the current legal historiography and the general intellectual historical background of legal evolution be ignored. This could *prima facie* be seen as a structuralist and an inner-oriented (legally positivistic) approach.

Donald H. J. Hermann, who still writes about legal historiography from the perspective of structuralist thought, thus claims that the evolution of law reflects the structural changes in the evolution of legal doctrines, which need to be researched in their mutual structural relationship:

> In a structural analysis of the development of legal doctrine, one begins with the premise that the significance of each opinion lies not in its surface formulations, but in the unconscious deep structures guiding the decision. Hints of these deep structures can be found both in the language of the decisions and in the terms in which the doctrinal postulates are cast. The focus of a structural analysis of legal doctrine is to discover

38 After previous attempts to find novel approaches as presented by the Critical Legal Studies and Critical Legal History movement. See Christopher Tomlins, "After Critical Legal History: Scope, Scale, Structure," *Annual Review of Law and Social Science* 8 (2012): 31–68.

39 Justin Desautels-Stein, "Structuralist and Poststructuralist Legal History," in *The Oxford Handbook of Legal History*, eds. Markus Dubber et al. (Oxford: Oxford University Press, 2018), 541–560.

and formulate the deep structures and rules of transformation that operate in judicial decision-making.[40]

In practice, according to Hermann, it is thus clear that changes in doctrine emerge once the previous doctrine proves insufficient to provide guidelines in cases where the solution under the prevailing doctrine is perceived as unjust. There is, hence, an apparent mutual interconnectedness between law, legal doctrine, people, and the actual legal practice being evaluated in both legal (doctrinal) as well as non-legal terms (e.g., of morality) that can be reconstructed in the traditional "structuralist" vein. Hermann's approach is thus much broader than that of J. Desautels-Stein. However, to what extent there is space for individualism in Hermann´s structuralist view remains unclear. Instead, it seems like a deterministic and collectivistic approach.

Better equipped to cope with the critique of the determinism of structuralism thus seems to be the theory of Justin Desautels-Stein,[41] who might, in fact, be rather post-structuralist in his thoughts when he claims:

> Rather than offer an account of structures progressively evolving over time, structuralist historiography denies the possibility of obtaining apodictic accounts of legal history, progressive or otherwise. There is simply no way for the historian to get out of the way of her own prefigured interpretive orientations that will necessarily shape the forthcoming historical narrative. Further, rather than work in evolutionary historicism's modern mode and offer an account of legal structures functionally emerging in response to preexisting social needs, structuralist legal history tends to emphasize the other half of the law-in-society dialectic: although it is certainly true that law is shaped by social needs and interests, it is also the case, and perhaps more important to understand, that law itself shapes social needs and interests. Law is constitutive of the social.[42]

This means the author is aware of the role of the individual historian in the line of narrative historiography (see, e.g., works by Hayden White[43]). Although there is a clear interconnectedness and interrelation between law and society, the author claims that this relationship is, in fact, mutual and goes both ways. There are changing ideas and evolution of values in legal doctrines, while subsequently the evolved doctrines and legal rules can influence and change

40 Hermann, "Phenomenology, Structuralism, Hermeneutics, and Legal Study," 397–398. Accessed March 31, 2024. https://repository.law.miami.edu/umlr/vol36/iss3/3.

41 Justin Desautels-Stein, "Structuralist Legal Histories," *Law and Contemporary Problems* 78 (2015): 37–59. Accessed March 31, 2024. https://scholarship.law.duke.edu/lcp/vol78/iss1/4.

42 Desautels-Stein, "Structuralist Legal Histories," 57.

43 E.g., Hayden White, *Tropics of Discourse: Essays in Cultural Criticism* (Baltimore: The Johns Hopkins University Press, 1978).

the society at large – especially when perceiving law as a mechanism that can efficiently regulate society.[44] Therefore, what J. Desautels-Stein claims to be structuralist legal historiography can, in fact, be read as a post-structuralist undertaking *par excellence* if further developed as basically pointing to the fact that it is necessary to examine the turning points and changes in the development of legislation, doctrines, and generally in legal thinking, on the example of the changes (Foucauldian ruptures[45]) of legal institutions, legal regulations, or legal practices, subsequently influencing the society at large. This can clearly be done mostly by using methods of individualism rather than purely collectivist methodology, as originally suggested by structuralists. No generalisations or specific predictions can be made, nor can determinism be claimed to be found in the multifaceted and mutually directed influences of the society, doctrine, and law. Even Desautels-Stein apparently recognises the influence of individuals and individual cases in shaping the doctrine and rules, and the role of individual cases and rules in shaping the society – which is, in fact, more in line with post-structuralist rather than structuralist thought.

J. Desautels-Stein´s theory can thus be possibly further elaborated in post-structuralist terms, as this chapter shall try to prove. Desautels-Stein summarises his ideas in four brief points: (i) structuralist legal history does not reject the search for context but directs the historian to contexts other than those searched for by the intellectual historian; (ii) the object of historical analysis is the legal concept; (iii) the structure of legal argument is constructed within the concept, and not taken from some external context; and (iv) the legal concept is always a linguistic creation and not a mirrored reflection of the natural world.[46] He thus suggests that legal context is to be searched for primarily in "legal thought," which in his view refers to the mechanics of legal argument – the techniques and styles jurists use in the process of putting legal rules into action, giving the rules momentum, and, when applied successfully, giving the rules a gloss of necessity. Thus, while he is very much in favour of putting rules into context, it is not about putting them into a political or a philosophical context, but rather the context of legal thought. In fact, what J. Desautels-Stein argues for is to situate the history of a legal institution (e.g., actual legal regulation of ownership) in the history of legal methodology. The method used by lawyers (or a specific lawyer) of the period can explain the context of the legal regulation (rules) and uncover the evolution of specific rules in their changing doctrinal and methodological context. The mutual relationship between the history of legal methodology and the history of a legal regulation is thus to be uncovered and researched as the main task of (post-)struc-

44 Justin Desautels-Stein, "International Legal Structuralism: A Primer," *International Theory* 8, no. 2 (2016): 201–235.

45 See, e.g., Arun Iyer, *Towards an Epistemology of Ruptures: The Case of Heidegger and Foucault* (New York: Bloomsbury, 2014).

46 Iyer, *Towards an Epistemology of Ruptures.*

turalist legal historiography aimed at explaining interconnected shifts in legal regulation and legal thought.

However, this naturally begs a number of questions. For example, couldn't this approach be applied to law and legal scholarship in general (outside legal historiography), including research on the current constant evolution of law towards post-positivism? Can one try to understand the shifts in current legal methodology towards the application of principles, values, human rights, and the ideals of justice by using the same approach as when researching the history of changing legal rules and changing legal thought? Could thus legal history and its post-structuralist pluralistic methodology contribute also to a better understanding of the shifts in current law? Could it possibly even provide for historically tested pre-positivist legal methods and legal tools different from those that were used in the positivistic paradigm of the 20th century? It is particularly important to note that, due to the shift in the legal paradigm towards post-positivism, law and jurisprudence currently do not have suitable methodological instruments developed for investigating principles, values, human rights, and the ideals of justice as tools aimed at attaining justice in the current era. Moving away from structuralism and positivism towards post-positivist and post-structuralist rhetorical-discursive approaches at the same time necessarily emphasises the role of unique events in law, such as ground-breaking decisions of the supreme judicial authorities or influential doctrinal works, going thus beyond the idea of methodological collectivism of 20th-century legal scholarship. Legal historiography, drawing on the methodological individualism or pluralism of general historiography, could thus effectively contribute to the understanding of this development of jurisprudence – precisely by pointing to the pluralistic methodology (individual and collectivist in combination) that is being used in post-positivist jurisprudence.

The post-positivist and post-structuralist methodologically pluralistic approaches hence allow at the same time a reevaluation of the functioning of both law and legal scholarship, as well as the meaning and role of legal historiography *per se*. Legal historiography can thus possibly contribute to a better methodological understanding of the functioning of law by understanding the individual driving forces and interactions behind the development of legal doctrines, legal rules, principles, values, human rights, and the ideals of justice, and the overall development and shifts in legal thought. It is at least here that one could probably identify some practical use for legal historiography nowadays, which could contribute with its knowledge of historical legal methodology (legal thought of the past) to a better understanding of recent mechanisms of creation, interpretation, and application of principles, values, human rights, and the ideals of justice, together with their constant development and transformations. This could offer some space especially for the so-called current legal history or contemporary legal history (also referred to in German as *Juristische Zeitgeschichte*[47]). The methodology of legal historiography, being indeed pluralistic and methodologically individualistic (emphasising the uniqueness of historical facts and personalities and the role of individual legislators, scientists, or judges), as well as methodologically collectivist (aware of the role of institutions, groups, and collective entities such as states, nations, and cultures), may be, in particular, better equipped than the traditional methodologically collectivist and positivist approach for the purpose of explaining the actual nature of law, its development, and its current form and content, as well as its continuous development.

This may sound innovative, but, in fact, it would mean nothing more than a return to the pre-positivist, "traditional" school of law, which was subverted by the positivists and their special branch of normativists at the turn of the 19th and 20th centuries. Since the historical school of jurisprudence was abandoned in the second half of the 19th century, giving priority to the positivistic school of law, the history of law (legal history) remained considered from that time to be "only" one of the legal disciplines, and gradually lost its appeal and use, especially in the period of dominance of positivism in the 20th century, when it played solely the role of an introduction to other legal disciplines. A similar process also took place in economics where the famous battle – the *Methodenstreit* -- between the historical school of national economics (represented, e.g., by the German economist Gustav von Schmoller) and the theoretical school of economics (the Austrian school established by Carl Menger) was finally settled only in the middle of the 20th century with the victory of the theoretical school of economics.[48] Interestingly, in the post-positivist era arising at the end of the 20th century, a post-positivist school of economics is being revived again, challenging the positivist approach to economics and calling for methodological pluralism (both individualism and collectivism) rather than the methodological collectivism used so far by the positivistic school of economics.[49] The trend of abandoning positivism thus seems to be indeed a common feature in all the social sciences (while never being fully embraced at all by the humanities). Such a shift in the evolution of the approach to social sciences certainly represents a challenge also for legal history as a separate legal discipline, which now can and should start searching for new footing where it can gain a more respectable position again in the world where principles, values, human rights, and the ideals of justice, together with the role of unique individual factors, are being appraised again.

47 Marcel Senn and Lukas Gschwend, *Rechtsgeschichte II: Juristische Zeitgeschichte*. 3. überarbeitete Auflage (Zürich: Schulthess Verlag, 2010), 1ff.

48 Robert E. Ekelund and Robert F. Hébert, *A History of Economic Theory and Method* (New York: McGraw Hill, 1975).

49 Bruce J. Caldwell, *Beyond Positivism: Economic Methodology in the Twentieth Century* (London: George Allen & Unwin, 1982). See also Nicholas Balabkins, *Not by Theory Alone: The Economics of Gustav von Schmoller and Its Legacy to Contemporary America* (Berlin: Duncker und Humblot, 1988).

It is precisely in this spirit and with these tools that it is possible to also understand the post-positivist transformations of the current legal concepts and doctrines due to the methodological shifts in searching for justice in law. Since justice is both a legal and a non-legal concept, it allows for both an intellectual historiographical analysis as well as for a legal historiographical analysis. The dividing line between the two approaches to justice is therefore very thin and very difficult to find, including based on the evolution from the legalist concept of justice to the class concept of justice, and finally the concept of justice as a legal goal enshrined in principles, values, human rights, and the ideals of justice which together can be perceived (in structuralist terminology[50]) as "empty principles" established by constitutions and international agreements,[51] waiting to be filled in by interpretation and application in the everyday practice of law and legal scholarship, including general perceptions of justice by the society. This shift in the perception of justice has gone hand in hand with shifts in the methodology of law, legal thought, and changes in legal doctrine, as well as legal rules. Certainly, it is a bit broader undertaking than the one advocated by Desautels-Stein, including also accounting for societal changes. However, it proves that it is not necessary to strictly omit broader intellectual history and background in explaining shifts in legal thought. The involvement of broader contexts might be necessary and useful in the methodology of post-structuralist legal historiography if it can help, e.g., to better understand the evolution of justice from a collectivist concept to an individualistic one, or even a pluralistic one, in the context of the changing legal and societal as well as economic thought of the 20th century. The same methodology can also help to better understand the actual role of justice in current European legal systems.

2.4 Conclusions

We are currently witnessing a general paradigm shift in all the sciences (including legal scholarship) tending to become post-positivist, post-modern, and

50 Especially coined by Czechoslovak interwar author Jaroslav Honza-Dubnický. See Ingrid Ciulisová, "Štrukturalista Jaroslav Dubnický a slovenský dejepis umenia [Structuralist Jaroslav Dubnický and Slovak Art History]," in *Československý štrukturalizmus a viedenský scientizmus [Czechoslovak Structuralism and Viennese Scientism]*, ed. Peter Michalovič (Bratislava: Stimul, 1992), 194–204.

51 For instance, Article 29 of the American Convention on Human Rights (ACHR) adopted by more than twenty countries of Latin America prohibits that convention from being interpreted in a way that suppresses, restricts, precludes, excludes, or limits the rights and freedoms recognised therein. Other similar provisions include Article 5.1 of the International Covenant on Civil and Political Rights (ICCPR) and the International Covenant on Economic, Social and Cultural Rights (ICESCR), and Article 17 of the European Convention on Human Rights (ECHR). See Hayde Rodarte Berbera, "The *Pro Personae* Principle of Interpretation and Its Application by Mexican Courts," *QMHRR* 4, no. 1 (2017): 6.

post-structuralist. This is manifested in embracing new post-positivist elements, such as principles, values, human rights, and the ideals of justice as tools to attain fairness and justice in law. This means a post-structuralist overcoming of the ideas of collectivist perception and determination of justice as advocated by structuralism as well as Marxism-Leninism. At the same time, it is also an overcoming of the legalist concept of justice as advocated by legal positivists and normativists.

In fact, the current shift means a need to search for new post-positivist footing of legal scholarship replacing the collectivist methodologies of the 20th century with a more pluralistic methodology (both individualistic as well as collectivistic). The same approach is being suggested nowadays also with regard to legal historiography, which should abandon the idea of searching for universal rules applied in the past and should, on the contrary, accept the role of individuals and individual events in the evolution of law. Such a reconsidering of the role of legal historiography can at the same time contribute to a generally better understanding of the driving forces and interactions behind the evolution of legal doctrines, law, and legal thought. Probably the same pluralist mechanism of evolution applies also with regard the actual day-to-day theory and practice of post-positivist law, which is faced with constant evolution via the "empty principles" of principles, values, human rights, and the intersubjective ideals of justice.

This diagnosis, in fact, represents nothing more than a revamped return to the pre-positivist, "traditional" perception of law, which was refused by positivists and normativists at the turn of the 19th and 20th centuries. They were eager to establish a truly positivistic legal scholarship and a truly scientific law, but apparently they failed in the effort, which possibly gives legal historians a chance to revive the competing views once again. Once the pluralist methodology of legal historical research is better researched and understood, the same approach and methodology can then be possibly tested also on the actual functioning of the current mechanism and techniques of post-positivist law.

References

Balabkins, Nicholas. *Not by Theory Alone: The Economics of Gustav von Schmoller and its Legacy to Contemporary America*. Berlin: Duncker und Humblot, 1988.

Balibar, Étienne. "Structuralism: A Destitution of the Subject?" *Differences* 14, no. 1 (2003): 1–21.

Barber, Sotirios A., and James E. Fleming. *Constitutional Interpretation: The Basic Questions*. Oxford and New York: Oxford University Press, 2007.

Barberis, Mauro. "For a Truly Realistic Theory of Law." *Revus* 29 (2016): 7–14.

Blackburn, Simon. "Structuralism." In *Oxford Dictionary of Philosophy*, 2nd rev. ed., edited by Simon Blackburn, 353. Oxford: Oxford University Press, 2008

Caldwell, Bruce J. *Beyond Positivism: Economic Methodology in the Twentieth Century*. London: George Allen & Unwin, 1982.

Campbell, Tom D. "Rights Without Justice." *Mind* 83, no. 331 (July 1974): 445–48.

Carbonell, Miguel. *Teoría del neoconstitucionalismo. Ensayos escogidos.* Madrid: Trotta-UNAM, Instituto de Investigaciones Jurídicas, 2007.

Chen, Daniel L. "This Morning's Breakfast, Last Night's Game: Detecting Extraneous Factors in Judging." *Pepperdine Law Review* 1, no. 2 (2016): 341–55.

Chesterman, Simon. *We, the Robots? Regulating Artificial Intelligence and the Limits of the Law (Introduction).* Cambridge: Cambridge University Press, 2021. Accessed March 31, 2024. https://papers.ssrn.com/sol3/papers.cfm?abstract_id=4231363.

Ciulisová, Ingrid. "Štrukturalista Jaroslav Dubnický a slovenský dejepis umenia [Structuralist Jaroslav Dubnický and Slovak Art History]." In *Československý štrukturalizmus a viedenský scientizmus [Czechoslovak Structuralism and Viennese Scientism]*, edited by Peter Michalovič, 194–204. Bratislava: Stimul, 1992.

Cohen, Adam, Michael Shengtao Wu, and Jacob Miller. "Religion and Culture: Individualism and Collectivism in the East and West." *Journal of Cross-Cultural Psychology* 47, no. 9 (2016): 1236–49.

Cornis-Pope, Marcel. "Introduction: Critical Theory and the Sociocultural Opening in Eastern Europe." *College Literature* 21, no. 1 (1994): 81–88.

Deleuze, Gilles. "How Do We Recognize Structuralism?" In *Desert Islands and Other Texts*, translated by Melissa McMahon and Charles J. Stivale and edited by David Lapoujade, 170–92. New York and Cambridge: Semiotexte and MIT Press, 2004.

Desautels-Stein, Justin. "International Legal Structuralism: A Primer." *International Theory* 8, no. 2 (2016): 201–35.

Desautels-Stein, Justin. "Structuralist Legal Histories." *Law and Contemporary Problems* 78 (2015): 37–59. Accessed March 31, 2024. https://scholarship.law.duke.edu/lcp/vol78/iss1/4.

Desautels-Stein, Justin. "Structuralist and Poststructuralist Legal History." In *The Oxford Handbook of Legal History*, edited by Markus Dubber et al., 541–60. Oxford: Oxford University Press, 2018.

Ekelund, Robert E., and Robert F. Hébert. *A History of Economic Theory and Method.* New York: McGraw Hill, 1975.

Frank, Jerome. *Law and the Modern Mind.* 6th ed. Garden City, NJ: Anchor Books, 1963.

Golanski, Alani: "Structuralist Concept of the Rule of Law." *British Journal of American Legal Studies* 10, no. 1 (2021): 121–53.

Gravett, Willem H. "The Myth of Rationality: Cognitive Biases and Heuristics in Judicial Decision-Making." *South African Law Journal* 134 (2017): 53–79.

Guastini, Riccardo. "A Realistic View on Law and Legal Cognition." *Revus* 27 (2015): 45–54.

Haferkamp, Hans-Peter. "Legal Formalism and its Critics." In *The Oxford Handbook of European Legal History*, edited by Heikki Pihlajamäki, Markus D. Dubber, and Mark Godfrey, 929–45. Oxford: Oxford University Press, 2018.

Heath, Joseph. "Methodological Individualism." In *Stanford Encyclopedia of Philosophy (Summer 2020 Edition)*, edited by Edward N. Zalta. Accessed March 31, 2024. https://plato.stanford.edu/entries/methodological-individualism/.

Hermann, Donald H. J. "Phenomenology, Structuralism, Hermeneutics, and Legal Study: Applications of Contemporary Continental Thought to Legal Phenomena." *University of Miami Law Review* 36, no. 3 (1982): 379–410. Accessed March 31, 2024. https://repository.law.miami.edu/umlr/vol36/iss3/3.

Iyer, Arun. *Towards an Epistemology of Ruptures: The Case of Heidegger and Foucault.* New York: Bloomsbury, 2014.

Kaufmann, Arthur. "The Ontological Structure of Law." *Natural Law Forum* 95 (1963): 79–96. Accessed March 31, 2024. http://scholarship.law.nd.edu/nd_naturallaw_forum/95.

Kennedy, David W. "Critical Theory, Structuralism and Contemporary Legal Scholarship." *New England Law Review* 21 (1986): 209–89.

Laszlo, Ervin. *Individualism, Collectivism, and Political Power. A Relational Analysis of Ideological Conflict.* Dordrecht: Springer, 1963.

Marmor, Andrei. *The Language of Law.* Oxford: Oxford University Press, 2014.

Nedzel, Nadia Elizabeth. "Fuller, Dworkin, Scientism, and Liberty: The Dichotomy between Continental and Common Law Traditions and Their Consequences." *Laws* 12, no. 3 (2023): 1–47.

Negishi, Yota. "The Pro Homine Principle's Role in Regulating the Relationship Between Conventionality Control and Constitutionality Control." *The European Journal of International Law* 28, no. 2 (2017): 457–81.

Pavlakos, George, ed. *Law, Rights and Discourse: The Legal Philosophy of Robert Alexy.* Oxford: Hart Publishing, 2007.

Pleasants, Nigel. "Free Will, Determinism and the 'Problem' of Structure and Agency in the Social Sciences." *Philosophy of the Social Sciences* 49, no. 1 (2019): 3–30.

Radbruch, Gustav. *Rechtsphilosophie III. Vol. 3 of the Gustav Radbruch Gesamtausgabe.* Edited by A. Kaufmann. Heidelberg: C.F. Müller, 1990.

Reimann, Matthias. "Nineteenth Century German Legal Science." *Boston College Law Review* 31 (1990): 837–97. Accessed March 31, 2024. http://lawdigitalcommons.bc.edu/bclr/vol31/iss4/2.

Rodarte Berbera, Hayde. "The Pro Personae Principle of Interpretation and its Application by Mexican Courts." *QMHRR* 4, no. 1 (2017): 1–27.

Schreier, Fritz. *Grundbegriffe und Grundformen des Rechts. Entwurf einer phänomenologisch begründeten formalen Rechts- und Staatslehre.* Berlin: Deuticke, 1924.

Senn, Marcel, and Lukas Gschwend. *Rechtsgeschichte II: Juristische Zeitgeschichte.* 3. überarbeitete Auflage. Zürich: Schulthess Verlag, 2010.

Spitzer, Steven. "Marxist Perspectives in the Sociology of Law." *Annual Review of Sociology* 9 (1983): 103–24.

Tomlins, Christopher. "After Critical Legal History: Scope, Scale, Structure." *Annual Review of Law and Social Science* 8 (2012): 31–68.

White, Hayden. *Tropics of Discourse: Essays in Cultural Criticism.* Baltimore: The Johns Hopkins University Press, 1978.

Williams, James. *Understanding Poststructuralism (Understanding Movements in Modern Thought).* London: Routledge, 2005.

Wintr, Jan, and Patrik Koželuha. "Teleological Interpretation In Czech Case Law." *The Lawyer Quarterly* 2 (2015): 133–49.

Zahle, Julie. "Methodological Holism in the Social Sciences." In *Stanford Encyclopedia of Philosophy (Winter 2023 Edition)*, edited by Edward N. Zalta and Uri Nodelman. Accessed March 31, 2024. https://plato.stanford.edu/entries/holism-social/.

Part 1

Law & Justice

3 The Concept of Justice in Polish Municipal Law in the 16th–18th Centuries[1]

Maciej Mikuła

3.1 Subject of the Study

Thinking about the legal culture of the early modern period, intuitive associations arise, such as the strong connection between law and morality, the rooting of Christian values in the law, the metaphysical rationalisation of punishments, including the harshest ones, and the belief in ensuring that of holy justice was carried out as a result of issuing a just verdict. Judicial offences were taken seriously and the punishments for issuing biased and unjust verdicts and for avoiding the pursuit of justice were particularly severe.[2] The concept of justice appears in many contexts and diverse types of sources, and even a cursory review of the discussion of this concept in the European legal culture of the 16th–18th centuries seems a task beyond the scope of the most comprehensive article. Nevertheless, it is still an open topic. An area that requires further exploration is the understanding of this concept by legal practitioners, especially the functions and purposes given to it in documents used in the practice of law.

In this chapter, I want to examine the extent to which the concept of justice played an important role in legal discourse in Polish cities of the early

1 This research has been supported by the National Science Centre (Poland) (project title "The Natural History of Law," UMO-21/42/A/HS5/00309).

2 Misappropriation of a judge's duties – biased adjudication or avoiding the pursuit of justice – led, in the light of the *Saxon Mirror*, to the sentencing of the judge to a punishment that threatened the original offender; Grzegorz M. Kowalski, "'Persony sądowi przynależące, jakie mają być'. Jurysta doskonały na podstawie wybranych dzieł dawnych polskich pisarzy-prawników" ['The Persons Affiliated with the Court. The Requirements that They Should Fulfill.' The Perfect Jurist as Outlined on the Basis of the Selected Works Written by Jurists of the Old Poland], *Krakowskie Studia z Historii Państwa i Prawa* 3 (2010): 60. Kacper Górski cites, among others, the words of the Jesuit preacher Piotr Skarga, who referred to judges as 'living justice" (Górski, "Wizerunek sędziego w polskich utworach literackich i pisanie politycznych XVI i XVII stulecia" [The Image of a Judge as Illustrated in Works of Polish Poets and Political Writers in the 16th–17th Centuries], *Krakowskie Studia z Historii Państwa i Prawa* 13/4 (2020): 483, foootnote 88).

DOI: 10.4324/9781003654131-5

modern era, in particular, whether justice was seen as an overriding value that was resorted to in specific situations, for example, when courts avoided the application of written law and turned to customs and unwritten customary law. I focus primarily on the sources of legal practice – the court books of the cities of southern Poland: Kraków, Dobczyce, Nowy Wiśnicz, Myślenice, Proszowice, the so-called Muszyna Kres (the property of the bishop of Kraków that included the city of Muszyna and adjacent villages), and Żywiec. Except for the manuscript from Proszowice,[3] I used critical editions.[4] However, before the results of the analysis of these sources are presented, I wish to indicate the contexts in which the term "justice" appears in the *Ius municipale Magdeburgense*, the collection of laws for cities used in practice, and I intend to address the meaning of the term "equity," whose semantic range in the analysed sources proves surprising.

First, a caveat is necessary. Reading court sources from the above-mentioned cities does not at all lead to clear conclusions as to who was the actual author of the wording found in them. Criminal court records, known in old Poland as tar (black) books,[5] often contain the contents of complaints, testi-

3 National Archives in Kraków, Akta Miasta Proszowice [Document of the City of Proszowice], no. 29/121: Variae civitates et villae, shelfmark 165.

4 Wacław Uruszczak, Maciej Mikuła, and Anna Karabowicz, eds., *Księga kryminalna miasta Krakowa z lat 1554–1625* [*Criminal Records of the City of Cracow from 1554–1625*], Fontes Iuris Polonici. Seria: prawo miejskie, vol. I (Kraków: Jagiellonian University Press, 2013); Wacław Uruszczak et al., eds., *Księga kryminalna miasta Krakowa z lat 1589–1604* [*Criminal Records of the City of Cracow from 1589–1604*], Fontes Iuris Polonici. Seria: prawo miejskie, vol. III (hereafter FIP III) Kraków: Societas Vistulana, 2016; Wacław Uruszczak, Maciej Mikuła, and Krzysztof Fokt, eds., *Księgi kryminalne miasta Krakowa z lat 1630–1633, 1679–1690* [*Criminal Records from Kraków City from 1630–1633, 1679–1690*], Fontes Iuris Polonici. Seria: prawo miejskie, vol. IV (Kraków: Societas Vistulana, 2016); Maciej Mikuła, ed., *Księga kryminalna miasta Dobczyc 1699–1737* [*Criminal Records of the City of Dobczyce 1699–1737*], Fontes Iuris Polonici. Seria: prawo miejskie, vol. II (Kraków: Jagiellonian University Press, 2013); Wacław Uruszczak and Irena Dwornicka, eds., *Księga złoczyńców sądu kryminalnego w Wiśniczu (1629–1665)* [*Book of Villains of the Criminal Court in Wiśnicz (1629–1665)*] (Kraków: Collegium Columbinum, 2003) (hereafter Wiśnicz I); Wacław Uruszczak et al., eds., *Księga czarna złoczyńców sądu kryminalnego w* Wiśniczu *(1665–1785)* [*Black Book of Villains of the Criminal Court in Wiśnicz (1665–1785)*] (Kraków: Archiwum Państwowe, 2010) (hereafter Wiśnicz II); Maciej Mikuła, ed., *Księga ławników myślenickich z lat 1700–1725* [*Jurors' Records of Myślenice 1700–1725*], Fontes Iuris Polonici. Seria: prawo miejskie, vol. 8 (Kraków, Jagiellonian University Press, 2022). Accessed March 25, 2024. https://iura.uj.edu.pl/dlibra/publication/3304#structure; Franciszek Piekosiński, ed., *Akta sądu kryminalnego kresu muszyńskiego 1647–1765* [*Records of the Criminal Court of the Muszyna Kres 1647–1765*] (Kraków: Akademia Umiejętności, 1889); Rafał Kosiński, ed., *Księga złoczyńców albo akta sądu koniecznego gajonego żywieckiego z lat 1589–1782* [*The Book of Villains, or the Records of the Necessary Court of Żywiec from 1589 to 1782*] (Żywiec: Towarzystwo Naukowe Żywieckie, 2014).

5 Marian Mikołajczyk, "O miejskich księgach czarnych i ich wydawaniu uwag kilka. W związku z edycją Acta maleficorum Wisniciae. Księga złoczyńców sądu kryminalnego w Wiśniczu (1629–1665), oprac. i wyd. W. Uruszczak, I. Dwornicka, 2004" [A Few Remarks on the Municipal "Black Books" and Their Publication. On the Edition of Acta maleficorum Wisniciae. Book of

monies of defendants and witnesses, and sometimes statements of attorneys, who, at least in the case of Kraków, were professional attorneys. The books were kept in the city chancelleries, in which scribes and their deputies played an important role.[6] They were among the intellectual elite of the locality and were responsible for giving the final shape to the entries in the books.[7] Therefore, it is not excluded that, relying on this type of source, we draw a picture of the legal culture of only a narrow group of educated burghers. We are not sure whether the recurring demand in the complaints in small Dobczyce for the administration of "holy justice" was a customary phrase reproduced by the scribes in the local chancellery or a faithful record of the content of the complainants' demand – or perhaps both.

3.2 The Meaning of the Concept of Justice in the Sources of Municipal Law

Collections of Saxon-Magdeburg law belonged to the sources of municipal law in medieval and early modern Poland. The *Ius municipale Magdeburgense* (Magdeburg Weichbild) was the primary collection in the Middle Ages and continued to play an important role in the early modern period.[8] Grzegorz M. Kowalski, publisher of the Polish translation of the *Ius municipale* (1581) by *Iuris Utriusque Doctor* ("Doctor of both laws," i.e., civil and church law) Paweł Szczerbic (1552–1609),[9] stressed that theoretical considerations of law were linked to justice: "Attention is drawn to the supremely modern principle – although not formulated *expressis verbis* – that something unjust cannot be

villains of the criminal court in Wiśnicz (1629–1665), edited by W. Uruszczak, I. Dwornicka, 2004], *Czasopismo Prawno-Historyczne* 57/2 (2005): 413–424.

6 Janusz Łosowski, *Kancelarie miast szlacheckich województwa lubelskiego od XV do XVIII wieku* [*Chancelleries of Noble Towns of Lublin Province from the 15th to the 18th century*] (Lublin: Agencja Wydawniczo-Handlowa Antoni Dudek, 1997), 191.

7 Łosowski's research on the environment of the employees of the chancellery of the noble towns of the former Lublin province in the early modern period shows that they were most often recruited from among craftsmen, organists, and bachelors of parish schools, sometimes also from among the impoverished nobility. The level of education of canvassers and their deputies varied greatly, from university education in large cities (Kraków, Poznań) to elementary education in smaller towns. Łosowski, *Kancelarie miast*, 197–201.

8 Stanisław Kutrzeba, *Historia źródeł dawnego prawa polskiego* [*History of the Sources of Old Polish Law*], vol. 2 (Lwów-Warszawa-Kraków: Zakład Narodowy im. Ossolińskich, 1926), 208–211; Wieland Carls, "Rechtsquellen Sächsisch-magdeburgischen Rechts," in Inge Bily, Wieland Carls, Katalin Gönczi, *Sächsisch-magdeburgisches Recht in Polen: Untersuchungen zur Geschichte des Rechts und seiner Sprache*, Ivs Saxonico-Maidebvrgense in Oriente, 2 (Berlin: De Gruyter, 2011), 86–88.

9 *Corpus Academicum Cracoviense (CAC)*, "Paweł Szczerbic of Krakow (Id: 2000313)." Accessed April 4, 2024. http://cac.historia.uj.edu.pl/osoba/2000313_Pawe%C5%82_Szczerbic_z_Krakowa.

referred to as law."[10] At the same time, he stated that typical of bourgeois legal culture was an intuitive understanding of the concept of justice.[11] This view is worth supplementing with testimonies that confirm the interest of practitioners in considering the meaning of the concept of justice. One can already find Ulpian's classic definition in the *Ius municipale Magdeburgense* itself. It appeared in the copies included in the so-called Silesian-Małopolska compilation, used in the Kingdom of Poland from the 14th to the mid-16th centuries. It was included in a prologue, probably constructed using a collection of excerpts of legal and theological maxims.[12] This prologue did not appear in all the surviving texts of the Silesian-Małopolska compilation, but, nevertheless, it was entered in the official text, published in 1506 in the so-called Statute of Jan Łaski.[13] The readers of the Statute were not indifferent to the essence of justice. This is evidenced by the handwritten marginal notes. Let us not be deceived by their succinct wording: "Iustitie laus, Iustitia quod"[14]; "Definitio iustitiae"[15]; "[I]usticia debet esse fortissima inter [omn]es virtutes"; "[I]ustitia quomodo est."[16] The brief notes in the margins were usually meant to highlight an important passage. These examples, however, lead us to believe that practitioners, and they were undoubtedly the users of the Statute of Jan Łaski, asked themselves: what is justice?

After 1535, a new edition of the *Ius municipale Magdeburgense*, based on the so-called Weichbild Vulgate rather than the Silesian-Małopolska compilation, began to supplant the latter. This new edition, prepared by Mikołaj Jaskier (1504–1539), was accompanied by a gloss prepared using Roman law.[17] The concept of justice was found in the following contexts. The king, the judge,

10 Grzegorz M. Kowalski, in: Paweł Szczerbic, *Ius Municipale to jest prawo miejskie Majdeburskie...* [*Ius municipale i.e. municipal Magdeburg law...*], ed. Grzegorz M. Kowalski, Bibliotheca Iagiellonica. Fontes et Studia, 20 (Kraków: Księgarnia Akademicka, 2011), XVIII.

11 Kowalski, *Ius Municipale*, XX.

12 Edition in: Maciej Mikuła, *Municipal Magdeburg Law (Ius municipale Magdeburgense) in Late Medieval Poland: A Study on the Evolution and Adaptation of Law*, Medieval Law and Its Practice, vol. 30 (Leiden–Boston: Brill, 2021), 388–390.

13 *Commune incliti Poloniae Regni privilegium constitutionum et indultuum publicitus decretorum approbatorumque...*, Cracoviae, MDVI.

14 *Commune incliti Poloniae Regni privilegium...*, in: Polish Academy of Sciences Kórnik Library, Cim.F.4119.

15 *Commune incliti Poloniae Regni privilegium...*, in: Jagiellonian Library, St. Dr. Cim. 8004.

16 *Commune incliti Poloniae Regni privilegium...*, in: National Library in Warsaw, SD.XVI.F.432.

17 Krystyna Bukowska, *Orzecznictwo krakowskich sądów wyższych w sporach o nieruchomości miejskie (XVI–XVIII w.). Studium z historii prawa rzymskiego w Polsce* [*The Caselaw of Cracow Higher Courts Concerning Disputes over Real Property in Towns (16th–18th Century): A Study in the History of Roman Law in Poland*] (Warsaw: Państwowe Wydawnictwo Naukowe, 1967), 13; Krystyna Kamińska, *Lokacje miast na prawie Magdeburskim na ziemiach polskich do 1370 r. Studium historyczno-prawne* [*Incorporation of Towns under Magdeburg Law in Poland until 1370: A Study in the History of Law*] (Toruń: Uniwersytet Mikołaja Kopernika, 1990), 62.

and the trial attorney were obliged to ensure justice was done by providing a fair trial. In addition, judicial complaints, oaths of evidence, judgements, and laws passed by the city council should be just. Performing a legal act in accordance with the requirements of the law, for example, selling something, was considered just. In contrast, taking a horse by force (Article CXXXIX), ignoring a curse (Article V), using falsified weights and measures (Articles XIX, XX), making claims that cause harm (Article XCL), and wrongful appropriation (CXL), including appropriating an undue portion of an inheritance (Article XXIII), were considered unjust. Violation of natural law – for example, the entitlement of children to inherit from their parents – was also considered a violation of justice. Jaskier's Latin translation, as well as the 1555 German edition of the Vulgate compiled by Christoph Zobel,[18] formed the basis of Paweł Szczerbic's Polish translation of 1581, which Kowalski wrote about. The examples cited conclusively confirm that, as Kowalski mentioned, the concept of justice was closely associated with law, but only unquestionable law consistent with natural law and divine law. Moreover, justice was a prerequisite for law.

Reflection on the concept of justice entered the canon of university studies, both philosophical and then legal. Both the scope of this reflection and the transfer of university knowledge beyond the universities to the bodies applying the law still require further analytical studies. Nevertheless, it is already worth noting that the discussion of *ius et iustitia* was the subject of in-depth study in the Polish-Lithuanian Commonwealth at the University of Vilnius, among others, to cite as an example the treatise *De iure et iustitia* (1647/1648) by Sigmundus Lauxmin (1596–1670), a professor there.[19] The treatise was based on two works of the same title, *De iustitia et iure*, by Leonardus Lessius (1605) and Juan de Lugo (1642), and it is part of a sequence of philosophical and legal considerations.[20] Lauxmin closely linked the concepts of justice and law. The editors of his work note that: "What is to be considered just, the so-called object of the virtue of justice, must be in harmony with the letter of the law (*cum lege consentit eique adaequatur*). Lauxmin thus rules out any account of justice that would override the laws and be independent of them."[21] Importantly, in his lecture, Lauxmin distinguishes between *iustitia* and *aequitas*, justice/law and justice/equity, the latter concept being assigned a wider range of meaning beyond the legal sphere.[22]

18 Christoph Zobel, *Magdeburgisch und Sechsisch Weichbild und Lehenrecht, auffs new an vielen orten...*, Leipzig, MDLV.

19 Sigismundus Lauxmin, *De iure et iustitia*, eds. Krzysztof Bekieszczuk et al. (Warsaw: Wydawnictwo Naukowe Sub Lupa, 2023), V–VII.

20 Zobel, *Magdeburgisch und Sechsisch*, X and n.

21 Zobel, *Magdeburgisch und Sechsisch*, XIX.

22 Zobel, *Magdeburgisch und Sechsisch*, XIX.

However, the complexity of the history of the terms "justice" and "equity" in the context of legal practice is shown by the following examples.[23] In the small town of Myślenice, near Kraków, a municipal book of records was kept (1700–1725). It mainly recorded transfers of real estate – plots of land, farms, gardens. Criminal cases were completely absent from it. Of the two terms mentioned, "equity" (fairness) appears far more frequently. The context for this term indicates that "lawful" could just as well have been used in place of "fairness." As it turns out, the translator of Saxon-Magdeburg law sources into Polish, Paweł Szczerbic, also equated the two terms. While the German text of 1499 and the Latin translation by Mikołaj Jaskier in Article LXV of *Ius municipale Magdeburgense* include the term "lawful" / "legally" ("mit den rechten" / "iure"),[24] Szczerbic replaced it with "słusznie" (fair) in his Polish translation. Thus, it is not excluded that the urban writer of Myślenice suggested the meaning proposed by Szczerbic, reducing the meaning of the concept of equity to compliance with the law, and therefore something quite different from the proposal of the Vilnius theorist. The concept of equity also accompanies the law in the justifications of municipal statutes (Ger. *Willkür*, Pol. *wilkierz*). The Poznań statute of 1598 prohibited the disposal of property in a will to the detriment of the legal heirs. Such disposal was considered a violation not only of divine, natural, and human law, but also of the principle of equity. This context makes it possible to believe that the authors of the statute treated the principle of equity as extralegal, which is closer to the view expressed by Lauxmin than the one expressed by Szczerbic. The examples cited encourage caution and suggest refraining from firmly attributing separate meanings to the terms "justice" and "equity" in legal sources.

3.3 The Term "Justice" in City Criminal Records

There are nearly a thousand criminal cases in the analysed court records. The term "justice" was mentioned almost 130 times, thus, on average in every ninth entry. In reality, however, this is not the case, since it appears only once in 560 records of various stages of trials in the Kraków records of 1630–1633 and 1679–1690, while it appears 30 times in 39 cases in Dobczyce (1700–1737). The term "justice" occurs in several repeated situations in the analysed sources, as presented in the following summary:

23 I explore this issue in detail in a separate article: "Praworządność, sprawiedliwość, słuszność. O kulturze prawnej w sądach małych miast u progu XVIII stulecia" [The Rule of Law, Justice, Equity: On Legal Culture in the Courts of Small Towns at the Dawn of the Eighteenth Century], in *Prawo i kultura: Księga jubileuszowa dedykowana Profesorowi Markowi Wąsowiczowi* [*Law and Culture: A Book Dedicated to Professor Marek Wąsowicz*], eds. Jarosław Kuisz and Anna Rosner (Warsaw: Wydawnictwo Naukowe Scholar, 2022), 157–168.

24 *Remissorium mit sambt dem weichbilde und lehenrecht* [Eike von Repgow, *Sachsenspiegel: Lehnrecht*. Add: *Weichbild*. Dietrich von Bocksdorf: *Remissorium*] (Augsburg: Johann Schönsperger, 1499), fol. Ciiii verso; Mikołaj Jaskier, *Iuris Municipalis Maideburgensis Liber vulgo Weichbild nuncupatur*... (Kraków: Hieronim Wietor, 1535), fol. LXV recto.

Table 3.1 Reference to the concept of justice in selected city criminal records (compiled by the author).

	"Demand for justice" in the lawsuit	*A fair hearing of evidence*	*Reference to justice in the judgement*
Dobczyce 1699–1737	26	4	
Kraków 1554–1625	6		
Kraków 1589–1614	7		3
Kraków 1630–1633, 1679–1690	1		
Muszyna Kres 1647–1765	22	3	1
Proszowice 1552–1685	13		2
Wiśnicz 1629–1665	18		3
Wiśnicz 1665–1785	9		4
Żywiec 1589–1772	1		
Total	103	7	13

These situations relate to the demand for justice, the fairness of the evidence, and the reasons for the verdict. Regarding the first, "holy justice" demanded by the accuser was most often mentioned. "Fair testimony" is an example of a phrase appearing in evidentiary proceedings. It probably concerned the accuracy and truthfulness of the testimony. Most relevant are the contexts of the invocation of justice in the sentences. In several of them, justice (or "holy justice") is achieved by the conviction. The city court of Kraków in 1591 sentenced Jan Zapart to death by beheading for the murder of his wife. The sentence was issued in accordance with the applicable written law. The justification stated that the condemned "is to be punished with the sword, as holy justice teaches." The application of the law was at the same time the administration of justice.[25]

3.4 Concept of Justice v Deviation from Written Law

Dating back to the mid-14th century, the gloss to the *Ius municipale Magdeburgense* provided guidelines according to which new laws should be enacted. These considerations were addressed to city councils, although it is known that the lawmaking process in the cities of the Kingdom of Poland was more complex and involved other authorities, including the king and other city owners.[26] The *Ius municipale Magdeburgense* required compliance with

25 FIP III, no. 41, 56.

26 Stanisław Kutrzeba, "Autonomia miast i władza ustawodawcza panów miast w dawnej Rzeczpospolitej" [Autonomy of Cities and the Legislative Power of City Lords in the Old Republic of Poland], in *Księga ku czci Oswalda Balzera* [Book in Honor of Oswald Balzer], vol. II (Lwów: Zakład Narodowy im. Ossolińskich, 1925), 95.

the enacted written law.[27] This obligation was pointed out by the Supreme Court of Magdeburg Law at the Wawel Royal Castle in Kraków. In a 1469 verdict, the judges stated that if a particular city did not have its own enacted and written regulations differing from Magdeburg law, the latter could not be waived.[28] In this formulation, we can see the primacy of written law and the exclusion of the application of unwritten customary law.

Nevertheless, Polish legal practice in cities in the early modern period provides many cases of non-application of written law. This issue is very well recognised for criminal law thanks to the research of Marian Mikołajczyk[29] and Grzegorz M. Kowalski. The latter emphasised that the deviation from the written law took place not only in the sentence itself (for example, the type of punishment), but also in the proceedings before the court (for example, the gathering of evidence).[30] Moreover, the *Saxon Mirror* (*Sachsenspiegel*)[31] itself provided for situations that justified the precedence of custom over written law. General custom was in accordance with natural law, and therefore superseded written law, which would have been contrary to natural law. What is at issue here are the requirements to be met by regulations (compliance with natural law) in order to be considered law. The second type of custom, a special one, if cultivated in a given territory for a long enough period of time, could exclude the validity of earlier written law.[32]

As can be seen, the juxtaposition of the excerpt from the Magdeburg Weichbild, the ruling of the Higher Court in Kraków, the consideration of the nature of custom in the *Saxon Mirror*, and the practice of deviating from written law in criminal courts created an extremely diverse legal culture. However, current research shows that custom and customary law played an important role in Polish cities of the second half of the 16th century until the 18th century. Practice allowed a deviation from written law in favour of unwritten

27 Maciej Mikuła, *Prawodawstwo króla i sejmu dla małopolskich miast królewskich (1386–1572). Studium z dziejów rządów prawa w Polsce* [*Royal and Parliamentary Legislation for the Royal Towns of the Province of Lesser Poland (1386–1572). A Study of the History of the Rule of Law*] (Kraków: Jagiellonian University Press, 2014), 40–41.

28 Ludwik Łysiak and Karin Nehlsen-von Stryk, eds. *Decreta iuris supremi Magdeburgensis castri Cracoviensis: Die Rechtssprüche des Oberhofs des deutschen Rechts auf der Burg zu Krakau 1456-1481* (Frankfurt/M: V. Klostermann, 1995), no. 1037.

29 Marian Mikołajczyk, "'Stosując się do prawa wyraźnego...'. Podstawy prawne wyroków kryminalnych grodziskiego sądu miejskiego w latach 1702–1756" ['Following the law clearly...' The legal basis of criminal convictions Grodzisk city court during 1702–1756], *Studia Iuridica Lubliniensia* 19 (2013): 201–203.

30 Grzegorz M. Kowalski, *Zwyczaj i prawo zwyczajowe w doktrynie prawa i praktyce sądów miejskich karnych w Polsce XVI–XVIII w.* [*Custom and Customary Law in Legal Doctrine and Practice of Municipal Criminal Courts in Poland in the 16th–18th Century*] (Kraków: Jagiellonian University Press, 2013), 127ff.

31 See the English translation of this collection of medieval Saxon law: *The Saxon Mirror: A "Sachsenspiegel" of the Fourteenth Century*, trans. Maria Dobozy (Philadelphia: University of Pennsylvania Press, 1999).

32 *The Saxon Mirror*, 89–90.

customary law. As a justification for this phenomenon, the literature pointed out, among other things, the anachronistic nature of the regulations of the Magdeburg law.[33] Some of the regulations still dated back to the 13th century (*Ius municipale Magdeburgense*), and, unfortunately, a comprehensive reform of municipal law in the Kingdom of Poland, which would have allowed its modernisation, failed. Moreover, the written law was very strict, especially because of the partial reception of the provisions of the *Constitutio Criminalis Carolina* of 1532.

Deviation from the written law in sentencing consisted primarily of mitigating punishment. The sources record two ways of deviation from the strict written law. The first was at the court's own initiative. In those cases, it levied a more lenient punishment than the written law would impose. This was characteristic, for example, in the jurisprudence of the municipal court in Kraków.[34] The second way required the initiative of third parties and was either "intercession" or a merciful dispensation from the death penalty (*wyproszenie od kary śmierci*)".[35] Intercession was the intervention of credible people, respected in the community. They asked the court to commute the sentence, sometimes even to waive the punishment. In contrast, a merciful dispensation from the death penalty was often requested by relatives of the condemned. Neither intercession nor a merciful dispensation from the death penalty was regulated by written law. According to Marcin Kamler's research, about 10% of the cases before the Kraków municipal court ended in commutation of the sentence as a result of various interventions, while in Lviv it was about 2%. Based on the sample studied, the author concluded that about 4% of sentences were subject to commutation, which he believes is a small percentage.[36] Even if we accept Kamler's cautious judgement, but at the same time take into account the cases of the court's imposition of lenient punishments contrary to the written law, in my opinion their joint share in the total of cases decided is already significant.

The collected sources contain numerous cases of deviation from written law, but only six judgements allow us to observe how the court used the argument of justice in a situation of deviation from written law.

33 Mikołajczyk, "Stosując się do prawa wyraźnego...," 202.

34 Marian Mikołajczyk, *Proces kryminalny w miastach Małopolski XVI–XVIII wieku* [*A Criminal Trial in Towns of Małopolska Region between the 16th and 18th Centuries*], Prace naukowe Uniwersytetu Śląskiego w Katowicach, 2979 (Katowice: Wydawnictwo Uniwersytetu Śląskiego, 2013), 476.

35 Exceptionally, the mitigation of an already imposed sentence was carried out by the court on its own initiative or at the request of the convicted person. Mikołajczyk, *Proces kryminalny*, 522–523.

36 Marcin Kamler, "Nadzwyczajne złagodzenia kar dla przestępców pospolitych w dużych miastach Korony w drugiej połowie XVI i pierwszej połowie XVII wieku" [Extraordinary Mitigations of Punishments for Common Criminals in the Large Cities of the Crown in the Second Half of the 16th and First Half of the 17th Centuries], *Czasopismo Prawno-Historyczne* 59/2 (2007): 189–190.

A. Deviation from written law: court's initiative. Bartłomiej Groicki (1519/1534–1605), a Kraków lawyer and writer,[37] was the author of, among other things, *Ten postępek wybran jest z praw cesarskich...* (*This Proceeding is Chosen from the Imperial Laws...*). That work was his excerpt from the *Constitutio Criminalis Carolina* of 1532 and, along with his other studies, was repeatedly printed and circulated in courts and bourgeois houses.[38] Article 80 of the *Proceeding*[39] was cited in the justifications for sentences. It described the crime of infanticide for which the punishment was to be buried alive and pierced with a stake. Alternatively, the punishment of drowning was allowed, which should be preceded by tormenting the body with kindling tongs. I mention this provision because infanticide cases were not rare.[40] In Wiśnicz, a small town about 50 kilometers southeast of Kraków, there were two verdicts in cases of infanticide where the female guilty parties were sentenced to death by beheading – in 1658[41] and 1773.[42] Records of other cases in the Wiśnicz criminal records prove that the punishment specified in Article 80 was known

37 Lesław Pauli, "Die polnische Literatur des Magdeburger Rechts im 16. Jahrhundert," in *Studien zur Geschichte des sächsisch-magdeburgischen Rechts in Deutschland und Polen*, Rechtshistorische Reihe, Bd. 10, eds. Dietmar Willoweit and Winfried Schich (Frankfurt am Main–Bern–Cirencester: Lang, 1980), 150–157; Grzegorz M. Kowalski, *Bartłomiej Groicki, prawnik polskiego odrodzenia: wystawa w 400-setną rocznicę śmierci, Biblioteka Jagiellońska 5-29 kwietnia 2005* [*Bartłomiej Groicki – A Jurist of the Polish Enlightenment: Special Exhibition on the 400th Centenary of His Death, Jagiellonian Library, April 5–12, 2005*] (Kraków: Księgarnia Akademicka, 2005), 11–13.

38 Karol Koranyi, "Wstęp" [Introduction], in Barłomiej Groicki, *Porządek sądów i spraw miejskich prawa majdeburskiego w Koronie Polskiej* [*Order of Courts and Municipal Affairs under the Magdeburg Law in the Polish Crown*], ed. Karol Koranyi (Warsaw: Wydawnictwo Prawnicze, 1953), XI–XII. Purchases for the needs of the chancellery in the towns of Lublin Province are confirmed by the town records of expenditures (J. Łosowski, *Kancelarie miast*, 203).

39 Bartłomiej Groicki, *Ten postępek wybran jest z praw cesarskich...* [This Proceeding Is Chosen from the Imperial Laws...], eds. Bartosz Gałucha and Maciej Mikuła, Kraków 2020. Accessed April 2, 2024. https://iura.uj.edu.pl/dlibra/publication/1281/edition/612/content?ref=desc. Infanticide cases in the jurisprudence of the Vistula court are analysed in G.M. Kowalski, *Zwyczaj i prawo zwyczajowe*, 152.

40 Wacław Rosa, *Przestępstwa z użyciem przemocy w świetle akt sądów kryminalnych wybranych miast dawnego województwa krakowskiego od połowy XVI do XVIII wieku* [*Violent Crimes in the Light of the Records of the Criminal Courts of Selected Cities of the Former Cracow Province from the Mid-16th to the 18th Century*] (Kraków: AFM Publishing House, 2023), 148–153; there is also earlier literature on the subject, in particular: Marcin Kamler, "Dzieciobójstwo w miastach Korony w drugiej połowie XVI i pierwszej połowie XVII wieku" [Infanticide in the Cities of the Crown in the Second Half of the Sixteenth and First Half of the Seventeenth Centuries], *Czasopismo Prawno-Historyczne* 38/1 (1986): 171–172; Małgorzata Delimata-Proch, "Cudzołóstwo w praktyce prawa miejskiego Rzeczypospolitej na przykładzie „Księgi czarnej złoczyńców sądu kryminalnego w Wiśniczu" (koniec XVII–XVIII wieku)" [Adultery in the Polish Urban Law Presented on the Example of "Acta Nigra Maleficorum Wisniciae" (from the End of the 17th and the 18th Century)], *Czasopismo Prawno-Historyczne* 69/1 (2017): 177.

41 Wiśnicz I, 1658, no. 38, 195.

42 Wiśnicz II, 15.03.1773, no. 31, 100.

and imposed.[43] Thus, the court departed from the written law in both cases by imposing the ordinary death penalty. Significantly, in the reasons for the second one, the court made it clear that the verdict was lawful and just.

B. Deviation from written law: intercession and merciful dispensation from the death penalty. In 1722, in one case, the court in Wiśnicz ruled out the possibility of mitigation of punishment due to the intervention of third parties. In accordance with "holy justice," adulterers and people who committed infanticide were sentenced to death.[44] In the same year,[45] the Wiśnicz court – also in a case of adultery and infanticide – sentenced a man to death, clearly emphasising that this was right according to the law and holy justice. However, the verdict was changed due to the intervention of "worthy" people, with a retraction of some of the man's incriminating testimony by his partner (she was sentenced to death).[46] Reading the transcript of this case gives the compelling impression that, although the custom of leniency was followed, judges were not in favour of it. The court in Wiśnicz did not rule consistently. It is possible that who was requesting the change of sentence was important.

The discrepancy between a "just sentence" and a lenient one was expressed in the justification of a ruling issued in 1784, also in Wiśnicz. A man accused of having sex with a cow was sentenced to death. As a result of an appeal to the Supreme Court of Appeals in Lviv, "the Wiśnicz Magistrate's Court, having learned of such a terrible deed that he should die by death [sic!], nevertheless taking into account his years, and acting more by the way of mercy than by the way of justice [...]" substituted the death penalty with the punishment of flogging.[47] Of course, this was already a different era. Wiśnicz was within the borders of the Austrian Empire and one can see a move towards leniency of punishment consistent with the concepts of humanitarianism. We can surmise that this radical opposition of justice to mercy stemmed both from dissatisfaction with the court whose original verdict had been overturned and from disapproval of a punishment that was too lenient. Based on the above examples, one might assume that the court in Wiśnicz was inconsistent concerning what it considered just when deciding to mitigate a sentence as a result of third-party intervention. This, however, is not true. One can cite the example of a verdict in which the conversion of a criminal sentence (*criminaliter*) into a civil one (*civiliter*) was considered justifiable by the court. In that 1653

43 Wiśnicz II, 17.06.1722, no. 26, 81. The ignorance of the written law by many judges was pointed out by Mikołajczyk, "Stosując się do prawa wyraźnego...," 203–204.

44 Wiśnicz II, 17.06.1722, no. 26, 81.

45 This was pointed out by Grzegorz M. Kowalski examining customary law in cities: Kowalski, *Zwyczaj i prawo zwyczajowe*, 152.

46 Wiśnicz II, 30.09.1722, no. 27, 83.

47 Wiśnicz II, 22.09.1784/26.01.1785, no. 42, 155. "[...] Sąd Magistracki Wiśnicki w tak strasznym uczynku poznawszy, iżby śmiercią ginąć powinien, jednakowoż zważając na lata jego, a bardziej postępując sobie bardziej drogą łaski, niż drogą sprawiedliwości [...]."

decision, the court, administering what it believed to be holy justice, spared a thief's life and ordered him to be flogged and banished instead.[48]

As it turns out, the reference to "holy justice" legitimised opposing situations: adherence to the written law, but also deviation from the written law in favour of more lenient punishment. A position strongly opposed to deviation from the written law was also expressed, as well as the idea that such a deviation would be a judicial mercy, but not the administration of justice.

3.5 Conclusion

The concept of justice was referred to in the justifications of normative acts, in legal literature, and in the records of judicial practice in municipal books. Practitioners of municipal law were not unfamiliar with the classical meaning of the term – handwritten notes in the margins of the official edition of the collection of laws in the Statute of Jan Łaski confirm practitioners' interest in the meaning of the term "justice." "Justice" and often "holy justice" appeared in city records in three main contexts, i.e., in the accuser's complaint, in evidentiary proceedings, and in the justifications of judgements (altogether in more than 10% of the records). The small number (in just over 1% of the entries) of instances where justice was mentioned in verdicts is significant because it was probably due to the widespread recognition that sentencing itself constituted the performance of justice. The Wiśnicz sources provided an opportunity to go beyond simply stating that the concept was mentioned in verdicts. The chronological span of Wiśnicz judgements is so large and their number so small that indicating any regularity is impossible. Instead, it is possible to note the variety of contexts and functions of mentioning the concept of justice.

Based on the source material, we can conclude that:

- the reference to this concept in the sentences of city criminal courts was rare;
- the application of unwritten customary law incompatible with written law did not usually involve additional axiological justification, including reference to the concept of justice;
- once the axiological justification was made by referring to the concept of justice, it supported completely different positions: the compatibility of judgements with the written law, as well as deviations from the written law.

In jurisprudence, justice was carried out through the application of municipal law, which was legitimised by its compliance with natural law and divine law. Testimony was found supporting the belief that deviation from unquestioned law should not be considered just but instead, at most, a judicial mercy. On the other hand, however, in cases of deviation from written law, either on the initiative or with the approval of judges, justice was cited as legitimising such actions. I do not think that such cases should be classified as instrumental use of this

48 Wiśnicz I, 1653, no. 34, 166.

concept. On the contrary, it was a justification for action in situations in which, in the opinion of the judges, the application of written law – due to, for example, its excessive severity or archaisms – would be unjust. In this context, justice was an overriding value[49] in the system of early modern Polish municipal law and was invoked in a subsidiary manner in justifications of pragmatic and common-sense decisions in the municipal courts of old Poland.

References

Primary sources

Archival primary sources

National Archives in Kraków, Akta Miasta Proszowice [Document of the City of Proszowice], no. 29/121: Variae civitates et villae, shelfmark 165.

Old prints and incunabula

Commune incliti Poloniae Regni privilegium constitutionum et indultuum publicitus decretorum approbatorumque..., Cracoviae, MDVI.
Commune incliti Poloniae Regni privilegium... in: Jagiellonian Library, St. Dr. Cim. 8004.
Commune incliti Poloniae Regni privilegium... in: National Library in Warsaw, SD.XVI.F.432.
Commune incliti Poloniae Regni privilegium... in: Polish Academy of Sciences Kórnik Library, Cim.F.4119.
Jaskier, Mikołaj. *Iuris Municipalis Maideburgensis Liber vulgo Weichbild nuncupatur....* Kraków: Hieronim Wietor, 1535.
Remissorium mit sambt dem weichbilde und lehenrecht, [Eike von Repgow. *Sachsenspiegel: Lehnrecht.* Add: *Weichbild.* Dietrich von Bocksdorf: *Remissorium*]. Augsburg: Johann Schönsperger, 1499.
Zobel, Christoph. *Magdeburgisch und Sechsisch Weichbild und Lehenrecht, auffs new an vielen orten....* Leipzig, MDLV.

Edited sources

Groicki, Bartłomiej. *Porządek sądów i spraw miejskich prawa majdeburskiego w Koronie Polskiej [Order of Courts and Municipal Affairs under the Magdeburg Law in the Polish Crown].* Edited by Karol Koranyi. Warsaw: Wydawnictwo Prawnicze, 1953.
Groicki, Bartłomiej. *Ten postępek wybran jest z praw cesarskich...* [*This Proceeding is Chosen from the Imperial Laws...*]. Edited by Bartosz Gałucha and Maciej Mikuła. Kraków, 2020. Accessed April 2, 2024. https://iura.uj.edu.pl/dlibra/publication/1281/edition/612/content?ref=desc.
Kosiński, Rafał, ed. *Księga złoczyńców albo akta sądu koniecznego gajonego żywieckiego z lat 1589–1782* [*The Book of Villains, or the Records of the Necessary Court of Żywiec from 1589 to 1782*]. Żywiec: Towarzystwo Naukowe Żywieckie, 2014.

49 Roman A. Tokarczyk, "Sprawiedliwość jako naczelna wartość prawa" [Justice as the Principal Value of Law], *Annales Universitatis Mariae Curie-Skłodowska Lublin*, LXVI, Section G (1997): 161, 164.

Lauxmin, Sigismundus. *De iure et iustitia*. Edited by Krzysztof Bekieszczuk, Steffen Huber, Konrad Kokoszkiewicz, Živilė Pabijutaitė, Maria Poszepczynska, and Anna Treter. Warsaw: Wydawnictwo Naukowe Sub Lupa, 2023.

Łysiak, Ludwik, and Karin Nehlsen-von Stryk, eds. *Decreta iuris supremi Magdeburgensis castri Cracoviensis. Die Rechtssprüche des Oberhofs des deutschen Rechts auf der Burg zu Krakau 1456–1481*. Frankfurt/M: V. Klostermann, 1995.

Mikuła, Maciej, ed. *Księga kryminalna miasta Dobczyc 1699–1737* [*Criminal Records of the City of Dobczyce 1699–1737*], Fontes Iuris Polonici. Seria: prawo miejskie, vol. II. Kraków: Jagiellonian University Press, 2013.

Mikuła, Maciej, ed. *Księga ławników myślenickich z lat 1700–1725* [*Jurors' Records of Myślenice 1700–1725*], Fontes Iuris Polonici. Seria: prawo miejskie, vol. 8. Kraków: Jagiellonian University Press, 2022. https://iura.uj.edu.pl/dlibra/publication/3304#structure (accessed on 25 March 2024).

Piekosiński, Franciszek, ed. *Akta sądu kryminalnego kresu muszyńskiego 1647–1765* [*Records of the Criminal Court of the Muszyna Kres 1647–1765*]. Kraków: Akademia Umiejętności, 1889.

The Saxon Mirror: A "Sachsenspiegel" of the Fourteenth Century. Translated by Maria Dobozy. University of Pennsylvania Press, 1999.

Szczerbic, Paweł, ed. *Ius Municipale to jest prawo miejskie Majdeburskie...* [*Ius municipale i.e. municipal Magdeburg law...*]. Edited by Grzegorz Kowalski, Bibliotheca Iagiellonica. Fontes et Studia, 20. Kraków: Księgarnia Akademicka, 2011.

Uruszczak, Wacław, and Irena Dwornicka, eds. *Księga złoczyńców sądu kryminalnego w Wiśniczu (1629–1665)* [*Book of Villains of the Criminal Court in Wiśnicz (1629–1665)*]. Kraków: Collegium Columbinum, 2003.

Uruszczak, Wacław, Bartłomiej Migda, Anna Karabowicz, and Adam Uruszczak, eds. *Księga czarna złoczyńców sądu kryminalnego w* Wiśniczu *(1665–1785)* [*Black Book of Villains of the Criminal Court in Wiśnicz (1665–1785)*]. Kraków: Archiwum Państwowe, 2010.

Uruszczak, Wacław, Maciej Mikuła, Krzysztof Fokt, and Anna Karabowicz, eds. *Księga kryminalna miasta Krakowa z lat 1589–1604* [*Criminal Records of the City of Cracow from 1589–1604*], Fontes Iuris Polonici. Seria: prawo miejskie, vol. III. Kraków: Societas Vistulana, 2016.

Uruszczak, Wacław, Maciej Mikuła, and Anna Karabowicz, eds. *Księga kryminalna miasta Krakowa z lat 1554–1625* [*Criminal Records of the City of Cracow from 1554–1625*], Fontes Iuris Polonici. Seria: prawo miejskie, vol. I. Kraków: Jagiellonian University Press, 2013.

Uruszczak, Wacław, Maciej Mikuła, and Krzysztof Fokt, eds. *Księgi kryminalne miasta Krakowa z lat 1630–1633, 1679–1690* [*Criminal Records from Kraków City from 1630–1633, 1679–1690*], Fontes Iuris Polonici. Seria: prawo miejskie, vol. IV. Kraków: Societas Vistulana, 2016.

Secondary studies

Bukowska, Krystyna. *Orzecznictwo krakowskich sądów wyższych w sporach o nieruchomości miejskie (XVI–XVIII w.). Studium z historii prawa rzymskiego w Polsce* [*The Caselaw of Cracow Higher Courts Concerning Disputes over Real Property in Towns (16th-18th Century): A Study in the History of Roman Law in Poland*]. Warsaw: Państwowe Wydawnictwo Naukowe, 1967.

Carls, Wieland. "Rechtsquellen Sächsisch-magdeburgischen Rechts." In Inge Bily, Wieland Carls, and Katalin Gönczi, *Sächsisch-magdeburgisches Recht in Polen.*

Untersuchungen zur Geschichte des Rechts und seiner Sprache, Ivs Saxonico-Maidebvrgense in Oriente 2, 86–88. Berlin: De Gruyter, 2011.

Corpus Academicum Cracoviense (CAC). "Paweł Szczerbic of Krakow (Id: 2000313)." Accessed April 4, 2024. http://cac.historia.uj.edu.pl/osoba/2000313_Pawe%C5%82_Szczerbic_z_Krakowa.

Delimata-Proch, Maria. "Cudzołóstwo w praktyce prawa miejskiego Rzeczypospolitej na przykładzie „Księgi czarnej złoczyńców sądu kryminalnego w Wiśniczu" (koniec XVII–XVIII wieku)" [Adultery in the Polish Urban Law Presented on the Example of "Acta Nigra Maleficorum Wisniciae" (from the End of the 17th and the 18th Century)]. *Czasopismo Prawno-Historyczne* 69, no. 1 (2017): 175–92.

Górski, Kacper. "Wizerunek sędziego w polskich utworach literackich i pisanie politycznych XVI i XVII stulecia" [The Image of a Judge as Illustrated in Works of Polish Poets and Political Writers in the 16th–17th Centuries]. *Krakowskie Studia z Historii Państwa i Prawa* 13, no. 4 (2020): 469–89.

Kamińska, Krystyna. *Lokacje miast na prawie Magdeburskim na ziemiach polskich do 1370 r. Studium historyczno-prawne* [*Incorporation of Towns under Magdeburg Law in Poland until 1370: A Study in the History of Law*]. Toruń: Uniwersytet Mikołaja Kopernika, 1990.

Kamler, Marcin. "Dzieciobójstwo w miastach Korony w drugiej połowie XVI i pierwszej połowie XVII wieku" [Infanticide in the Cities of the Crown in the Second Half of the Sixteenth and First Half of the Seventeenth Centuries]. *Czasopismo Prawno-Historyczne* 38, no. 1 (1986): 171–84.

Kamler, Marcin. "Nadzwyczajne złagodzenia kar dla przestepców pospolitych w dużych miastach Korony w drugiej połowie XVI i pierwszej połowie XVII wieku" [Extraordinary Mitigations of Punishments for Common Criminals in the Large Cities of the Crown in the Second Half of the 16th and First Half of the 17th Centuries]. *Czasopismo Prawno-Historyczne* 59, no. 2 (2007): 187–203.

Koranyi, Karol. "Wstęp [Introduction]." In Bartłomiej Groicki, *Porządek sądów i spraw miejskich prawa majdeburskiego w Koronie Polskiej* [*Order of Courts and Municipal Affairs under the Magdeburg Law in the Polish Crown*], edited by Karol Koranyi, XI–XII. Warsaw: Wydawnictwo Prawnicze, 1953.

Kowalski, Grzegorz M. *Bartłomiej Groicki, prawnik polskiego odrodzenia: wystawa w 400-setną rocznicę śmierci, Biblioteka Jagiellońska 5-29 kwietnia 2005* [*Bartłomiej Groicki – A Jurist of the Polish Enlightenment: Special Exhibition on the 400th Centenary of His Death, Jagiellonian Library, April 5–12, 2005*]. Kraków: Księgarnia Akademicka, 2005.

Kowalski, Grzegorz M. "'Persony sądowi przynależące, jakie mają być'. Jurysta doskonały na podstawie wybranych dzieł dawnych polskich pisarzy-prawników" ['The Persons Affiliated with the Court. The Requirements that They Should Fulfill.' The Perfect Jurist as Outlined on the Basis of the Selected Works Written by Jurists of the Old Poland]. *Krakowskie Studia z Historii Państwa i Prawa* 3 (2010): 51–62.

Kowalski, Grzegorz M. *Zwyczaj i prawo zwyczajowe w doktrynie prawa i praktyce sądów miejskich karnych w Polsce XVI–XVIII w.* [*Custom and Customary Law in Legal Doctrine and Practice of Municipal Criminal Courts in Poland in the 16th–18th Century*]. Krakow: Jagiellonian University Press, 2013.

Kutrzeba, Stanisław. "Autonomia miast i władza ustawodawcza panów miast w dawnej Rzeczpospolitej" [Autonomy of Cities and the Legislative Power of City Lords in the Old Republic of Poland]. In *Księga ku czci Oswalda Balzera* [*Book in Honor of Oswald Balzer*], vol. II, 95. Lwów: Zakład Narodowy im. Ossolińskich, 1925.

Kutrzeba, Stanisław. *Historia źródeł dawnego prawa polskiego* [*History of the Sources of Old Polish Law*], vol. 2. Lwów-Warszawa-Kraków: Zakład Narodowy im. Ossolinskich, 1926.

Łosowski, Janusz. *Kancelarie miast szlacheckich województwa lubelskiego od XV do XVIII wieku* [*Chancelleries of Noble Towns of Lublin Province from the 15th to the 18th century*]. Lublin: Agencja Wydawniczo-Handlowa Antoni Dudek, 1997.

Mikołajczyk, Marian. "'Stosując się do prawa wyraźnego...'. Podstawy prawne wyroków kryminalnych grodziskiego sądu miejskiego w latach 1702–1756" ['Following the Law Clearly...' The Legal Basis of Criminal Convictions Grodzisk City Court during 1702–1756]. *Studia Iuridica Lubliniensia* 19 (2013): 201–16.

Mikołajczyk, Marian. "O miejskich księgach czarnych i ich wydawaniu uwag kilka. W związku z edycją Acta maleficorum Wisniciae. Księga złoczyńców sądu kryminalnego w Wiśniczu (1629–1665), oprac. i wyd. W. Uruszczak, I. Dwornicka, 2004" [A Few Remarks on the Municipal "Black Books" and Their Publication. On the Edition of Acta Maleficorum Wisniciae. Book of Villains of the Criminal Court in Wiśnicz (1629–1665), edited by W. Uruszczak, I. Dwornicka, 2004]. *Czasopismo Prawno-Historyczne* 57, no. 2 (2005): 413–24.

Mikołajczyk, Marian. *Proces kryminalny w miastach Małopolski XVI–XVIII wieku* [*A Criminal Trial in Towns of Małopolska Region between the 16th and 18th Centuries*], Prace naukowe Uniwersytetu Śląskiego w Katowicach, 2979. Katowice: Wydawnictwo Uniwersytetu Śląskiego, 2013.

Mikuła, Maciej. *Municipal Magdeburg Law (Ius municipale Magdeburgense) in Late Medieval Poland. A Study on the Evolution and Adaptation of Law, Medieval Law and Its Practice*, vol. 30. Leiden and Boston: Brill, 2021.

Mikuła, Maciej. *Prawodawstwo króla i sejmu dla małopolskich miast królewskich (1386–1572). Studium z dziejów rządów prawa w Polsce* [*Royal and Parliamentary Legislation for the Royal Towns of the Province of Lesser Poland (1386–1572). A Study of the History of the Rule of Law*]. Kraków: Jagiellonian University Press, 2014.

Mikuła, Maciej. "Praworządność, sprawiedliwość, słuszność. O kulturze prawnej w sądach małych miast u progu XVIII stulecia" [The Rule of Law, Justice, Equity: on Legal Culture in the Courts of Small Towns at the Dawn of the Eighteenth Century]. In *Prawo i kultura: Księga jubileuszowa dedykowana Profesorowi Markowi Wąsowiczowi [Law and Culture: A Book Dedicated to Professor Marek Wąsowicz]*, edited by Jarosław Kuisz and Anna Rosner, 157–68. Warsaw: Wydawnictwo Naukowe Scholar, 2022.

Pauli, Lesław. "Die polnische Literatur des Magdeburger Rechts im 16. Jahrhundert." In *Studien zur Geschichte des sächsisch-magdeburgischen Rechts in Deutschland und Polen*, Rechtshistorische Reihe, Bd. 10, edited by Dietmar Willoweit and Winfried Schich, 150–57. Frankfurt am Main-Bern-Cirencester: Lang, 1980.

Rosa, Wacław. *Przestępstwa z użyciem przemocy w świetle akt sądów kryminalnych wybranych miast dawnego województwa krakowskiego od połowy XVI do XVIII wieku* [*Violent Crimes in the Light of the Records of the Criminal Courts of Selected Cities of the Former Cracow Province from the Mid-16th to the 18th Century*]. Kraków: AFM Publishing House, 2023.

Tokarczyk, Roman A. "Sprawiedliwość jako naczelna wartość prawa" [Justice as the Principal Value of Law]. *Annales Universitatis Mariae Curie-Skłodowska Lublin* LXVI, Section G (1997): 137–67.

4 Good Morals as the Yardstick of Cartels' Validity in Hungarian Private Law at the Turn of the 20th Century[1]

Norbert Varga

4.1 Introduction

The process of codification of Hungarian private law and the lack of a written code resulted in the fact that it was primarily case law and customary law that determined the development of Hungarian private law even in the period between the two world wars. This does not mean, of course, that there were no legislative acts in the field of Hungarian private law (e.g., the Trade Act of 1875 and the Marriage Act of 1891), but the fact remains that there was no uniform code of private law. In order to examine the history of Hungarian private law, it is essential to analyse the relevant literature and, in the absence of legislation, the rulings issued by the courts, especially the Curia (Hungarian Supreme Court), in the context of their unifying efforts. Without relevant legislation, cartels were considered to be unfair because of restrictions on freedom of competition. This chapter will first describe the system of principles of private law, basically the principles of justice and equity, as well as the social norms that are closely related to them and which are the yardsticks of private law. In doing so, this chapter will pay special attention to the concept of good morals, on the basis of which – in the absence of statutory regulations – cartel agreements could be found to be valid or invalid by the Curia. With no applicable legislation, a true picture of the validity of cartel agreements can be obtained only by systematically examining judicial practice. Therefore, the study will present the judicial practice on cartel agreements in the period before the first Hungarian Cartel Act of 1931 entered into force. The most important question is what judges could do with agreements regulating economic competition before the entry into force of this act in 1931.

1 This research has been supported by the National Research, Development and Innovation Fund of the Ministry of Innovation and Technology (Hungary) and financed by the K 21 grant programme (project title "The Development of Private Law between the Two World Wars," K 138618).

DOI: 10.4324/9781003654131-6

In particular, on what basis could the Curia decide whether or not agreements regulating economic competition were valid? As will be shown, in this respect, what judges could do, in the absence of a written code, was to go back to the principles that had appeared early in Hungarian private law and apply them. The period under examination is the end of the second half of the 19th century and the first half of the 20th century between the two world wars. The classification of cartels by the courts requires an examination of the 19th-century history of cartel agreements.

4.2 Brief Description of Hungarian Private Law Principles

The point of departure for our topic is the examination of the principles of Hungarian private law. This is still missing in the majority of 19th- and 20th-century summaries of Hungarian private law.[2] There was no systematic debate and discussions of the principles applicable in particular contexts can be found only in the relevant sections within different areas of private law. A comprehensive and one of the most thorough presentations of the principles of Hungarian private law was published in the monumental work of law professor Károly Szladits (1871–1956). It is in the general part of his six-volume work titled *A magánjog fogalma, fejlődése és tudománya* (*The Concept, Development and Science of Private Law*) that Károly Szladits discussed the topics of justice and equity. These two principles, however, can be understood only in the context of the system of ideas and norms prevailing in Hungarian private law at that time. The subchapter titled "Guiding Ideas in Private Law" included an analysis of reasonableness, justice, and legal certainty.[3] Professor Szladits stated as follows:

2 Ármin Fodor, ed., *Magyar magánjog. Általános rész, Személyi jog* [*Hungarian private law. General part, Personal law*] (Budapest: Signer és Wolfner, 1899); Dezső Márkus, *Magyar magánjog mai érvényben: Törvények, rendeletek, szokásjog, joggyakorlat. I. kötet. Jogforrások, személyjog, családjog* [*Hungarian private law in force today: Laws, Regulations, Customary law, Case Law. Volume I. Legal sources, Personal law, Family law*] (Budapest: Grill Károly Könyvkiadóvállalata, 1906); Lajos Vadász, *Magánjogunk főbb elvei és az új jogfejlődés. I. kötet* [*The main principles of our private law and the new legal developments. Volume I*] (Szeged: Endrényi Lajos Nyomda, 1926); Andor Sárffy, *Magánjog alapismeretek* [*Basic knowledge of private law*] (Budapest: Zemplén Vármegye, s.l. 1933); László Villányi, *A magyar magánjog rövid tankönyve* [*A short textbook of Hungarian private law*] (Budapest: Grill Károly Könyvkiadóvállalata, 1941); Bálint Kolozsváry, *A magyar magánjog tankönyve* [*Textbook on Hungarian private law*] (Budapest: Grill Károly Könyvkiadóvállalata, 1911).

3 Károly Szladits, "A magánjog fogalma, fejlődése és tudománya" [*The concept, development and science of private law*], in *Magyar magánjog: Első kötet: Általános rész, Személyi jog* [*Hungarian private law. Volume 1: General part, Personal law*], ed. Károly Szladits (Budapest: Grill Károly Könyvkiadóvállalata, 1941), 40; József Benke, *Bevezetés a magyar magánjog általános elveibe* [*Introduction to the general principles of Hungarian private law*] (Budapest: HVGOrac, 2019), 53–74.

> For the most part, the laws that have developed are only frameworks; they hold society together with iron tires, but they provide only the basic framework of the private legal order. These frameworks are filled with ever-changing content as life continuously evolves. It is this rich variety of life that must be adapted to the frameworks. This is the task of all those who deal with the law in any way, whether in the field of legislature, the application of law, or jurisprudence.[4]

According to Szladits, there were three basic ideas that should be the leitmotifs of Hungarian private law. These are reasonableness, justice, and legal certainty. The tenets of reasonableness were not arbitrary commands demanding blind obedience. Law seeks to establish reasonableness; in this respect, its tenets must be understood and applied in accordance with their purpose. In many cases, Szladits goes back to one of the most important sources of Hungarian private law in the late feudal era, István Werbőczy's (1465–1541) *Tripartitum* (printed in 1517), for an interpretation of the principles of private law. The law, says Werbőczy after St. Thomas Aquinas, "est ordinatio rationis ad bonum commune."[5] Furthermore, "finis vero juris civilis est bonum publicum," i.e., the purpose of law is the common good.[6] Therefore, all legislation must be presumed to be intended to achieve a rational result.

Szladits also referred to no less a Hungarian statesman than Baron József Eötvös (1813–1871), the first Hungarian minister of education: "do not believe in an idea which your heart contradicts,"[7] which Károly Szladits interpreted as: "do not believe in an explanation of law that contradicts reason."[8] Szladits relied on his literary erudition as he also referred to Goethe. Goethe accused law of turning reason into nonsense ("*Vernunft wird Unsinn*"), whereas the lawyer's noblest calling is to make certain that this does not happen.[9] This is also what the well-known proverb, "summum ius summa iniuria," hints at. This saying is not intended to mean that the law should be applied literally

4 Szladits, "A magánjog fogalma, fejlődése és tudománya," 40.

5 Istvan Werbőzcy, *Werbőzcy Hármaskönyve* [*Werbőczy's Tripartitum*] (Pecs: Pécsi Szikra Kiadó, 1989), Prol. tit. 6 § 11. In connection with morals, Dezső Márkus also referred to Werbőczy. Márkus, *Magyar magánjog mai érvényben*, 3; Vadász, *Magánjogunk főbb elvei*, 5; Artur Meszlényi, *Magyar magánjog. Törvények, rendeletek, szokásjog, joggyakorlat, magánjogi törvénykönyv szövegével és rendszerében* [*Hungarian private law. Laws, Decrees, Customary law, Case law, text and system of the private law code*] (Budapest: Grill Károly Könyvkiadóvállalata, 1928), 28.

6 Istvan Werbőzcy, *Werbőzcy Hármaskönyve* [*Werbőczy's Tripartitum*] (Pecs: Pécsi Szikra Kiadó, 1989), Prol. tit. 10 § 3.

7 The following reference is found in a letter written by József Eötvös to Pál Gyulai on 12 September 1863: "Thoughts offered to the memory of my mother. The motto: 'do not believe in an idea which your heart contradicts' (from my mother's letters). In my mother's letter, this is written as follows: *Glaube keinen Gedanken, dem dein Herz widerspricht*" In: József Eötvös, *Levelek* [Letters]. Accessed June 4, 2024. https://mek.oszk.hu/05400/05480/05480.htm.

8 Szladits, "A magánjog fogalma, fejlődése és tudománya," 41.

9 Szladits, "A magánjog fogalma, fejlődése és tudománya," 41.

even if it is manifestly unjust; on the contrary, it is intended to warn against overinterpreting blind application of provisions of law.

Szladits said that justice is, in general, the ideal of private law. Justice is the achievement of a social order that best serves the universal purpose of society and thus of human existence. It is the task of justice to remedy breaches of interest by applying an equal measure, proportionately, by subordinating the greater interest to the lesser one. Ignác Frank (1788–1850), royal counsellor, professor of law, and member of the Hungarian Academy of Science, called private law "the law of distributive justice,"[10] that is, the branch of law which "distributes" conflicting private spheres between the parties concerned in accordance with justice. Frank's formulation also appeared in the work of Lajos Vadász (1881–1948) on private law, where he drew attention to the importance of the application of the law. "In concrete cases, therefore, it is necessary to consider whether it is compatible with the principles of distributive justice and fairness, as well as with the moral conception of the common man, to introduce the dead letters of the law into pulsating, vigorous life, when the simple layman's logic and pure heart cry out against it."[11]

Károly Szladits said that justice, as a guiding principle, has always played a major role in the application of the law. A rule of private law may have had different meanings and a rule formulated in general terms may have had different applications and interpretations in particular cases. According to Szladits, these doubts must be resolved by applying the idea of justice in the context of legal interpretation in order to determine the correct meaning of a specific legal rule. This guiding role of justice was not a mere wish of natural law, but a command of statutory law itself. István Werbőczy, in several of his theses in *Tripartitum* (for example: Prol. tit. 1–2. 4), identified justice as the guiding principle for judges when ruling on a specific case. This is confirmed in many statements of principle in our judicial practice, which always set justice (and its concrete manifestation: fairness) as the guiding principle for reaching the right decision.[12]

Justice requires taking into account the individual circumstances of a case, whereas legal certainty, on the contrary, requires the standardisation of the variations of life, according to Szladits. Legal certainty is itself a requirement of justice. Above all, the aspect of legal certainty places various demands on legislators. First and foremost, it required the construction of a legal system that describes legal institutions as precisely and concretely as possible. This was the aim of systematic codification. Legal certainty also required uniformity

10 "Distributive justice, as it distributes to everyone his own" – Ignácz Frank, *A közigazság törvénye Magyarhonban. I. rész* [*The law of public administration in Hungary. Part I*] (Buda: Magyar Királyi Egyetem betűivel, 1845), 17; Attila Menyhárd, *A jóerkölcsbe ütköző szerződések* [*Contracts that are contrary to good moral*] (Budapest: Gondolat, 2004), 26.

11 Vadász, *Magánjogunk főbb elvei*, 43.

12 Szladits, "A magánjog fogalma, fejlődése és tudománya," 42–43.

in the application of the law and the creation of legal unity. Therefore, case law aimed at preserving legal unity has been an important safeguard of legal certainty.[13]

From the point of view of the legal assessment of cartel agreements, it is more important to analyse the so-called extra-legal social norms that are found within the rules referring to the extra-legal axioms.

A group of life relations governed by law often appears so richly varied in its concrete form that a specific provision of law cannot cope with it. In such cases, the law refers to some other normative principle in society as a substitute. The social norm thus invoked therefore becomes the indirect source of the law. According to Károly Szladits, they can subsequently serve as such normative principles.

The rules of morality (good morals) generally declared a legal transaction having immoral content as null and void. Social custom prevailed, especially in the commercial sphere; in an even narrower sense, it was to be understood as business custom, which was the basic value of all industrial and commercial life. Customary practice is not yet law, but it may be the basis for the development of customary law. However, custom, as it has developed in economic life, is an excellent means of explaining and supplementing people's values and of being a yardstick for proper conduct (e.g., the performance of an obligation). Often it was the combination of a moral requirement and custom that provided a basis for indirect legal regulation. Commercial fairness and good faith are such values, in particular, that are generally accepted as the main guiding principles for the performance of obligations. They can be demonstrated in the business conduct of a party who takes into account the interest of the other party. A similar guideline was unfair conduct in business competition (Act V of 1923 on Unfair Competition). Lastly, the principle of equity (*aequitas*) should be mentioned as one of the main standards of indirect law. Equity is generally a method of reconciling conflicts of interest. It is characterised by a benevolent, lenient, humane balancing of conflicting interests. Equity in the application of rules thus ensures that the outcome is appropriate to the circumstances of the case. Equity was equalising justice itself.[14]

Bernát Besnyő (1876–1944) also analysed separately the validity of contracts that were contrary to good morals and public order in the light of the Hungarian Private Law Bill of 1928.[15] Article 973 of the proposed law

13 Szladits, "A magánjog fogalma, fejlődése és tudománya," 43–44.

14 Károly Szladits, "Jogszabálytan" [*Doctrine of the law*], in *Magyar magánjog. Első kötet: Általános rész, Személyi jog* [*Hungarian private law. Volume 1: General part, Personal law*], ed. Károly Szladits (Budapest: Grill Károly Könyvkiadóvállalata, 1941), 147–151.

15 The bill was submitted by the Minister of Justice to the National Assembly on 1 March 1928. The impending global economic crisis prevented the adoption of the proposal. The MPs also wanted Hungarian private law to prevail in the territories that had seceded after the First World War. If this proposal had been accepted, the unity of private law would have been destroyed. The MPs were still confident of the reattachment of the lost territories.

provided that a contract contrary to good morals or public order was null and void. In his view, the proposal did not define when a contract was contrary to good morals, which was a matter of judicial practice. "Judicial practice has already declared many contracts void on the grounds of ***turpis causa***, which cannot be regarded as having an immoral content or an immoral object even according to common usage, and yet they have been correctly declared void."[16] The second part of the passage cited, which also declared a contract contrary to public order as void, is important from the point of view of cartel law. The question is what can be regarded as a contract contrary to public order. Immoral transactions could be more easily identified because, from time to time and from place to place, contracts for certain purposes and for certain services were regarded by society as immoral and contrary to society's moral standards. According to Besnyő, however, the concept of a breach of public order is more difficult to formulate. He considered it inappropriate to include within this scope such contracts that were contrary to the freedom of industry or freedom of association, such as cartel agreements. In his view, the protection of public order did not mean the protection of freedom since public order was precisely a restriction of freedoms. As Besnyő stated, "Obviously, public order can only be infringed by a contract which is prohibited by and contrary to a rule of law."[17] A cartel agreement could be contrary to public order only if its conclusion was prohibited by a law or decree. In such a case, however, it would be contrary to a statutory prohibition, which would in itself be sufficient to render it invalid. In Besnyő's view, therefore, the category of contracts contrary to public order was unnecessary. Moreover, the lack of a definition of the concept created legal uncertainty.[18] A legal transaction which was expressly prohibited by law was prohibited, null and void, but one whose content was contrary to good morals and public order was also void without a specific prohibition by law.[19] In addition to good morals, Szladits also considered it important that cartel agreements were contrary to public order as well, which he defined as follows: "In particular, an agreement regulating economic competition (cartels and the like) is contrary to public order if it 'jeopardises the interests of the economy or the common good'; namely, if it regulates the production, distribution or pricing of goods to the detriment of

16 Bernát Besnyő, "A jó erkölcsbe és a közrendbe ütköző szerződések a magánjogi törvénykönyv javaslatában" [Contracts contrary to good morals and public policy in the proposal for a private law code], *Jogállam* 28, nos. 7–8 (1929): 361. See also: Antal Almási, *A tilos cselekmények a magánjogban* [*Prohibited actions in private law*] (Budapest: Grill Károly Könyvkiadóvállalata, 1907), 92.

17 Besnyő, "A jó erkölcsbe és a közrendbe," 363.

18 Besnyő, "A jó erkölcsbe és a közrendbe," 636.

19 H. Sz. (Szigfrid Holitscher?), "A tilos és a jó erkölcsbe ütköző szerződésekről [*On prohibited contracts and contracts contrary to good morals*]," *Közjegyzők Közlönye* 11, no. 4 (1908): 113. Cf. Lajos Vadász, ed., *Magánjogi törvénykönyvünk és elő tételes jogunk. 2. Kötet* [*Our private law code and our preliminary law. Volume 2*] (Budapest: Attila Nyomda, 1930), 15.

the consuming public or the producers (either within the trade or other entrepreneurs) in a manner not justified by the economic situation."[20]

Contracts contrary to good morals or the law must be placed within the scope of what is legally permissible and possible in the context of legal transactions.[21] János Suhayda (1818–1881) also stated that "the condition of being contrary to law or good morals renders the legal transaction null and void."[22] Andor Sárffy (1889–1951) also emphasised this in his discussion of impossible contracts.[23] On the basis of the legal literature, it can be concluded that a legal transaction aimed at achieving an aim contrary to good morals would not be protected by the courts due to being invalid.[24] László Villányi (1903–1945) analysed separately transactions contrary to good morals and transactions contrary to public order. He also referred to agreements regulating economic competition and stressed that the legislature intended to combat cartels by means of private law sanctions, on the one hand, and by means of criminal law provisions, on the other. Systematically, he placed cartels within the category of prohibited transactions and described them in the framework of specific rules.[25]

4.3 Judicial Decisions Rejecting the Validity of Cartel Agreements

Hungarian judicial practice, mainly that of the Curia, initially considered cartel agreements, which appeared in the second half of the 19th century, as contrary

20 Szladits, "A magánjog fogalma, fejlődése és tudománya," 341.

21 Imre Zlinszky and János Reiner, *A magyar magánjog mai érvényben különös tekintettel a gyakorlat igényeire* [*Hungarian private law as it stands today with particular reference to the needs of practice*] (Budapest: Franklin-Társulat, 1902), 185; Mór Katona, Mór Kiss, and János Reiner, "Kötelmi jog [Law of obligation]," in *Magyar magánjog. III. Kötet* [*Hungarian private law. Volume III*], ed. Fodor Ármin (Budapest: Singer és Wolfner, 1898), 132; Dezső Márkus, *Magyar magánjog mai érvényben: Törvények, rendeletek, szokásjog, joggyakorlat. III. kötet. kötelmi jog. öröklési jog* [*Hungarian private law in force today: Laws, Regulations, Customary law, Case law. Volume III. Contract law. Law of succession*] (Budapest: Grill Károly Könyvkiadóvállalata, 1906), 26; Béni Grosschmid, *Fejezetek kötelmi jogunk köréből. II. Kötet* [*Chapters on our law of obligations. Volume II*] (Budapest: Grill Károly Könyvkiadóvállalata, 1933), 1098.

22 János Suhayda, *A magyar polgári anyagi magánjog rendszere az országbírói értekezlet által megállapított szabályokhoz és azóta a legújabb időig hozott törvényekhez alkalmazva* [*The system of Hungarian private civil law applied to the rules laid down by the Conference of the Judges and to the laws enacted since then until recent times*] (Budapest: Magyar Királyi Egyetemi Könyvnyomda, 1874), 85.

23 Sárffy, *Magánjog alapismeretek*, 126.

24 Antal Almási, *A bírói gyakorlat jelentősége a magyar magánjogban* [*The importance of judicial practice in Hungarian private law*] (Budapest: Jogállam Kiadóhivatala, 1935), 12.

25 Villányi, *A magyar magánjog rövid tankönyve*, 63-66; Kálmán Személyi, *Magánjogunk fejlődésének utolsó két évtizede* [*The last two decades of the development of our private law*] (Kolozsvár: Nagy Ny, 1941), 9–10.

to good morals. After the turn of the century, however, the practice of the Curia suggests that not all cartel agreements were considered to be contrary to good morals. The substance of good morals, i.e., what is considered contrary to good morals, has been determined by judicial practice.[26] Bálint Kolozsváry (1875–1954) rightly stated that "good morals are determined by the prevailing social perception, and therefore this is not a legal question."[27]

In the absence of legislation, "only judicial practice has provided information on the legal assessment of cartels."[28] Few cartel cases have been brought before the courts as they have been mostly settled through arbitration. On the basis of the judicial practice, it can be stated at the outset that cartel agreements were generally considered to be contrary to good morals in the second half of the 19th century and even in the years after the turn of the century. As the economic interests of the state changed, so did the judicial practice. The courts started to examine the purpose of cartels. Another important factor to bear in mind when examining the judicial practice is that it is difficult to determine whether a judgement concerned a cartel agreement or a simple non-compete clause. With regard to non-compete clauses, the courts were no longer dismissive because such a contract could be considered invalid only if it was contrary to good morals, i.e., if it imposed an excessive burden on one of the parties or was intended to exploit that party.

The first case in which a Hungarian court declared a cartel agreement legally invalid was when the Curia, in its judgement no. 2554 of 6 June 1883, ruled that "an agreement between merchants, whereby they bind themselves and each other under penalty of a fine not to sell certain goods below a price which they regulate, constitutes a *turpis causa* directed to the injury of consumers, and does not give rise to a right of action against the party not keeping the agreement in respect of the fine."[29] In the case against G. B. Jakab, the district court of Szarvas, in its judgement no. 667 of 22 March 1883, was confronted

26 Gergely Deli, *A generális klauzulák dogmatikai, történeti és összehasonlító elemzése, különös tekintettel a jóerkölcsbe ütköző szerződések tilalmára (doktori értekezés)* [*A dogmatic, historical and comparative analysis of general clauses, with special reference to the prohibition of contracts contrary to good morals (doctoral dissertation)*] (Budapest: PPKE JÁK, 2009), 178.

27 Kolozsváry, *A magyar magánjog tankönyve*, 104; Mária Homoki-Nagy, "Megjegyzések a kartellmagánjog történetéhez" [Notes on the history of private cartel law], *Versenytükör* 12, special issue II (2016): 46–47.

28 Károly Dobrovics, "Kartelszerződés és a versenytilalom a bírói gyakorlatban a karteltörvény életbelépte előtt" [Cartel agreements and non-competition in judicial practice before the entry into force of the Cartel Act], in *Kartel, Árelemzés, Külföldi törvények* [*Cartel, Price Analysis, Foreign Laws*], ed. Károly Dobrovics and Endre Kőházi (Budapest: Monopol Könyvkiadó, 1938), 299. According to Kolozsváry, the validity of cartel agreements has not been recognised by the Hungarian courts. Kolozsváry, *A magyar magánjog tankönyve*, 106.

29 No. 2554, in: Döntvénytár [Case book], *A M. K. Curia, A Budapesti Kir. Itélő Tábla és a Pénzügyi Közigazgatási Biróság elvi jelentőségű határozatai. Uj folyam. IX. Kötet* [*Decisions of Principle of the Royal Hungarian Curia, the Royal Budapest Court of Appeal and the Financial Administrative Court. New issue. Volume IX*] (Budapest: Franklin-Társulat, 1884), 309.

with a case where the defendant did not deny that he had personally signed the contract submitted by the plaintiff, whereby they mutually undertook "to sell sugar and kerosene for 3 years at a price mutually agreed upon."[30] The court found that the defendant was not coerced into concluding the contract, and, moreover, since he signed it he was bound by its provisions. In the absence of a private law code, in 1883, the Curia referred back to Article 17 of the *Decretum Maius* of Matthias I, issued in 1486, which meant the application of the principle of *pacta sunt servanda*.[31] On appeal by the defendant, the Budapest Royal Court of Appeal reversed the judgement of the court of first instance and dismissed the plaintiff's action due to the fact that the disputed contract "contains an agreement which completely excludes free competition in the interests of consumers, and is thus aimed at harming the interest of the public and, therefore, cannot be the basis of a claim before the courts since it is contrary to moral concepts (*turpis causa*)."[32] The Curia upheld the judgement of the court of appeal.

A similar decision was reached by the Curia in 1893 in the case of *János Pfeifer v. Jakab Heger and János Hollák*, which concerned the use of threshing machines. In a summary judgement, the Royal District Court of Szabadka, acting as the court of first instance, ruled that the statement of claim showed that the defendants had agreed with the plaintiff that they would undertake threshing with their threshing machines only under certain conditions. The agreement also stated that, if either party breached their undertakings, they would have to pay a stipulated liquidated damages. The defendants did not contest the substance of the agreement. However, they also stated that they had agreed with the plaintiff that machine owners from Merovicza and Pacsér would join the contract, and the contract would enter into force only thereafter. The machine owners from Merovicza, however, undertook the threshing on different terms. The court stated that "even if this claim of the defendants were to be accepted as true, they could not escape from their obligations under the contract. [...] They have an obligation towards the contracting parties."[33] On the basis of the above, the court of first instance found for the plaintiff. The Szeged Royal Court of Appeal, however, reversed the judgement and dismissed the claim of the plaintiff on the following grounds. The purpose of the contract in question was to allow the use of threshing machines by farmers'

30 Döntvénytár, vol. IX, 309.

31 Decree of 1486 of King Mathias I (VI): 1. "And as to obligations, the rule shall be, that he who is bound shall receive law and justice according to the first eighth part of the statute, after a legal action, and shall be bound thereto by this decree."

32 Döntvénytár, vol. IX, 310.

33 No. 8377/P, in. Döntvénytár [Case book], *A M. K. Curia, A Budapesti Kir. Itélő Tábla és a Pénzügyi Közigazgatási Biróság elvi jelentőségű határozatai. Uj folyam. XXXVII. Kötet* [*Decisions of Principle of the Royal Hungarian Curia, the Royal Budapest Court of Appeal and the Financial Administrative Court. New issue. Volume XXXVII*] (Budapest: Franklin-Társulat, 1894), 104.

associations under certain conditions. "Since the conditions laid down in the contract preclude free competition in the interests of the farming community, and, further, since the contract in question is intended to harm the farming community, and is therefore not only contrary to the free exercise of the industry but also to the concept of morality, the contract in question cannot be relied on as a basis for a claim before the courts."[34] The Curia upheld the decision of the court of appeal in this case as well.

The background to the Curia's judgement no. 965/1903 of 6 September 1904 was as follows. The Court of Trade and Exchange dismissed the plaintiff's action. The plaintiff alleged that he had acted as an intermediary in the formation of a contract for the transport of stone and had agreed with the defendant not to compete with the defendant. On the basis of the intermediation and the non-compete agreement, the defendant promised to pay the plaintiff three crowns per cubic metre for the quantity to be delivered. The court found that "the plaintiff had facilitated the conclusion of the contract by not entering into competition, and without having carried out any other promotional activity."[35] The plaintiff demanded from the defendant the amount stipulated in exchange for not competing, which was deemed to be contrary to good morals. The defendant did not engage in an economic activity worthy of remuneration, but sought to enrich himself at the expense of others. As a result, buyers were forced to buy the goods at a higher price to cover the intermediary's fees. "Therefore, no justiciable claim can arise from the collusion not to compete, which is a transaction contrary to good morals."[36] The Budapest Court of Appeal upheld the dismissal of the defendant's plea in its judgement no. 3872/902 of 1 April 1903, which was confirmed by the Curia in its ruling no. 965/903.[37]

The Curia, in its judgement no. 1476/1903 of 27 June 1904, considered a bakers' cartel agreement to be contrary to public interest. It is clear from the judgement of the Győr Court of Appeal that the plaintiff admitted in his reply that the defendant had granted the bill of exchange in order to secure the cartel agreement between himself and the other master bakers. He thereby admitted that he knew the details of the contract. The court ruled that the parties had entered into "a cartel agreement to make cakes more expensive. This contract, which raised the price of a foodstuff meeting a primary need,

34 Döntvénytár, vol. XXXVII, 104. See also: Károly Szladits and László Fürst, eds. *A magyar birói gyakorlat. Magánjog. II. Kötet* [*The practice of Hungarian judges. Private law. Volume II*] (Budapest: Grill Károly Könyvkiadó Vállalata, 1935), 27.

35 Dezső Márkus, ed., *Felső bíróságaink elvi határozatai A M. Kir. Curia és a Kir. Ítélő Táblák elvi jelentőségü döntéseinek rendszeres gyüjteménye. XV. Kötet* [*Decisions of principle of our higher courts. The Regular collection of decisions of principle of the Royal Hungarian Curia and the Royal Courts of Appeal. Volume XV*] (Budapest: Grill Károly Könyvkiadó Vállalata, 1903), 63–64.

36 Márkus, *Felső bíróságaink elvi határozatai*, 64.

37 Márkus, *Felső bíróságaink elvi határozatai*, 65.

was intended to exploit consumers and as such was founded on an immoral basis, and therefore did not give rise to rights and obligations which could be enforced by judicial process."[38] The Curia upheld the ruling of the Court of Appeal, stating that "craftsmen may not contractually restrict their freedom to exercise their trade to the substantial detriment of the public interest."[39] The cartel agreement between the master bakers was intended to increase the price of cakes and, as such, was detrimental to consumers and therefore contrary to the public interest.

In its judgement no. 666/1904 of 7 November 1905, the Curia considered a cartel-like agreement null and void, stating that "the mere fact that the agreement to fix the selling price is concluded with the aim of fixing the price between the producer and the consumer, i.e., the public at large, deprives agreements of the above nature of their legal validity."[40] The increase or decrease in price is in itself sufficient to render such agreements null and void. The competent royal court (it is not clear from the text of the judgement which court) took into consideration the judicial practice and referred to the Curia judgement no. 2554/1883, already cited. It held that it was contrary to good morals to have an agreement which depresses the price or makes more expensive the availability of some goods that are the subject of industrial or commercial trade, or of products or raw materials necessary for their production, and which restricts free competition with the object of harming consumers. Such an agreement was contrary to good morals and the public interest. The applicant admitted in the course of the proceedings that in 1891 he had purchased from butchers in Budapest leather from calves, lambs, and cattle at a certain price, and he had resold the leather at a fixed price. The plaintiff and the defendant were motivated by the desire to drive down the purchase price of raw materials and then to drive up the prices when reselling those raw materials to tanners. The Curia upheld the judgement of the court of appeal.[41]

In another case, the Marosvárásrhely Court of Appeal upheld the judgement of a lower court, in which the claim for damages in the amount of 20,000 crowns by the plaintiff was rejected on the following grounds. On 14 November 1908, an agreement was concluded between the defendants and K. Bank és Takarékpénztár Rt., the purpose of which was that the defendants, as lessees of the "Salutaris" mineral water flowing from the main well in Kászon, transferred the exclusive right to sell this water to the bank "in order

38 Márkus, *Felső bíróságaink elvi határozatai*, 66–67.

39 Judgment no. 1476/903 in: Márkus, *Felső bíróságaink elvi határozatai*, 67. Szladits and Fürst, *A magyar birói gyakorlat*, 28.

40 Felsőbíróságaink elvi határozatai, *A M. Kir. Curia és a Kir. Itélő Táblák elvi jelentőségű döntéseinek rendszeres gyűjteménye. XVI. Kötet* [*Decisions of principle of our higher courts. The Regular collection of decisions of principle of the Royal Hungarian Curia and the Royal Courts of Appeal. Volume XVI*] (Budapest: Grill Károly Könyvkiadó Vállalata, 1907), 352–353; Szladits and Fürst, *A magyar birói gyakorlat*, 27.

41 Szladits and Fürst, *A magyar birói gyakorlat*, 27.

to increase the demand for their spring water."[42] The reason for plaintiff filing a claim was that the defendants had withdrawn from their agreement alleging that the plaintiff was in breach. The plaintiff undertook to distribute the mineral water in question and, on payment of a penalty of 20,000 crowns, also undertook to keep the water in distribution and to its increase consumption in the quantities specified in the contract. A framework for the promotion of the mineral water was also established. On their own side, the defendants subleased the spring water at a low price and undertook not to infringe the bank's exclusive right to distribute it. If plaintiff breached these obligations, it had to pay a penalty of 20,000 crowns to the defendants. The plaintiff distributed not only "Salutaris" mineral water, but also 15 other brands of mineral water, which could happen only to the detriment of the defendants' interests. The court of appeal found that the plaintiff had set the sales price of the mineral water by circumventing the economic laws of supply and demand. This was sufficient reason for the defendants to withdraw from the contract. Because of the plaintiff's breach of contract, the defendants rightfully terminated their business relationship. The Curia also accepted the reasoning of the court of second instance and upheld its judgement.[43]

4.4 Judicial Decisions Supporting the Validity of Cartel Agreements

Still, not all cartel agreements were considered invalid by the Curia. In its judgement no. 6630/1898 of 15 June 1898, the Curia ruled the opposite and declared a cartel agreement to be valid. The Budapest Court of Appeal ruled that the parties' "clauses to the effect that neither of them is allowed to keep or sell in trade such articles of commerce as the other holds or sells cannot be considered null and void."[44] The court's reasoning behind this finding was that the clauses protected the commercial interests of the contracting parties against each other, which were not intended to restrict free competition or harm consumers. For this reason, the contract in question was also recognised as valid by the Curia in its judgement no. 6630 of 1898.[45]

42 Béla Gallia, ed., *Hiteljogi döntvénytár (Váltó-, csőd-, kereskedelmi és tőzsde ügyekben). VI. Kötet* [*Credit law case book (In bill of, bankruptcy, commercial and stock exchange cases). Volume VI*] (Budapest: Franklin-Társulat, 1913), 300.

43 Gallia, *Hiteljogi döntvénytár*, 302.

44 Márkus, *Felső biróságaink elvi határozatai*, 48.

45 Márkus, *Felső biróságaink elvi határozatai*, 48. Referring to the same: Szladits and Fürst, *A magyar birói gyakorlat*, 27; Károly Grecsák, ed., *Magyar döntvénytár. A Magyar Kir. Curia, Kir. Itélőtáblák, nemkülönben más legfelsőbb foku itélőhatóságok elvi jelentőségü határozatai. VIII. Kötet* [*Hungarian Case Book. Decisions of principle of the Royal Hungarian Curia, the Royal Courts of Appeal, and other higher courts. Volume VIII*] (Budapest: Politzer Zsigmond és Fia, 1906), 647–648; Károly Szladits, Miklós Ujlaki, and László Villányi, eds., *Magyar magánjog mai érvényben: Törvények, rendeletek, joggyakorlat III. rész. Kötelmi jog I. kötet* [*Hungarian private law in force today: Laws, regulations, case law Part III. Law of obligations,*

The Curia declared a carpenters' cartel agreement valid in its judgement no. 363/1911 of 14 November 1911. This judgement is also important because it established, on the basis of substantiated practice, what constituted *turpis causa* in the case of cartel agreements. The judicial practice did not take the view that cartel agreements were in general contrary to good morals and therefore invalid, but examined in each case whether or not the aim and the operation of the cartel in question was contrary to good morals. In the case of cartel agreements, "the Court found that the *turpis causa* was, on the one hand, the exclusion or greater restriction of free competition from the point of view of the contracting parties and, on the other, the resulting exploitation of consumers, and, in fact, that the latter was sufficient in itself."[46] Having examined these two important elements, the competent court held that the contract was not so restrictive as to be impermissible from the point of view of individual freedom or the freedom of trade and industry, and that it did not go beyond what was necessary to safeguard the commercial interests of the parties. As regards the aim of exploiting consumers, the court also found that the primary purpose of the cartel agreement was to ensure the even distribution of work and not to influence pricing. The competent royal court upheld the judgement of the lower court since the purpose of the one time association of master carpenters in Budapest was to prevent the harmful consequences of competition between master carpenters and to maintain normal market prices. "If, however, those engaged in a trade unite for the purpose of maintaining the normal market price of their work by preventing offers below a price which would endanger the economic operation of the industry, a contract concluded for this purpose and not for an unreasonably long period cannot be regarded as contrary to the interests of either the participants or the public and contrary to good morals."[47] The judgement of the court of second instance was upheld on the basis of the reasons given. This was a milestone in the judging of cartel agreements.

Volume I] (Budapest: Grill Károly Könyvkiadóvállalata, 1942), 50. From among the works presenting the judicial practice, special mention should be made of the collection of rulings edited by Jenő László and Péter Pár Szende, who refer to the above-mentioned decision of the Curia in connection with Section 973 of the Hungarian Private Law Bill ("A contract which is contrary to morality or public policy is null and void"). Jenő László and Péter Pál Szende, eds., *Magyar magánjog mai érvényben: Törvények, rendeletek, szokásjog, joggyakorlat "Magyarország magánjogi törvénykönyve" javaslatának rendszerében. III. kötet. első rész* [*Hungarian private law in force today: Laws, decrees, customary law, case law in the system of the proposed "Hungarian Code of Private Law," Volume III, part 1*] (Budapest: Grill Károly Könyvkiadóvállalata, 1928), 45.

46 Károly Grecsák and Sándor Aladár, eds., *Magyar döntvénytár XIX. Kötet* [*Hungarian Case Book. Volume XIX*] (Budapest: Grill Károly Könyvkiadóvállalata, 1913), 160.

47 Grecsák and Aladár, *Magyar döntvénytár*, 163.

4.5 Conclusion

On the basis of the judicial practice presented above, it can be said that, in the absence of statutory regulations, cartel agreements were judged by Hungarian courts on the basis of general principles of private law, with particular attention given to the fact that contracts contrary to good morals were considered invalid. The Hungarian judiciary initially took the position that cartel agreements were fundamentally invalid. After the turn of the 20th century, however, the approach to cartels changed and the courts examined on a case-by-case basis whether or not the contract in question was contrary to good morals or the public interest. The real change in jurisprudence came with the adoption of the Hungarian Cartel Act in 1931, after which only cartels engaged in activity that was contrary to the public interest were found to be in breach of the law. Thus, the courts acted against cartels only if their activities were against the public interest. Thereafter, cartel agreements were judged by the courts under the Cartel Act. The infringement of the public interest was the basis for the proceedings. In all other cases, cartels' activities were authorised by the Hungarian state. The Cartel Act legalised cartels and placed them under supervision, justified by the need to protect consumers. In the absence of statutory regulations, the development of Hungarian cartel law has been characterised by the enforcement of classic private law principles, the main reason for which is the need for justice in the interests of the development of law.

References

Primary sources

Döntvénytár [Case book]. *A M. K. Curia, A Budapesti Kir. Itélő Tábla és a Pénzügyi Közigazgatási Biróság elvi jelentőségű határozatai. Uj folyam. IX. Kötet* [*Decisions of Principle of the Royal Hungarian Curia, the Royal Budapest Court of Appeal and the Financial Administrative Court. New Issue. Volume IX*]. Budapest: Franklin-Társulat, 1884.

Döntvénytár [Case book]. *A M. K. Curia, A Budapesti Kir. Itélő Tábla és a Pénzügyi Közigazgatási Biróság elvi jelentőségű határozatai. Uj folyam. XXXVII. Kötet* [*Decisions of Principle of the Royal Hungarian Curia, the Royal Budapest Court of Appeal and the Financial Administrative Court. New Issue. Volume XXXVII*]. Budapest: Franklin-Társulat, 1894.

Eötvös, József. "Levelek [Letters]." Accessed June 4, 2024. https://mek.oszk.hu/05400/05480/05480.htm.

Felsőbiróságaink elvi határozatai. *A M. Kir. Curia és a Kir. Itélő Táblák elvi jelentőségű döntéseinek rendszeres gyűjteménye. XVI. Kötet* [*Decisions of principle of our higher courts. The Regular collection of decisions of principle of the Royal Hungarian Curia and the Royal Courts of Appeal. Volume XVI*]. Budapest: Grill Károly Könyvkiadó Vállalata, 1907.

Gallia, Béla, ed. *Hiteljogi döntvénytár (Váltó-, csőd-, kereskedelmi és tőzsde ügyekben). VI. Kötet* [*Credit Law Case Book (In Exchange, Bankruptcy, Commercial and Stock Exchange Cases). Volume VI*]. Budapest: Franklin-Társulat, 1913.

Grecsák, Károly, ed. *Magyar döntvénytár. A Magyar Kir. Curia, Kir. Itélőtáblák, nemkülönben más legfelsőbb foku itélőhatóságok elvi jelentőségü határozatai. VIII. Kötet [Hungarian Case Book. Decisions of principle of the Royal Hungarian Curia, the Royal Courts of Appeal, and Other Higher Courts. Volume VIII]*. Budapest: Politzer Zsigmond és Fia, 1906.

Grecsák, Károly, and Sándor Aladár, eds. *Magyar döntvénytár XIX. Kötet [Hungarian Case Book. Volume XIX]*. Budapest: Grill Károly Könyvkiadóvállalata, 1913.

Márkus, Dezső, ed. *Felsőbiróságaink elvi határozatai. A M. Kir. Curia és a Kir. Táblák elvi jelentőségü döntéseinek rendszeres gyűjteménye. X. kötet [Decisions of Principle of Our Higher Courts. The Regular Collection of Decisions of Principle of the Royal Hungarian Curia and the Royal Courts of Appeal. Volume X]*. Budapest: Grill Károly Cs. és Kir. Udv. Könyvkereskedése, 1900.

Márkus, Dezső, ed. *Felső biróságaink elvi határozatai A M. Kir. Curia és a Kir. Itélő Táblák elvi jelentőségü döntéseinek rendszeres gyüjteménye. XV. Kötet [Decisions of Principle of Our Higher Courts. The Regular Collection of Decisions of Principle of the Royal Hungarian Curia and the Royal Courts of Appeal. Volume XV]*. Budapest: Grill Károly Könyvkiadó Vállalata, 1903.

Márkus, Dezső. *Magyar magánjog mai érvényben. Törvények, rendeletek, szokásjog, joggyakorlat. I. kötet. Jogforrások, személyjog, családjog [Hungarian Private Law in Force Today. Laws, Regulations, Customary Law, Case Law. Volume I. Legal Sources, Personal Law, Family Law]*. Budapest: Grill Károly Könyvkiadóvállalata, 1906.

Márkus, Dezső. *Magyar magánjog mai érvényben. Törvények, rendeletek, szokásjog, joggyakorlat. III. kötet. kötelmi jog. öröklési jog [Hungarian Private Law in Force Today. Laws, Regulations, Customary Law, Case Law. Volume III. Contract Law. Law of Succession]*. Budapest: Grill Károly Könyvkiadóvállalata, 1906.

Meszlényi, Artur. *Magyar magánjog. Törvények, rendeletek, szokásjog, joggyakorlat, magánjogi törvénykönyv szövegével és rendszerében [Hungarian Private Law. Laws, Decrees, Customary Law, Case Law, Text and System of the Private Law Code]*. Budapest: Grill Károly Könyvkiadóvállalata, 1928.

Szladits, Károly, Miklós Ujlaki, and László Villányi, eds. *Magyar magánjog mai érvényben. Törvények, rendeletek, joggyakorlat III. rész. Kötelmi jog I. kötet [Hungarian Private Law in Force Today. Laws, Regulations, Case Law Part III. Law of Obligations, Volume I]*. Budapest: Grill Károly Könyvkiadóvállalata, 1942.

Werbőzcy, Istvan. *Werbőzcy Hármaskönyve [Werbőczy's Tripartitum]*. Pecs: Pécsi Szikra Kiadó, 1989.

Secondary studies

Almási, Antal. *A bírói gyakorlat jelentősége a magyar magánjogban [The Importance of Judicial Practice in Hungarian Private Law]*. Budapest: Jogállam Kiadóhivatala, 1935.

Almási, Antal. *A tilos cselekmények a magánjogban [Prohibited Actions in Private Law]*. Budapest: Grill Károly Könyvkiadóvállalata, 1907.

Benke, József. *Bevezetés a magyar magánjog általános elveibe [Introduction to the General Principles of Hungarian Private Law]*. Budapest: HVGOrac, 2019.

Besnyő, Bernát. "A jó erkölcsbe és a közrendbe ütköző szerződések a magánjogi törvénykönyv javaslatában [Contracts Contrary to Good Morals and Public Policy in the Proposal for a Private Law Code]." *Jogállam* 28, no. 7–8 (1929): 361–67.

Deli, Gergely. *A generális klauzulák dogmatikai, történeti és összehasonlító elemzése, különös tekintettel a jóerkölcsbe ütköző szerződések tilalmára (doktori értekezés)* [*A Dogmatic, Historical and Comparative Analysis of General Clauses, with Special Reference to the Prohibition of Contracts Contrary to Good Morals (Doctoral Dissertation)*]. Budapest: PPKE JÁK, 2009.

Dobrovics, Károly. "Kartelszerződés és a versenytilalom a bírói gyakorlatban a karteltörvény életbelépte előtt [Cartel Agreements and Non-competition in Judicial Practice Before the Entry into Force of the Cartel Act]." In *Kartel, Árelemzés, Külföldi törvények* [*Cartel, Price Analysis, Foreign Laws*], edited by Károly Dobrovics and Endre Kőházi, 299–335. Budapest: Monopol Könyvkiadó, 1938.

Fodor, Ármin, ed. *Magyar magánjog. Általános rész, Személyi jog* [*Hungarian Private Law. General Part, Personal Law*]. Budapest: Signer és Wolfner, 1899.

Frank, Ignác. *A közigazság törvénye Magyarhonban. I. rész* [*The Law of Public Administration in Hungary. Part I*]. Buda: Magyar Királyi Egyetem betűivel, 1845.

Grosschmid, Béni. *Fejezetek kötelmi jogunk köréből. II. Kötet* [*Chapters on Our Law of Obligations. Volume II*]. Budapest: Grill Károly Könyvkiadóvállalata, 1933.

H. Sz. (Holitscher, Szigfrid?). "A tilos és a jó erkölcsbe ütköző szerződésekről [On Prohibited Contracts and Contracts Contrary to Good Morals]." *Közjegyzők Közlönye* 11, no. 4 (1908): 113–21.

Homoki-Nagy, Mária. "Megjegyzések a kartellmagánjog történetéhez [Notes on the History of Private Cartel Law]." *Versenytükör* 12, special issue II (2016): 46–47.

Katona, Mór, Mór Kiss, and János Reiner. "Kötelmi jog [Law of obligation]." In *Magyar magánjog. III. Kötet* [*Hungarian Private Law. Volume III*], edited by Fodor Ármin, 44–64. Budapest: Singer és Wolfner, 1898.

Kolozsváry, Bálint. *A magyar magánjog tankönyve* [*Textbook on Hungarian Private Law*]. Budapest: Grill Károly Könyvkiadóvállalata, 1911.

László, Jenő and Péter Pál Szende, eds. *Magyar magánjog mai érvényben. Törvények, rendeletek, szokásjog, joggyakorlat "Magyarország magánjogi törvénykönyve" javaslatának rendszerében. III. kötet. első rész* [*Hungarian Private Law in Force Today. Laws, Decrees, Customary Law, Case Law in the System of the Proposed "Hungarian Code of Private Law," Volume III, Part 1*]. Budapest: Grill Károly Könyvkiadóvállalata, 1928.

Menyhárd, Attila. *A jóerkölcsbe ütköző szerződések* [*Contracts That Are Contrary to Good Morals*]. Budapest: Gondolat, 2004.

Sárffy, Andor. *Magánjog alapismeretek* [*Basic Knowledge of Private Law*]. Budapest: Zemplén Vármegye, s.l. 1933.

Suhayda, János. *A magyar polgári anyagi magánjog rendszere az országbírói értekezlet által megállapított szabályokhoz és azóta a legújabb időig hozott törvényekhez alkalmazva* [*The System of Hungarian Private Civil Law Applied to the Rules Laid Down by the Conference of the Judges and to the Laws Enacted Since Then Until Recent Times*]. Budapest: Magyar Királyi Egyetemi Könyvnyomda, 1874.

Személyi, Kálmán. *Magánjogunk fejlődésének utolsó két évtizede* [*The Last Two Decades of the Development of Our Private Law*]. Kolozsvár: Nagy Ny, 1941.

Szladits, Károly. "A magánjog fogalma, fejlődése és tudománya [The Concept, Development and Science of Private Law]." In *Magyar magánjog. Első kötet: Általános rész, Személyi jog* [*Hungarian Private Law. Volume 1: General Part, Personal Law*], edited by Károly Szladits, 5–121. Budapest: Grill Károly Könyvkiadóvállalata, 1941.

Szladits, Károly. "Jogszabálytan [Doctrine of the law]." In *Magyar magánjog. Első kötet: Általános rész, Személyi jog* [*Hungarian Private Law. Volume 1: General*

Part, Personal Law], edited by Károly Szladits, 121–83. Budapest: Grill Károly Könyvkiadóvállalata, 1941.

Szladits, Károly, and László Fürst, eds. *A magyar birói gyakorlat. Magánjog. II. Kötet* [*The Practice of Hungarian Judges. Private Law. Volume II*]. Budapest: Grill Károly Könyvkiadó Vállalata, 1935.

Vadász, Lajos, ed. *Magánjogi törvénykönyvünk és elő tételes jogunk. 2. Kötet* [*Our Private Law Code and Our Preliminary Law. Volume 2*]. Budapest: Attila Nyomda, 1930.

Vadász, Lajos. *Magánjogunk főbb elvei és az új jogfejlődés. I. kötet* [*The Main Principles of Our Private Law and the New Legal Developments. Volume I*]. Szeged: Endrényi Lajos Nyomda, 1926.

Villányi, László. *A magyar magánjog rövid tankönyve* [*A Short Textbook of Hungarian Private Law*]. Budapest: Grill Károly Könyvkiadóvállalata, 1941.

Zlinszky, Imre, and János Reiner. *A magyar magánjog mai érvényben különös tekintettel a gyakorlat igényeire* [*Hungarian Private Law as it Stands Today with Particular Reference to the Needs of Practice*]. Budapest: Franklin-Társulat, 1902.

Part 2

Law & Equity

5 Legitimacy and Equity in the 11th Century? Age-Old Messages from Susali

Adrian Schmidt-Recla

5.1 Introduction

Legal history's most valuable benefit is to show that ever since people have been writing about conflicts and interests they have been using common methods and reasoning. This applies to legitimacy and equity as well as to law or even to the concepts of good and evil. This chapter will attempt to prove that point with regard to the earliest beginnings of medieval Saxon law. In his *Chronicon* the cleric and historiographer Thietmar, Bishop of Merseburg (975–1018), recorded information concerning an act, a contract, or last will of Count Friedrich I (960–1017) of Eilenburg, a county in the Saxon Siusili or Susali district (what is nowadays the north of the federal state of Saxony in Germany). This note, more than 1,000 years old, is surely one of the first legal messages concerning Saxon law, which until then (and for centuries to come – the *Sachsenspiegel* is 200 years younger) had not been written down in any writ, law book, law, or statute. Thietmar's report shines a light on the ideas and beliefs of the people involved and on cleric writing by a contemporary at a time when legal sources were scarce. Those ideas included sovereignty, family relationships (cognatic kinship), inheritance, prudence, as well as perhaps judiciousness and – probably most relevant – gender, which are still present in political and ethical discourse. Thietmar tied all these concepts together into a single word: legitimacy. He thus contributed to the eternal discussion concerning ethical and normative concepts. What could have motivated him, however, in those long gone times without written law? If the balance of interests is taken into account, one possibly could prove whether the concept of *aequitas* (equity) was present at the dawn of law. Religion and the pursuit of power were definitely not.

This chapter will take the reader on a journey to a dark age – "dark" in the sense of a lack of written sources of law – to a land then called "Siusili" or (more commonly) "Susali,"[1] which is known nowadays as the Leipzig lowlands. It is a land where woods stretched along the banks of the rivers Elbe

1 "Siusili" and "Susali" are words of Sorbian, not of Saxon, origin.

DOI: 10.4324/9781003654131-8

and Mulde, where farmers in far distant villages lived together with their sheep and pigs under roofs of straw and where they grew rye, barley, and einkorn wheat. It was a land where a man possessing and able to use sword and shield was deemed to be a ruler and where a Catholic priest whose church was not a wooden, but a single-naved building of stone was said to be even a "bishop." The farmers were Sorbs or Wends, which means they were ethnically of Sorbian, not German, origin, and they spoke a Slavonic language. They had been occupying the region following a population of German origin, which had left the Elbe region during the 5th century. These facts are confirmed by archaeology.[2] No written records exist, however.

Our current knowledge concerning events occurring around the year 1000 is limited. Written sources (of any origin and purpose) are rather rare. This also applies to sources of law. The age of the so-called *leges barbarorum* (ca. 490–850) had long since faded into the past. More than four generations of men had lived and died since those few scriptures were produced in abbeys far away from Susali, and there is no evidence that those texts were known at all. For people living around the year 1000, the age of the so-called *Rechtsbücher* or law books (for which the *Sachsenspiegel* – the Saxon Mirror – stands as a historical landmark) would have been at best a distant imagination. In this regard, it is of special interest to us today to examine individual messages for the information they contain about the legal behaviour of men and women living and arguing cases without texts or books of law.

5.2 The Case

5.2.1 Background

In that place and time when legal disputes were resolved orally, without written law codes, there lived a man called Friedrich I, count of Wettin and Eilenburg. Eilenburg (or "Ilburg," "Eulenburg") around the year 1000 was more than a single building, more than a *villa*, more than a *curtis*, even more than a castle: it was said to be a *civitas*, which means a place where people settled who were more privileged than the people living in the surrounding settlements. In those days, Eilenburg was the central settlement of the Susali county and today it is a small town 10 miles north of Leipzig. The fact that scholars have any knowledge at all about Friedrich I is due only to a special person, a cleric from nearby who was called Thietmar, bishop of Merseburg, who died one year after Friedrich. This Thietmar was one of the very few people able to read and write at that time. He left behind a chronicle – the

2 Cf. Judith Oexle, ed., *Sachsen: archäologisch. 12.000 v. Chr. – 2.000 n. Chr.* (Dresden: Sächsisches Druck- und Verlagshaus, 2000); Felix Biermann, *Slawische Besiedlung zwischen Elbe, Neiße und Lubsza: Archäologische Studien zum Siedlungswesen und zur Sachkultur des frühen und hohen Mittelalters* (Bonn: Habelt, 2000).

Chronicon[3] – which today is still the primary source of information about the life and acts of people living in the duchy of Saxony as part of the Ottonian Empire around the year 1000.

Friedrich I was the son of Dietrich I, count of Wettin. He was born around 960 and had a brother, Dedi I, also Count of Wettin, who had a child, too, a son, later called Dietrich II (after his grandfather). Dietrich II was Friedrich's nephew and his next (and as far as we know only) male relative. In 997, Emperor Otto III granted the entire county of Susali to Friedrich I. Friedrich acted as burgrave of Meissen several times and was granted the county of Hassegau in 1009 by Emperor Heinrich II, whom Friedrich supported during the election process in 1002[4] (while other rulers did not). Friedrich was said to be a Christian, which first of all means that he was not a pagan Sorb. Friedrich's wife was Ida, daughter of a Magdeburg burgrave. With her, he fathered three children, all girls, named Oda, Ida, and Milda (whom we know almost nothing about except the fact that Oda later married the nobleman Schenck von Summersberg). Nearly all the knowledge we have concerning these people comes from Thietmar's *Chronicle.* If Thietmar had not been the man he was (a man of letters), nobody today would know about the persons and events discussed in this article. There is no contemporaneous image, painting, or tomb slab to get any personal impression of Friedrich as an important Saxon ruler around 1000. He was probably one of the sword-bearers who exercised Ottonian kingship in those days when the area was still dominated by Sorbian influence. Saxon rulers or conquerors like Friedrich were involved in violent and bloody conflicts with the (unknown) leaders of the Sorbs and their pagan followers (who were probably the majority). They fought wars and battles every year and it is very likely that they enriched themselves at the cost of the Susali Sorbs. Some of them considered the Sorbs as "fair game" and carried out terrible butcheries among them.[5] During the 10th century, the Saxon upper class began to successfully dominate the majority of the Sorbs. Those were the times and conditions in which Friedrich I lived.

5.2.2 *What Happened*

Sometime in the year 1017 Count Friedrich I felt close to death. According to Thietmar[6] (when discussing Friedrich's deeds and thoughts one always should

3 Robert Holtzmann, ed., *Thietmari Merseburgensis episcopi chronicon: Die Chronik des Bischofs Thietmar von Merseburg und ihre Korveier Überarbeitung*, Monumenta Germaniae Historica, Scriptores rerum Germanicarum, Nova Series IX (Berlin: Weidmann, 1935).

4 Cf. Adrian Schmidt-Recla, *Kalte oder warme Hand: Verfügungen von Todes wegen in mittelalterlichen Referenzrechtsquellen* (Köln–Weimar–Wien: Bohlau, 2011), 366.

5 Thomas Westphalen, "Zwischen Prag und Meißen – Die Slawen in Sachsen," in *Sachsen: Archäologisch. 12.000 v. Chr.–2.000 n. Chr.*, ed. Judith Oexle (Dresden: Sächsisches Druck- und Verlagshaus, 2000), 74.

6 The case is reported in Holtzmann, *Thietmari Merseburgensis episcopi chronicon*, 50.

consider that it is Thietmar's clerical and learned mind that recounted them), he made up his mind and concluded that his three daughters should inherit all his belongings, all the wealth and fortune he had inherited or acquired or, in Latin, his *predium omne*. Moreover, Friedrich decided to transfer (*tradere*) this *predium* to his daughters by himself while still living. But – and here is where the law came into play – he obviously had to take certain things into consideration. As a result, he gave Eilenburg to his nephew Dietrich. In Thietmar's words:

> et in sacra nocte[7] eadem Fritherícus comes fidelis Christo et seniori suo obiit in civitate sua Ilburg dicta. Hic, quia sapiens erat et sibi finem huius vitae iam appropinquare cernebat, predictam civitatem fratris suimet filio nomine Thidrico ea racione dedit, ut cum laude sua, quia heres suimet fuit et aliter hoc legitime fieri non potuit, liceret sibi tribus suis filiabus predium omne, quid remansit, tradere. [And in the holy night Count Friedrich died as a follower of Christ and of his predecessors in his town Eilenburg. But before that – because he was a wise man who had felt his death coming soon – he gave that town to his brother's son called Dietrich. He did so because he was thus able to give away all his remaining belongings to his three daughters with the permission of Dietrich. Otherwise (without this permission), this could not have been done legitimately.]

Friedrich did not wait for death to distribute his possessions and belongings with cold hands. Today, we do not know what principles of non-testamentary inheritance were applied by the Saxons in Susali. Nevertheless, it is apparent that law, or at least thinking in terms of law, is entering the scene. This is proven by the use of the Latin word *legitime* – "legitimately."

5.3 The Law

5.3.1 Sources

The law of that time and place is completely unknown. The world would have to wait another 200 years for the *Sachsenspiegel*. There were earlier books concerning law or rules that were 200 years older, but it is very unlikely that they would have been known in Susali. The so-called *Lex Saxonum*, for example, was written around the year 802 in Aachen[8] and is known only from two manuscripts produced in Corvey (an abbey 150 miles away from Eilenburg) that have probably never left that abbey. Citations of and references to these manuscripts are rare and do not date from the 11th century. The *Lex Saxonum*

7 Thietmar meant the 6th January 1017.

8 Gerhard Theuerkauf, *Lex, Speculum, Compendium iuris. Rechtsaufzeichnungen und Rechtsbewußtsein in Norddeutschland vom 8. bis zum 16. Jahrhundert* (Köln: Böhlau, 1968).

is presumed to have had hardly any influence on the ability to know right from wrong[9] more than 200 years after the Aachen Reichstag. Thus, research concerning Saxon (or German) law of the 10th to the 12th centuries faces a characteristic lack of norms and decisions. Only documents are passed on, and documents as a basis of legal history have a disadvantage: one cannot learn a lot about the reasons for the disposals of property recorded in documents because documents of the Early and High Middle Ages are rather formal and impersonal. Individual cases which allow conclusions to be drawn about mutual obligations, claims, aspirations, and objections thus provide very useful information when searching for legal or judicial thinking "before the law."

5.3.2 Thinking and Opinions

At this point, one should note how Friedrich was characterised by Thietmar. Thietmar did not and could not write such that Friedrich would have been able to use, know, or ponder the (written) law. There was none: there is not a single reference to written law in Thietmar's *Chronicle*. Moreover, he did not write anything about counsellors, notaries, or in any possible way people who were *iurisperiti* (men skilled at law) and could give advice to a ruler wishing to dispose of his fortune. One can thus assume that such people did not exist at that time in that place. Therefore, Thietmar wrote of Friedrich as a person who was *sapiens* [wise]. And as such, a wise (or a clever or a prudent) man Friedrich – in Thietmar's words – knew that his primary wish concerning his daughters would be feasible – but only if Dietrich II gave his permission. That's why Friedrich gave Dietrich the best reason to consent: Eilenburg. That alone would not be sufficient to attract our attention, but Friedrich's reasoning is.

5.4 The Reasoning, or: A Wise Man's Wisdom

It has just been mentioned that Thietmar described Friedrich as having been a wise man (*sapiens*). One should not suppose, however, that Thietmar wanted to describe Friedrich as a learned man who would have been able to read and write (maybe a ruler's book or a law book). More probably, Friedrich was illiterate. *Sapiens* could have been used to describe Friedrich as smart, clever, prudent, wise, and/or discreet. But as a *vir sapiens* [wise man] he was said to have known that his disposition in favour of his daughters could not happen *legitime* without the consent of Friedrich's heir or heirs. *Sapiens* is said to have been (again, 200 years before Friedrich and Thietmar) a label for men who could read and find law in the Frankish empire of Charlemagne.[10] I doubt whether this was a proper label for Saxon sword-bearers in pagan environ-

9 Theuerkauf, *Lex, Speculum, Compendium iuris*, 96.
10 Theuerkauf, *Lex, Speculum, Compendium iuris*, 54, 67.

ments fighting the Sorbs. At the beginning of the 11th century, there were only a few books circulating in those areas (and those which were circulating were held in recently founded monasteries to which a man like Friedrich did not have access; Thietmar's *Chronicon* was one of those rare books, but the *Lex Saxonum* was not – its two manuscripts never left Corvey). Nevertheless, the legitimacy argument was (according to Thietmar) part of Friedrich's wisdom, prudence, or – according to Peter Landau who also wrote about the Susali case – judiciousness.[11] Such a conclusion seems excessive, however, and certainly not supported by Thietmar's words. Nonetheless, what this chapter attempts to prove is that, due to the concept of equity, people were thinking lawfully before laws were written down.

In any event, Friedrich's reasoning must have taken into account the following conflicting interests: (1) sovereignty – as far as Eilenburg as the Susali ruler's seat is concerned (whoever was subject to the Susali count's rule); (2) family relationships (cognatic kinship) and gender – Friedrich was a count's son with a brother who had a son, fathered none by himself, but with his noble wife had three daughters; and (3) inheritance, since he decided to dispose of his possessions while still alive.

What legal support did he have to back up his reasoning? There were no contemporary writs or any kind of written law that he could use as sources. Moreover, even if Friedrich knew of the *Lex Saxonum*, he would have found that female paternal relatives (agnates) could inherit all goods and belongings (*omnis hereditas*) only if there was no son (cf. Tit. 41, 44 LSax).[12] He would have also found that dispositions by living people were void once they made any living heirs (i.e., relatives) *exhereditati* (Tit. 62 LSax).[13] It is, as mentioned before, very unlikely that Friedrich knew the 200-year-old provisions of the *Lex Saxonum* (not to mention the provisions of the *Corpus Iuris Civilis*). And

11 Peter Landau, "Thietmar von Merseburg in Zusammenhang mit der Überlieferung von Lex Saxonum und Lex Thuringorum: Eine Studie zum Erbrecht der Ottonenzeit," *Zeitschrift der Savigny-Stiftung für Rechtsgeschichte, Germanistische Abteilung* 124 (2007): 298ff.

12 Tit. 41 LSax: De haeredibus et viduis: Pater aut mater defuncti filio non filiae hereditatem relinquent [Of heirs and widows: Father and mother leave their heritage to the son, not to the daughter]. Tit. 44 LSax: Qui defunctus non filios sed filias reliquerit ad eas omnis hereditas pertineat; tutela vero earum fratri vel proximo paterni generis deputetur [If the bequeather does not leave a son but daughters only, all the heritage goes to them]; see Claudius Freiherr v. Schwerin, ed., *Leges Saxonum und Lex Thuringorum, Fontes Iuris Germanici antiqui in usum scholarum ex Monuments Germaniae Historicis separatem editi* (Hannover–Leipzig: Hahn, 1918), 28ff.

13 Tit. 62 LSax: Nulli liceat traditionem hereditatis suae facere praeter ad ecclesiam vel regi ut heredem suum exheredem faciat nisi forte famis necessitate coactus ut ab illo qui hoc acceperit sustentetur; mancipia liceat illi dare ac vendere [Nobody is allowed to make a delivery of possession of his heritage unless to the Church or to the King by which the heir would be disinherited unless the disposer is driven by necessity of hunger and the recipient promises to keep the disposer. Vassals are free to be disposed of and to be sold]; see v. Schwerin, *Leges Saxonum und Lex Thuringorum*, 32. For this, cf. Schmidt-Recla, *Kalte oder warme Hand*, 368ff.

it is even more unlikely that Friedrich positively knew what Frankish noblemen were accustomed to doing, knowing that – according to the 500-year-old Frankish *Lex Salica* (dating back to the beginnings of the 6th century) – daughters by law had no right to any part of their father's real property.[14] The Franks could voluntarily bequeath property to their daughters while the former were still alive providing the latter with a substitute for their equal share. This is likely since there were notary instruments to record such transactions, as proven by a Frankish document, the so-called *Formula Markulfi* II.12 (edited by Karl Zeumer in 1886).[15] It is interesting that that document (dating back to the end of the 7th century) declared a traditional custom to be "impious." Whatever the Frankish author may have understood by the terms "impiety" or "equity" (there is no clarification in the wording of the text), one can assume that there must have been a need to provide daughters with "equal shares" of the paternal heritage. It is tempting to assume that there was a common understanding of equity concerning inheritance in law or custom throughout medieval Europe ever since the 6th century. This is only conjecture, however. Nobody will ever be able to prove how often documents like the *Formula Markulfi* II.12 were used in practice, or – moreover – if there was a notarial practice at all.

14 Cf. Tit. 59.6 LSal: De terra uero Salica nulla in mulieri portio aut hereditas est, sed ad uirilem sexum, qui fratres fuerint, tota terra pertineat [From Salic land no portion or heritage goes to the wife. All land belongs to the male relatives, which are brothers]; see Karl August Eckhardt, ed., *Pactus Legis Salice*, Monumenta Germaniae Historica, Legum Sectio I, vol. 4, part 1 (Hannover: Hahn, 1962), 223. For this, cf. Schmidt-Recla, *Kalte oder warme Hand*, 216.

15 Markulf II.12: Carta, ut filia cum fratres in paterna succedat alode. Dulcissima filia mea illa illi. Diuturna, sed impia inter nos consuetudo tenetur, ut de terra paterna sorores cum fratribus porcionem non habeant; sed ego perpendens hanc impietate, sicut mihi a Deo aequales donati estis filii, ita et a me setis aequaliter diligens et de res meas post meum discessum aequaliter gratuletis. Ideoque per hanc epistolam te, dulcissima filia mea, contra germanos tuos, filios meos illos in omni hereditate mea aequalem et legitimam esse constituo heredem, ut tam de alode paterna quam de conparatum vel mancipia aut presidium nostrum, vel quodcumque morientes relinquaeremus, equo lante cum filiis meis, germanis tuis, dividere vel exequare debias et in nullo paenitus porcionem minorem quam ipse non accipias, sed omnia vel ex omnibus inter vos dividere vel exaequare debeatis. Si quis vero et quod sequitur [Letter by which a daughter inherits together with her brothers. Dear daughter [...], Common among us there is a long but impious custom providing that a daughter should not have a patrimony alongside brothers. Pondering this impiety and concerning that you were donated to me equally with your brothers by God almighty, I want you to get an equal share after my death. Hence, I appoint you, my dear daughter, my equal and legitimate heir with your brothers to all my belongings and you shall have an equal share of all paternal land, acquiree, people and all faculty I will leave behind dying. And you shall divide equally with my sons, your brothers and you shall not accept a smaller share anyway. You all shall share everything equally amongst you]; see Karl Zeumer, ed., *Formulae Merovingici et Karolini Aevi*, Monumenta Germaniae Historica, Legum Sectio V (Hannover: Hahn, 1886), 83. For this, cf. Schmidt-Recla, *Kalte oder warme Hand*, 216–219. Markulf is said to have been a Frankish monk who collected notary instruments, *cartae*, for educational purposes at the end of the 7th century.

Returning to Friedrich, there is no proof that either Friedrich or Thietmar had knowledge of the *Lex Saxonum*, the *Lex Salica*, or any legal instrument or record. It is (as mentioned) very likely that Friedrich was an illiterate man. Moreover, one cannot even prove why Friedrich considered Dietrich to be his heir (as Thietmar wrote). But he obviously did. And what he did as a result and what Thietmar calls "legitimate" was that, as a "wise" man, he gathered all the people possibly involved or affected around his table (or his deathbed, in his castle or his court). There he dealt with Oda, Ida, Milda, and Dietrich together. Finally, he obviously found the easiest solution: Oda, Ida, and Milda got (after Friedrich's soon expected death) all his belongings (that means his movable and immovable property). Dietrich would not contest his first cousins' inheritance and was compensated for this with the Susali ruler's seat. This was an intelligent solution considering all the interests involved. One could thus label Friedrich's wise deed an example of *ars boni et aequi.*

5.5 Legitimacy and Equity before the Law

At this point, it should again be considered what Thietmar could have had in mind when he spoke about legitimacy. The bishop never mentioned or referred to an act, writ, *lex Barbarorum*, or anything scholars would call a legal or normative source of secular law in his *Chronicle*. Of course, he took into account the *lex divina*, the *lex Dei*, and the *lex Moysi*.[16] That is irrelevant to this discussion, however, and Friedrich's compromise solution did not refer to earlier written Saxon law. This is also due to a substantial comparison of Friedrich's disposition and Tit. 62 LSax.[17] On the contrary, "legitimacy" according to Friedrich and Thietmar must refer to the fact that the validity of the transaction was, according to Thietmar's information (which ends 1018), not disputed afterwards among the remaining parties: Oda, Ida, Milda and Dietrich.

This leads us potentially back to the dawn of the law – and of course into the open arms of equity, which is, according to the classic statement of Eugen Wohlhaupter, "the dynamic principle of development of law in general."[18] One does not have to assume that equity is primarily or only a principle or matter to rectify or to amend law to achieve greater justice. Equity in medieval law has to be regarded as *iustitia*,[19] as the law itself, too, because the law can be described as a system of rules that produce equitable results when obeyed. That's precisely what one can see in Friedrich of Eilenburg's case and in Thietmar's description of it as "legitimate." Is it speculative to assume that

16 Schmidt-Recla, *Kalte oder warme Hand*, 369ff.

17 Schmidt-Recla, *Kalte oder warme Hand*, 368–371.

18 Eugen Wohlhaupter, *Aequitas Canonica: Eine Studie aus dem kanonischen Recht* (Paderborn: Schöningh, 1931), 41.

19 Hans Hattenhauer, "Minne und recht," *Zeitschrift der Savigny-Stiftung für Rechtsgeschichte, Germanistische Abteilung* 80 (1963): 340.

Thietmar took the Eilenburg case as an example to illustrate his understanding of equitable or lawful thinking? I believe so.

Moreover, this case shows that agreements and contracts are the foundation of European law. Before the law was written into books, writs, or acts, people found nonviolent solutions only if they treated themselves equally and respected their mutual interests, which is what the five Saxons we have been discussing did (as did Frankish noblemen earlier). Friedrich respected the physical (or military) power Dietrich would have been able to exercise. He gave a now unknown mass of his movable and immovable belongings as a whole to his three daughters. Oda and her sisters acquired certain wealth and a ruler closely related to them and with a claim to their belongings, a sword-bearer with close ties to the king, gave his consent, the "heir's consent" (or in German: the *Erbenlaub*) to their future position. Dietrich for his part consolidated his position as the king's direct vassal with a second county under his command. No one knows whether Oda's, Ida's, and Milda's share was an equal share (when compared with Dietrich's share, Eilenburg). One can assume, however, that the transaction created a set of rules governing relations between the parties and, thus, nothing short of law. A future unilateral violation of this consent would appear inequitable, unjust, or illegitimate (as Thietmar probably would have called it).

The "heir's consent" respected by Friedrich and his daughters is a perfect means of bringing the scales of justice into equilibrium. It made, and makes, dispositions legitimate because of and by themselves. It is almost needless to say that the institution of the "heir's consent" formed a precedent for later Saxon law. Hence, the "heir's consent" proves to have been a method of protecting and taking into consideration the interests of persons who expect to inherit soon or someday, right from the early beginning of reasoning and writing about law. Equity called for it; Friedrich knew it intuitively because he was "wise"; Dietrich, Oda, Ida, and Milda agreed to it; Thietmar wrote it down as the first person ever in a short story about lawful thinking.

And finally, 200 years later, the law (written once again but now in a law book by the famous Eike von Repgow) recognised it. Eike von Repgow, who has (with a wink) to be considered to have been a wise man, too, for his sake called it "erven gelof" when working on his famous law book around 1225/1235 (cf. *Sachsenspiegel Landrecht* I.52.1[20]), from which the German word "Erbenlaub" took its origin. For how long the heir's consent was obeyed

20 Sachsenspiegel Landrecht I, 52, 1: Ane erven gelof unde ane echte dink ne mut neman sin egen noch sine lute geven. (...) Gift he it weder rechte sunder erven gelof, de erve underwinde't sek met ordelen, also of he dot si, jene de it dar gaf, so he is nicht ne geven mochte [Without the heir's consent and outside of court nobody is allowed to dispose of his land and his vassals. ... If a man disposes [of his possessions] against the law without his heir's consent, the heir is entitled to demand it by replevin as if the disposer was dead already and was unable to dispose [of his possessions]; see Karl August Eckhardt, ed., *Das Landrecht des Sachsenspiegels* (Göttingen: Musterschmidt, 1952), 52ff.

by people, learned lawyers, rulers, and courts in Susali, Saxony (upper and lower), and Germany is another story.

References

Primary sources

Edited sources

Eckhardt, Karl August, ed. *Pactus Legis Salice*, Monumenta Germaniae Historica, Legum Sectio I, vol. 4, part 1. Hannover: Hahn, 1962.
Holtzmann, Robert, ed. *Thietmari Merseburgensis episcopi chronicon. Die Chronik des Bischofs Thietmar von Merseburg und ihre Korveier Überarbeitung*, Monumenta Germaniae Historica, Scriptores rerum Germanicarum, Nova Series IX. Berlin: Weidmann, 1935.
Schwerin, Claudius Freiherr v., ed. *Leges Saxonum und Lex Thuringorum, Fontes Iuris Germanici antiqui in usum scholarum ex Monuments Germaniae Historicis separatem editi*. Hannover/Leipzig: Hahn, 1918.
Zeumer, Karl, ed. *Formulae Merovingici et Karolini Aevi*, Monumenta Germaniae Historica, Legum Sectio V. Hannover: Hahn, 1886.

Secondary studies

Biermann, Felix. *Slawische Besiedlung zwischen Elbe, Neiße und Lubsza. Archäologische Studien zum Siedlungswesen und zur Sachkultur des frühen und hohen Mittelalters*. Bonn: Habelt, 2000.
Eckhardt, Karl August, ed. *Das Landrecht des Sachsenspiegels*. Göttingen: Musterschmidt, 1952.
Hattenhauer, Hans. "Minne und recht." *Zeitschrift der Savigny-Stiftung für Rechtsgeschichte, Germanistische Abteilung* 80 (1963): 325–44.
Landau, Peter. "Thietmar von Merseburg in Zusammenhang mit der Überlieferung von Lex Saxonum und Lex Thuringorum. Eine Studie zum Erbrecht der Ottonenzeit." *Zeitschrift der Savigny-Stiftung für Rechtsgeschichte, Germanistische Abteilung* 124 (2007): 296–300.
Oexle, Judith, ed. *Sachsen: archäologisch. 12.000 v. Chr. – 2.000 n. Chr.* Dresden: Sächsisches Druck- und Verlagshaus, 2000.
Schmidt-Recla, Adrian. *Kalte oder warme Hand. Verfügungen von Todes wegen in mittelalterlichen Referenzrechtsquellen*. Köln/Weimar/Wien: Böhlau, 2011.
Theuerkauf, Gerhard. *Lex, Speculum, Compendium iuris. Rechtsaufzeichnungen und Rechtsbewußtsein in Norddeutschland vom 8. bis zum 16. Jahrhundert*. Köln: Böhlau, 1968.
Westphalen, Thomas. "Zwischen Prag und Meißen – Die Slawen in Sachsen." In *Sachsen: archäologisch. 12.000 v. Chr. – 2.000 n. Chr.*, edited by Judith Oexle, 74. Dresden: Sächsisches Druck- und Verlagshaus, 2000.
Wohlhaupter, Eugen. *Aequitas Canonica. Eine Studie aus dem kanonischen Recht*. Paderborn: Schöningh, 1931.

6 Visions of Equity

Guido Rossi

6.1 Equity: A Multifaceted Concept

Historically, the way equity came to be applied within a normative "system" (to use a misleading word for want of a better one) is not uniform. This chapter will focus on the medieval and the first early modern period, providing three examples of well-known but different uses of the same term: equity in common law, equity in civil law, and equity in mercantile transactions. In England, an increasingly formalistic approach led to a progressive rigidity, which called for some correction[1]; on the Continent, on the contrary, equity was quickly absorbed into law. Among merchants, equity was applied not as a way of correcting rules, but as their very essence. In general introductions on the development of the concept of equity, the English concept of equity is often dealt with only cursorily or by way of comparison. Therefore, this chapter will do the opposite, giving more space to the English approach to equity and being more succinct with respect to the other approaches.

6.2 Equity in the Common Law

6.2.1 Fairness and Equity

Any account of English law highlights the divide between equity and the common law.[2] This, however, does not mean that common law has never made use of the concept of fairness. From time to time, the justices of common law courts have shown an appreciation for the consequences of their decisions and well understood that, sometimes, the application of a general rule to a certain case may lead to unfair results. Such cases are attested even before the establishment of a separate court whose jurisdiction would be defined by its equitable nature. Medieval sources sometimes describe how common law justices

1 Cf. Jan Halberda's contribution in this book.

2 See, e.g., A. Gambaro, R. Sacco and L. Vogel, *Traité de droit compare – Le droit de l'Occident et d'ailleurs* (Paris: LGDJ, 2011), 87–90.

DOI: 10.4324/9781003654131-9

would deliberately choose to follow a more equitable interpretation of the law to avoid unfair solutions. In such cases, the justices were fully conscious of the two different paths which lay before them, and of their preference for the equitable solution as opposed to the more legalistic one. It is even more important that they indicated the fairer choice as the equitable one, that is, the one grounded in "equity."[3] During this formative period of the common law, some equitable features were even included in the law itself.[4]

Progressively, however, because of the highly formalistic nature of the writ system, during the late Middle Ages justices would increasingly refrain from intervening to correct the harshness that the application of a rule in a certain case might have.[5] Inflexible procedures often make for unfair results. Because of the procedural strictness of the common law, it was not uncommon to witness some cases of perfectly legal injustice, the result of a legalistic approach which requires certain means to achieve equitable ends; but, in so doing, it crystallises the means, leaving no alternative but to follow them strictly. Hence, the maxim that it was "better to suffer a mischief than an inconvenience," attested already by the early 15th century.[6] It is possible to think of the development of the Court of Chancery as a reaction to – or rather, the correction of – an exceedingly formalistic legal system. Yet, even more than in the issuing of equitable remedies, the true novelty of the Chancery as a court of equity lay in the systematic use of an equitable solution before a specific court, as if the notion of equity was no longer a way to interpret the rules in a more conscionable manner but was itself crystallised into new and different rules.

6.2.2 *Equity and the Chancery*

As it is well known, during the 15th century the Chancellor began to exercise jurisdictional functions no longer in the name of the king but in his own. This was doubtless an effect of the ever-increasing number of petitions by bill which were addressed to the king throughout the late Middle Ages, and which gave rise to different courts, the most important of which was that of the Court of Chancery.[7] For a long time, the Chancery was an office, not a law court. However, both because of the wide remit of the Chancellor's powers

3 P. Brand, "The Equity of the Common Law Courts," in *Law & Equity: Approaches in Roman Law and Common Law*, eds. E. Koops and W.J. Zwalve (Leiden: Nijhoff, 2014), 45.

4 See, for instance, the formation and the development of the action of account as examined by the same Brand, "The Equity," 45–52.

5 J.H. Baker, *The Oxford History of the Laws of England*, vol. 6 (1483–1558) (Oxford: Oxford University Press, 2003), 41, text and esp. fn 214. See more, in general, N. Doe, *Fundamental Authority in Late Medieval English Law* (Cambridge: Cambridge University Press, 1991), 155–174.

6 J.H. Baker, *An Introduction to English Legal History*, 5th ed. (Oxford: Oxford University Press, 2019), 111.

7 See, e.g., Baker, *An Introduction*, 106–108.

and because it was the Chancery that issued the writs to initiate litigation in the common law courts, the Chancellor's jurisdictional functions were perhaps easy enough to accept. This was also due to the simple fact that the Chancellor was also the Keeper of the Great Seal, which was used to authenticate most royal documents: thus, its holder was the person who could represent the Crown in the absence of the sovereign.[8] In retrospect, it is easy to see why petitioners began to address the Chancellor directly, in the hope that their bill would thus attract more attention than that which could be expected from a general petition to the king. Perhaps because of this function, the Chancery was also the only court before which the crown could be sued, for the king could not be sued by his own writ in a common law court. It was precisely because of the link with the crown that the Chancery retained the king's residuary jurisdiction to do justice to his subjects.[9] It is from the same residuary function that the jurisdiction of the Chancery as a court of equity stemmed.

The Chancellor began to provide remedies in equity on a rather *ad hoc* basis. Indeed, it took a rather long time for the jurisdictional activity of the Chancery (the so-called English side of the Chancery) to be seen as the activity of an institution and not the sum of many individual, one-off interventions by the Chancellor. As the whole jurisdiction of the Chancery was progressively created around the figure of the Chancellor and in a way adapted to him (and to his jurisdictional prerogatives), juries never played any role in it. The absence of a jury, in a system wholly informed by it, is of great importance[10]: the parties did not have to persuade a number of their peers, but instead they only had to persuade the Chancellor. This aspect should not be underestimated when assessing the nature of the early remedies sought and provided by the Chancery: in a system accustomed to having both a judge and a jury, doing without the latter meant vesting the former with a twofold role. This way, the judge was no longer just an umpire of sorts – by and large, responsible for overseeing the correctness of the procedure employed – but also a jury, called to decide whether some facts alleged by one party were true, and also (the two things usually worked together) whether they deserved some special consideration. The Chancellor, in other words, had to be persuaded. And the object of this persuasion was not that the pleadings of the parties were correct (which is what most litigation *in banc* in common law boiled down to),[11] but rather that their cause – taking into account all its facets – was indeed a worthy one. Thus, from the very beginning, the aim of the litigants in the Chancery was to

8 Thus, by the late 14th century, it is possible to find petitions nominally addressed to the king and his council but, in fact, meant for the Chancellor alone. Baker, *An Introduction*, 109, text and fn 24.

9 Baker, *An Introduction*, 109.

10 Cf. Baker, *The Oxford History*, 40–41.

11 Common law justices would express themselves "in banc" by ruling on a question of law whenever dealing with a hypothetical formula before trial, or on some legal consequences of the facts as established by the jury. Cf. Baker, *An Introduction*, 89.

persuade the Chancellor to grant them an *ad hoc* remedy. At the same time, the Chancellor did not have to follow any particular procedure and, moreover, was not tied to the specific requests of the parties. The approach followed in the Chancery was more reminiscent of a Continental law court and, thus, was more easily identifiable with the inquisitorial than the accusatorial procedure.[12] The peculiar combination of judge and jury is probably also the reason why in the development of the Chancery there was no clear-cut distinction between fact and law; this, in turn, was another reason for the slow development of a set of legal principles, as opposed to a number of *ad hoc* remedies devised for specific, individual instances. Unlike the common law courts, where the court did not have to take facts into account but only verify the correctness of the procedure, the Chancellor had to look at the whole matter being litigated before him as a single, unitary issue which required a comprehensive solution.[13]

6.2.3 Conscience and Equity

It is common knowledge that the Court of Chancery is known as a court of equity, and that, initially, it was designated more typically as a court of conscience. Using the concept of conscience or equity as the common denominator of the Chancellor's jurisdiction, however, is of little help in making sense of the features of his remedies. What is equity? A century ago Maitland observed how the concept of equity would point to the feeling of fairness that a layperson would have when confronted with a practical legal issue, as opposed to the specific remedies available (or not) at common law.[14] This divide between commonsense solutions and "technical" (i.e., based on the common law) solutions may perhaps help explain the fact that the term "equity" was also employed in different contexts altogether, for instance among merchants, and it was used to describe courts that would not rely on the common law to resolve a dispute. In this sense, 16th-century merchants could easily say that mercantile courts were "courts of equity."[15] Perhaps this was the reason

12 So much so that its origins have not infrequently been searched for in the Continental Romano-canonical procedure followed first of all in ecclesiastical courts: see esp. H. Coing, "English Equity and the *Denunciatio Evangelica* of the Canon Law," *Law Quarterly Review* 71 (1955): 223–241; J.L. Barton, "Equity in the Medieval Common Law," in *Equity in the World's Legal System*, ed. R.A. Newman (Brussels: Bruylant, 1973), 144–149; see also the introduction to T.F.T. Plucknett and J.L. Barton, eds., *St. German's Doctor and Student* (London: Selden Society, vol. 91, 1974), xxxiv. One fact, however, remains quite significant: at no time did the doctors of law plead there.

13 The presence of a jury as a factor that inhibited – or at any rate did not favour – a more equitable approach by common law justices can be found as early as in the biography of Thomas More written by his son-in-law, William Roper, *The Lyfe of Sir Thomas Moore, Knight*, ed. E.V. Hitchcock (Bloomington: Indiana University Press, 1935), 44–45.

14 F.W. Maitland, *Equity, Also, the Forms of Action at Common Law* (Cambridge: Cambridge University Press, 1929), 1.

15 British Library, Ms. Additional 48020, *fol.* 356*r* (a document of 1575).

why the term "equity" was increasingly used to identify the approach of the Chancellor and to distinguish it from that of the common law courts. The novelty, as already pointed out, lay in its systematic approach: the notion of equity was no longer used to advocate for a special application of a certain rule in a particular situation; rather, it was now invoked as the standard approach to any given situation. Thus, as Lord Chancellor Ellesmere famously put it in an early-16th-century case, the Court of Chancery existed precisely because[16]

> men's actions are so diverse and infinite that it is impossible to make a general law which may aptly meet with every particular and not fail in some circumstances. The office of the chancellor is to correct men's consciences for frauds, breaches of trust, wrongs, and oppressions of what nature soever they be, and to soften and mollify the extremity of the law.

By the early 16th century, equity and conscience were still treated as coterminous. This does not mean that equity had some subjective or arbitrary meaning; rather, it suggests that the term "conscience" itself had rather objective connotations, especially in its usage during the Middle Ages.[17] The shift from conscience to equity can be ascribed to a complex process, some of whose features will not be dealt with here even summarily, as they would require a complex and altogether different study. One of them is the Reformation and its impact on English society: the influence that the English Reformation had on the notion of conscience is very considerable and has been studied in depth.[18] Thus, the perception that the notion of conscience was more prone to personal views[19] might have been encouraged by religious factors. The fact that the Chancellor who oversaw the beginnings of the Reformation in England (Thomas Wolsey) was a cardinal and in all but name a prime minister, and that, more specifically, he made a point in antagonising common lawyers by relying on his own personal sense of justice surely did not help. A famous treatise, prudently published after Wolsey's death, purportedly highlighted the subjective

16 *Earl of Oxford's Case* (1615) 1 *Reports in Chancery* 1, 6.

17 D.R. Klinck, *Conscience, Equity and the Court of Chancery in Early Modern England* (Aldershot: Ashgate, 2010), 13–40; T. Haskett, "Conscience, Justice and Authority in the Late-Medieval English Court of Chancery," in *Expectations of the Law in the Middle Ages*, ed. A. Musson (Martlesham: The Boydell Press, 2001), 151–164, 159. Cf. also T.C. Potts, *Conscience in Medieval Philosophy* (Cambridge: Cambridge University Press, 1980).

18 Klinck, *Conscience, Equity and the Court of Chancery*. Klinck's excellent work shows a significant evolution of the concept of conscience – more objective in medieval times and more open to subjective interpretations once the Reformation began to exert a significant influence on English society. It would be wrong, however, to assume a rather brisk shift in the meaning ascribed to the term "conscience": as late as in the 1570s, the panels of arbiters in charge of settling mercantile controversies in London were required to decide according to "their conscience" – that is, on the basis of (objective) good faith.

19 Baker, *An Introduction*, 115.

undertones of the term "conscience" to show Wolsey's arbitrariness.[20] Surely, the term "equity" sounded more objective and less open to personal interpretations than that of "conscience." Hence, the famous quip by John Selden that taking the Chancellor's conscience as the standard for conscience was no better than opting for his foot as the standard length of one foot.[21] It is from the early reactions to Wolsey's chancellorship that the use of equity in opposition to the common law seems to date.[22] By the early 1540s, the divide was already apparent enough for John Hales to write of "two manner of equities," namely, an arithmetic one and a geometric one.[23]

The shift from conscience to equity can also be seen within the institutional development of the Chancery. The 16th century saw an exponential increase in litigation before the Chancery, which had in the meanwhile become one of the major courts in England. This great increase in the volume of litigation required an institutionalisation of its practice because it forced its clerks to repeat the same procedure time and again, and the Chancellor to decide on multiple occasions on cases very similar to each other. During the 17th century, this process was accompanied by another, no less important one – the reporting of Chancery cases. By the late 16th century all we have is just some references to common lawyers taking notes of what the Chancellor said, but by the middle of the following century this process had become regular practice. Thus, it was now possible for a Chancellor to affirm that his personal conscience and the conscience according to which he was supposed to decide a case were two very different things[24] because the latter kind of conscience was, in fact, no conscience at all but rather equity[25]. This objectivisation of conscience into equity also led to its embodiment in a set of rules. The development of the Chancery during the 16th century should be seen as one of the main reasons for the shift in the vocabulary adopted to describe that court – from a court of conscience to a court of equity.

20 *Replication of a Serjeant at Law*, (partial) transcription in J.H. Baker, *Baker and Milsom Sources of English Legal History: Private Law to 1750*, 2nd ed. (Oxford: Oxford University Press, 2019), 125. The full transcription may be read in J.A. Guy, ed., *Christopher St German on Chancery and Statute* (London: Selden Society, 1985), 99–105.

21 S.W. Singer, ed., *The Table-Talk of John Selden* (London: John Russell Smith, 1856), 49.

22 Cf. Baker, *The Oxford History*, 44.

23 John Hales, *Oration in Commendation of Lawes, fol.* 42, as reported in Baker, *The Oxford History*, 47.

24 *Coke v Fountaine* (1676) 3 Swanston's Chancery Reports 585, 600 (*per* Lord Nottingham C). On this important case, see M. Macnair, "*Coke v Fountaine* (1676)," in *Landmark Cases in Equity*, eds. C. Mitchell and P. Mitchell (Oxford: Hart, 2012), 33–62.

25 *Honywood v Bennett* (1675), *Lord Nottingham's Chancery Cases*, vol. 2 (D.E.C. Yale ed., London: Selden Society, vol. 73, 1954), 214.

6.2.4 *Equity, Fairness, and ἐπιείκεια*

From the beginning, however, it was difficult to provide a clear (i.e., rational) explanation as to what conscience/equity was, and thus, indirectly, the basis for having a different and separate Court of Chancery alongside those of common law. St German's treatise on the subject,[26] despite its celebrity, was not particularly clear on the point either. The treatise, a dialogue between a student of the common law and a doctor of divinity, focused on one of the classic examples where the formalism of the common law could result in an unequitable solution: a debtor who, upon receiving the money lent to him, issued a sealed bond in which he promised to pay back twice as much by a certain date. This was meant only as a fine for the case of non-repayment within a specific period. Sealed bonds were an ordinary way to lend money, as they offered greater security to the lender than a mere credit: not only there was no need of a jury to determine whether the claim was true or not, but also the amount of damages to be awarded was already quantified in the instrument itself (and it totaled an amount equivalent to the original debt).[27] The problem was that, at the moment of repaying the debt, the debtor needed to make sure to receive the bond from the creditor and destroy it. Otherwise, the instrument would still remain enforceable: under the common law procedural rules, it constituted incontrovertible written evidence of the existence of a debt.[28] So, after a long discussion, the student of the common law had to concede to the doctor of divinity that leaving the creditor able to claim his credit (plus the fine) once he had already collected it was against conscience, and some remedy had to be devised in order to prevent such a situation.[29] The example was a straightforward case of Chancery intervention,[30] but the way St German explained it was not very satisfactory as it was not a case in which a rule should be interpreted in a more equitable way to achieve a more balanced result; rather, it was a case in which a rule ought to be disregarded entirely for the outcome to be fair.[31] In defending the need of equity, St German recalled Aristotle's notion of

26 T.F.T. Plucknett and J.L. Barton, eds., *St German's Doctor and Student* (London, Selden Society, 1974). On St German's thought, see the recent study of I. Williams, "Christopher St German: Religion, Conscience and Law in Reformation England," in *Great Christian Jurists in English History. Law and Christianity*, eds. M. Hill and R.H. Helmholz (Cambridge: Cambridge University Press, 2017), 69–92.

27 Baker, *An Introduction*, 345–347.

28 Baker, *The Oxford History*, 41–42.

29 D.J. Ibbetson, "A House Built on Sand: Equity in Early Modern English Law," in *Law & Equity: Approaches in Roman Law and Common Law*, eds. E. Koops and W.J. Zwalve (Leiden: Nijhoff, 2014), 57–58.

30 See, e.g., E.G. Henderson, "Relief from Bonds in the English Chancery: Mid-Sixteenth Century," *The American Journal of Legal History* 18 (1974): 298–306.

31 G. Behrens, "An Early Tudor Debate on the Relation between Law and Equity," *Journal of Legal History* 19 (1998): 143–161.

epieikeia (ἐπιείκεια), highlighting its similarity to the equity of the Chancery.[32] *Epieikeia*, as it is well known, is the equitable application of a general rule to a specific case: as general rules are abstract, they cannot take into account all the peculiarities of each and every specific case. What Aristotle suggested in such cases was simply to put oneself in the place of the lawmaker and think of what he would have done not in general, but in that specific circumstance.[33]

To the common lawyer, interpreting the law according to its rationale and not on the sole basis of its letter was hardly a new concept: the fairness of the common law, for instance, is described as "equity" in the earliest treatise on the common law – that of Glanvill, written in the late 12th century.[34] As early as the late 13th century, the common law courts would at times prove willing to reach a more equitable (i.e., fair) conclusion, and not the one more in accordance with (and grounded on) the letter of the law.[35] Common law records show an increasing familiarity with the idea of the "equity of a statute" from the early 14th century onwards.[36] This "equity" is what a Continental jurist would call the rationale of the law, and both the civil and the common lawyer would not hesitate to oppose the equity/rationale of a rule to its mechanical application.[37]

In its meaning as the rationale of a rule, therefore, the concept of equity could hardly justify the existence of a separate court – a court of equity – issuing different remedies from those of the common law. St German suggested further reasons why equity should temper the rigour of the (common) law, especially the need to harmonise human law with natural and divine law. In so doing, he was following Aquinas's reading of Aristotle,[38] which admittedly narrowed down the Stagyrite's approach. Apart from not providing a theoretical justification for the court of equity, this and other meanings of equity found in St German were not necessarily all compatible with each other.[39]

32 See, e.g., D. Klimchuk, "Aristotle at the Foundations of the Law of Equity," in *Philosophical Foundations of the Law of Equity*, eds. D. Klimchuk, I. Samet, and H.E. Smith (Oxford: Oxford University Press, 2020), 32–51.

33 *Nicomachean Ethics*, V.10.

34 Glanvill, see: *The Treatise on the Laws and Customs of the Realm of England Commonly Called Glanvill*, ed. G.D.G. Hall (London: Clarendon Press, 1965; reprint, 1993), prologue; ii. 7; vii. 1. Cf. Baker, *An Introduction*, 114, fn 55 (comparing the meaning of equity in the late-12th-century work of Glanvill with that of the early-13th-century treatise of Bracton, II, 25).

35 See, e.g., Brand, "The Equity," 39–53.

36 Doe, *Fundamental Authority*, 104–106; Ibbetson, "A House Built on Sand," 56–57, text and notes 8–11. See already S.E. Thorne, "The Equity of a Statute and Heydon's Case," *Illinois Law Review* 31 (1936): 202–216.

37 Cf. Baker, *The Oxford History*, 45–46.

38 *Summa Theologiae*, 1ª 2ªᵉ, 96.1.1.

39 Ibbetson, "A House Built on Sand," 58–59. On the (considerable) influence of Gerson on St German, see Z. Rueger, "Gerson's Concept of Equity and Christopher St Germain," *History of Political Thought* 3 (1982): 1–30.

Despite its pitfalls, St German's work proved a great success and the basis for all future discussions on equity and the Chancery as it gave an authoritative foundation to what might otherwise be labelled as a mere historical accident. A series of later treatises written during the second half of the 16th century and the beginning of the 17th (namely, Edward Hake's *Epieikeia*, Thomas Ashe's *Epieikeia*, an anonymous and unpublished short work on equity,[40] the small tract *On Equitie* by Thomas Egerton (Chancellor in the years 1603–1616), William Lambarde's *Archeion*, Samuel Daniel's *Epistle to the Lord Keeper*, and a few pages in William West's *Symboleography* – a long and complex work whose core did not concern equity) would use St German and his notion of equity to explain the activity of the Chancery. Few of such treatises were particularly convincing.[41] The circularity of the concept of the Chancery as a court of equity,[42] therefore, is a petition of principle with a long historical pedigree.

6.3 Equity in the Civil Law

6.3.1 Equity and Strict Law

If the relationship between equity and the law in England became the dialectic between different institutions, the same relationship on the Continent remained internal to the law and did not bring about the forking of the law courts. This might be due, at least partially, to the fact that jurists had been dealing with this dialectic for a long time in the effort to square a legal circle. In the compilation of Justinian there are two different passages, one stating that equity should always be preferred to strict law (C.3.1.8.),[43] the other reserving the power to resolve contradictions between strict law and equity to the emperor alone (C.1.14.1). The attempts to find a solution date to the dawn of teaching law at Bologna. One attempt, by the 12th-century jurist Martinus Gosia, was to restrict C.1.14.1 to those cases in which the interpretation was both necessary – that is, binding – and general (and so, applicable to all cases). Thus, not only the interpretation of a jurist (which is neither necessary nor general), but also that of a judge (which is necessary but not general) would escape the monopoly of the emperor. By narrowing down the scope of C.1.14.1, it became possible to follow C.3.1.8 and so opt for

40 Cambridge University Library Ms. gg 2.31, *fols.* 12–17.

41 See the thorough analysis in Ibbetson, "A House Built on Sand," 62–74. A different treatise is that written by a lawyer, Anthony Ben, in defence of the jurisdiction of the Court of Chancery: that work, short and far more technical, should be placed within the more restricted context of the (legal and political) struggle leading to the clash between Coke and Ellesmere in 1616: J.H. Baker, "The Common Lawyers and the Chancery: 1616." *Irish Jurist* 4, no.2 (1969). 382. Ben's *Defence* may be found in British Library, Ms. Lansdowne 174 *fols.* 205ff.

42 W.H. Bryson, *Cases concerning Equity and the Courts of Equity, 1550–1660*, vol. 1 (London: Selden Society, 2000), xviii.

43 This was strengthened by D.50.17.90.

the equitable interpretation of a rule, especially by the judge when deciding a practical case.[44]

6.3.2 Written and Unwritten Equity

What would become the most popular solution, however, was that of a contemporary of Martinus (and his fellow student of the founder of the Bologna law school, Irnerius) – the jurist Bulgarus. For Bulgarus, the two provisions of the Code of Justinian dealt with two different kinds of equity: the more permissive provision (C.3.1.8) referred to "established equity" (*aequitas constituta*), while the more stringent provision (C.1.14.1) pointed to "unwritten equity" (*nondum constituta aequitas*, or *aequitas rudis*).[45] Unwritten equity may be applied only by the legislator – and, thus, by the emperor, who alone has the power to change the law; written equity, on the other hand, is that which has already been put into law so as to correct the harshness of the law itself. This way, having largely sidelined the strict rule, it became possible to focus only on C.3.1.8 and invoke it whenever two different provisions of written law were applicable to a same case, opting for the more equitable one.[46]

44 For a good and up-to-date synthesis of the scholarly debate on the subject, see L. Maniscalco, *Equity in Early Modern Legal Scholarship* (Leiden: Brill, 2020), 16–18.

45 H. Kantorowicz, *Studies in the Glossators of the Roman Law* (Aalen: Scientia Verlag, 1969), 233–235.

Translating into English the terms "constituta" and "nondum constituta" presents some ambiguity: the obvious translation would be "written" and "unwritten" equity, yet this would make it more problematic to explain the difference between *constituta* and *scripta*. Perhaps the best way to identify the difference is to look at the other form employed by medieval jurists to describe unwritten equity: *aequitas rudis*, literally "raw equity." The "raw" condition of this equity is the very opposite of *constituta* – equity that has been shaped into clear provisions. *Constituere* conveyed the meaning of establishing something, and it was perfectly suited to a legal discourse. The Institutes of Gaius famously open with the tripartition of the law into *ius civile*, *ius naturale*, and *ius gentium* (Gai. Inst. I.1). There, to define what *ius civile* is Gaius uses the same verb constituere: *quod quisque populus ipse sibi ius constituit, id ipsius proprium est vocaturque ius ciuile* ("what every people establishes as law for itself is peculiar to itself, and is called the civil law," Samuel Parsons Scott, *The Civil Law*, vol. 1 (Cincinnati: The Central Trust Company, 1932), 81). Thus, *sibi constituere* is "to establish for oneself." This also explains why the better antonym of *aequitas constituta* is not *aequitas scripta*, but *aequitas rudis*: it is not so much a question of putting into writing a rule of equity but rather of shaping it into a precise – established – form. Hence the reason why equity "nondum constituta" (literally, "not yet established") is used as coterminous with "rudis" ("raw"). What lacks a precise form is something that is not yet put into shape, but that it may well be moulded. It is, however, already *aequitas*; only, it lacks a precise juridical vest – and, as we shall see, the lack of a legal shape creates an obstacle to its practical application.

46 See the in-depth research of E. Cortese, *La Norma Giuridica: Spunti teorici nel diritto comune classico*, vol. 2 (Milan: Giuffré, 1964), 295–362. See also E. Cortese, "Equité et justice, la dynamique bipolaire du droit au Moyen Age," in *Mélanges en l'honneur d'Anne Lefebvre-Teillard*, eds. B. D'Alteroche, F. Demoulin-Auzary, O. Descamps, and F. Roumy (Paris: Éditions Panthéon-Assas, 2009), 299–313.

Such equitable provisions of the law were considered as *aequitas scripta* (written equity): tangible manifestations of the equitable approach to the law crystallised into specific provisions.[47]

The same approach, perhaps more refined in its form, may be found in the *Enodationes questionum super Codice*, a dialogue written by a student of Bulgarus – the Glossator Rogerius. In it, Rogerius explained how equity may prevail over strict law only if enshrined into a (written) legal rule: from a legal viewpoint, the only equity that a judge can take into account is "that equity which is itself not *rudis* [raw] but written law."[48] By contrast, whenever equity remains only a principle and is not embodied in a legal provision, then written law must be applied. The clash between equity and the law, in other words, was relevant only as a conflict between specific and discrete written normative propositions.[49] Bulgarus's (and Rogerius's) approach was then also advocated by Bulgarus's most famous student, Johannes Bassianus, who endorsed it and thus contributed to its popularity.[50] The same dialectic between strict law and equity, as observed by the preeminent law professor of Bologna Azo (in his turn, a student of Bassianus) a few years later, also applies within specific legal principles: every legal rule (*regula iuris*) has some exceptions.[51] In other words, it was precisely to avoid some harsh conclusions in specific circumstances that exceptions were introduced to a legal principle; such exceptions are themselves tangible manifestations of the same *aequitas constituta* (written equity).

This solution, and crucially, the incorporation of equity into the law, avoided the possibility of any "equitable" approach different from the application of the law, thereby preventing any corrective approach seeking to amend

47 Cortese, *La Norma Giuridica*, vol. 2, 334, fn 73.

48 "[H]anc equitatem, que ipsa non rudis est sed ius scriptum, cum iuri scripto strictoque similiter contradicat, omnes iudices investigare diligenter a iurisque rigore propria secernere interpretatione ac secundum eam iudicare precipiuntur", Rogerius, *Enodationes questionum super Codice*, § 2; Kantorowicz, *Studies in the Glossators*, 282.

49 Kantorowicz, *Studies in the Glossators*, 282.

50 Esp. Bassianus's *Summula* on the *l. Placuit* (C.3.1.8), Paris, Bibliothèque Nationale, Ms lat. 4546, *fol.* 40*va-b*, on which see esp. E. Cortese, "La Summula Placuit piacentiniana e le aggiunte di Giovanni nel Ms. parigino 4546," in *Scritti*, vol. 1, eds. I. Birocchi and U. Petronio (Spoleto: Fondazione Centro italiano di studi sull'alto medioevo, 1999), 233–247. Allowing for *aequitas rudis* to be taken into account, argued Bassianus, would have given excessively broad powers to the judge, who should decide according to the law and not after the "aequitas of his mind" ("secundum equitatem animi sui"), Paris, Bibliothèque Nationale, Ms lat. 4546, *fol. 40vb*; Cortese, "La Summula Placuit," 244.

51 Azo, gl. *Aequitatisque* ad 1. *Placuit*, C. *De iudiciis* (C.3.1.8) (Parisiis, 1581, 167, n. 1–3): "Pone ergo sic, quia quandoque aequitas et iustitia est ab una parte, strictum ius ab alia, et contradicit: tunc sequendum est praecipue iustitae aequitatisque rationem quam strict ius … Item poni potest fere in omni regula, cum quaelibet patiatur exceptionem, ut dicit regula iuris, et exceptiones sunt de aequitate."

the application of a rule,[52] and also, *a fortiori*, the establishment of separate jurisdictions dealing specifically with equity.[53]

6.3.3 The Scope of Equity

At the same time, however, incorporating equity into the law also created exegetical problems: if the *aequitas* that may be taken into account is only that already provided for by the law itself, then the jurist (whether a law professor or a judge) may only favour the more equitable rules already found in the sources, not create new ones. Yet this *favor* towards equitable provisions created interpretative issues: if exceptions to the rules are introduced out of fairness (*ex aequitate*), and if *aequitas* ought to be favoured over the strictness of the law, then is it possible to interpret them extensively? The answer to this question was not easy to elaborate on fully. On the one hand, as the *aequitas* of the exception ought to be favoured, its scope could be widened somewhat, thereby carving out a broader scope compared to what should remain a case where the rule fails to apply; on the other hand, the exception being, after all, just an exception to the actual rule, it could not be extended by way of analogy.[54]

When does equity apply? A classic example is found in the second title of book 47 of the Digest of Justinian, devoted to the subject of theft. One of its texts (D.47.2.21pr) describes the case in which a thief steals part of a whole (a portion of a heap of corn). In such a case, is the thief liable for the whole or just for the portion actually stolen? In Roman law, theft lay not in the unlawful removal of someone else's property but, more broadly, in its unlawful handling. This is why the case made sense: strictly speaking, the thief had been meddling with the whole heap of corn, though he took away only a portion of it. It was therefore possible to punish him for the theft of the whole amount. At the same time, however, the text itself allowed for the narrowing down of the theft to the portion actually removed. In dealing with this text, medieval civil lawyers associated the possibility of punishing someone for stealing the whole heap of corn with the application of strict law, and considered the alternative solution (limiting the punishment to the theft of the corn actually stolen) to be the more equitable one.[55] Punishing the thief only for the smaller amount was as an application of *aequitas* – yet, crucially, an application already present in the text of the Digest, and not an alternative conclusion which the

52 Maniscalco, *Equity*, 16–17.

53 Other interpretations, such as that (proposed by the Glossator Guilelmus de Cabriano) based on chronology, did not have much success: A. Padoa-Schioppa, "Equità nel diritto medievale e moderno: Spunti della dottrina." *Rivista di storia del diritto italiano* 87 (2014): 11.

54 Cortese, *La Norma Giuridica*, vol. 2, 339–340. Cf. Cortese, *La Norma* Giuridica, vol. 1, 50–51.

55 See the Accursian Gloss, gl. *videtur fur esse* and gl. *verum est*, l. *Vulgaris*, ff. *De furtis* (D.47.2.21pr) – Accursius, *Pandectarum Iuris Civilis*, vol. 3 (Paris, 1566), col. 1279.

interpreter could arbitrarily make.[56] Similarly, in other instances in which the civil lawyers held that a solution found in the sources was dictated by equity, they often did so in order to clarify some inconsistency. Such is the case, for instance, of two rules in which a guarantor kills the thing which the promisor undertook to deliver: in the first case (D.4.3.19, an animal), the guarantor may be sued for his behaviour with an *actio de dolo*; in the second case (D.45.1.88, a slave), however, the guarantor can be sued on the basis of the promise itself – whose fulfilment he had intentionally made impossible. In the first case, argued medieval civil lawyers, the solution was based on strict law; in the second, on equity.[57]

Distinguishing between written and non-written equity, it became possible to consider equity as part of the law and not as a way of correcting it. Any reference to equity, as Azo famously put it, should be understood as "equity which is found in the law, not which may be found in one's heart."[58] If this *favor* towards written equity leaned towards the more lenient approach found in the sources and avoided the application of the harsher solution in certain instances, it also tied the hands of the jurists since the opposite of favouring written equity was neglecting unwritten equity. As the 14th-century jurist Bartolus de Saxoferrato had it, "written law is to be preferred to unwritten equity."[59]

6.3.4 Equity and Canon Law

If the position of Bulgarus prevailed among civil lawyers over that of Martinus from the outset, the concept of *aequitas* as understood by canon lawyers – the so-called *aequitas canonica* – was initially interpreted in a broader way: whenever following the law would lead to unfair results, equity ought to prevail. The concept of equity was soon coupled with that of mercy (*misericordia*). This term was often used in the ecclesiastical sources of the High Middle Ages, and it was then employed also among canon lawyers to interpret and apply the idea of *aequitas*, colouring it with a shade of leniency which is not to be found among civil lawyers.[60] Thus, in the late 12th century Uguccio of Pisa, one of the greatest canon lawyers of his time, could argue in favour of unwritten

56 Cf. Maniscalco, *Equity*, 19; H. Lange, "Ius aequum und ius strictum bei den Glossatoren," *Zeitschrift der Savigny-Stiftung für Rechtsgeschichte* 71 (1954): 341.
57 Maniscalco, *Equity*, 19.
58 Azo, gl. *Aequitatisque, ad l. Placuit*, C. *De iudiciis* (C.3.1.8) (Parisiis 1581, 167): "intellige de aequitate quae in lege reperitur, non quod de corde suo liceat invenire."
59 Bartolus, *ad l. Inter equitatem*, C. *De legibus* (C.1.14.1) (Basileae 1588, 86, n. 1).
60 See, e.g., P. Landau, "'Aequitas' in the 'Corpus Iuris Canonici,'" *Syracuse Journal of International Law and Commerce* 20 (1994): 95–104. Cf. also P.G. Caron, "I fondamenti romanistici e patristici del concetto di "aequitas canonica" dalle origini alla dottrina dei decretisti," *Annali della Facoltà giuridica di Camerino* 34 (1984): 119–180.

equity (*aequitas non scripta*).[61] But this approach did not last long, as already in the Ordinary Gloss to the *Liber Extra* (written in the 1240s), Bernardus Parmensis stated clearly that the *aequitas non scripta* could be invoked only in the absence of written law, otherwise "written law is to be preferred to equity."[62] Bernardus was far from being an exception, as the most important canon lawyers of the 13th century, from Sinibaldus de Fieschi (Pope Innocent IV) to Henricus de Segusio, would argue as much.[63] Written law, thus, prevailed over unwritten equity in both civil and canon law.

Unlike civil law, however, canon law gave more importance to equity and fairness when the "salvation of the souls" (*salus animarum*) was concerned: as the ultimate aim of canon law was eschatological, whenever the strict application of the letter of the law would result in a sin, the ecclesiastical judge could dispense with the written *ius* and follow unwritten *aequitas*.[64] Thus, for instance, even if a promise was not actionable without certain formal requirements, nonetheless in canon law it was considered actionable so as not to encourage sin.[65]

6.4 Equity and Commerce

6.4.1 Fairness and Good Faith among Merchants

A third approach to equity was that of merchants. This approach is markedly different both from the diverging paths of law and equity followed in England and from their merging together by Continental civil lawyers. By and large, the approach of merchants, whenever possible, was to rely on equity alone – judging *ex bono et aequo*. This meant first and foremost relying on good faith[66]: if the bargain could be kept, then it should be. Clearly, there were many situations in which a deal could not be honoured, but such situations tended to be typified and accepted on the basis of sheer experience. Thus, the kinds of circumstances that allowed parties to walk away from a deal would be limited to a given set of facts. Other than that, *pacta sunt servanda* ("agreements must be kept"). The violation of the *pactum* (agreement) had to be justified,

61 On this point, see esp. C. Lefebvre, *Les pouvoirs du juge en droit canonique* (Paris: Librairie du Recueil Sirey, 1938), 185.

62 "[I]us scriptum sit preferendum equitati", gl. *Aequitate, ad X., De transactionibus*, c. *ex parte tua* (X.1.36.11), see Bernardus Parmensis, *Decretales Gregorii noni seu Liber Extra* (Basileae: Sebastianus Brant, 1500).

63 Padoa-Schioppa, "Equità nel diritto," 75.

64 See, e.g., C. Lefebvre, "Aequitas canonica et periculum animae dans la doctrine de l'Hostiensis," *Ephemerides Iuris Canonici* 13 (1952): 305–321.

65 Padoa-Schioppa, "Equità nel diritto," 75–76.

66 E.g., F. Macino, "L'applicazione del principio di aequitas nella prassi giudiziaria dei mercanti (xiv–xv sec.)," in *Les documents du commerce et des marchands entre Moyen Âge et époque moderne (XII–XVII s.)*, eds. C. Mantegna and O. Poncet (Rome: Publications de l'École française de Rome, 2018), 15–33.

and this justification would turn the approach upside down: a strong justification would make the enforcement of the agreement unequitable. Fairness and equity, however, are based on the widespread (i.e., socially accepted) attitude about certain conduct: repetition generates the expectation that a given behaviour will be followed also in the future.[67] This is particularly visible in the liability for the execution of a commercial contract: whenever a contracting party did not follow the expected conduct, it was *prima facie* to blame for any mishap that might thereafter arise.[68] Thus, even within an approach to liability that is chiefly based on good faith, an agreement incompatible with the usual (i.e., socially accepted) path may create problems.

6.4.2 Good Faith and Equity: A Practical Case

An example might clarify the point. In 16th-century English customary insurance practice, policies had to state their beneficiary. Elsewhere, that was not the case. Thus, for instance, during the same period in Antwerp it was possible to insure some goods in favour of whoever owned them, without adding more information about the beneficiary of the policy. During the siege of Calais by the French, in 1558, an English merchant sought to insure his merchandise for a certain period of time. Few insurers would have covered such a risk had they known of the actual danger of confiscation, and surely they would have asked for a huge premium. But the insured person managed to cover the risk through an intermediary who executed the policy in Antwerp with some English merchants. The policy was executed in the name of the intermediary acting in his own name as the insured or whoever else was the actual owner of the merchandise. When the French occupied Calais and seized English property there, the actual insured party demanded payment from the merchants in London, who refused to pay. The reasons supporting each party's case were quite straightforward. The insured insisted on the simple good faith principle: since the insurers had agreed to do something (covering the risk of some goods, no matter who their actual owner was), they had to stand by their word and pay up. Doing otherwise would have been unfair. On the other side, the insurers argued for the very opposite solution: making up for the loss would have been unfair to them since they had relied on the usual approach

67 On the nature and development of customs, it might be useful to refer more to economic rather than legal scholarship. See, e.g., M.C. Becker, "The Past, Present and Future of Organizational Routines: Introduction to the Handbook of Organizational Routines," in *Handbook of Organizational Routines*, ed. M.C. Becker (Cheltenham and Northampton: Edward Elgar Publishing, 2008), 3–14; R. Ellickson, "The Market for Social Norms," *American Law and Economics Review* 3 (2001): 1–49 (with the caveat that their focus is on the common law).

68 E.g., G. Rossi, "Early Modern Maritime Insurance between Mercantile Customs and *Ius Commune*: Some Remarks on the Liability of the Shipmaster," in *Le Droit face à l'économie sans travail*, vol. 2, *L'approche international*, eds. L. Brunori, S. Dauchy, O. Descamps, and X. Prévost (Paris: Garnier, 2020), 241–245.

to insurance policies followed in London. Thus, while one party highlighted the unfairness of reneging on a deal, the other party stressed the unfairness of interpreting a deal in a way that defied legitimate expectations. Because either solution could have been criticised as unequitable, the arbiters who decided on the matter asked a large number of preeminent London merchants to endorse their decision – which they did. The arbiters found for the insured merchant because they reasoned that, in accepting the unusual terms of the policy, the insurers ought to have realised the possible outcome – and so, they should stick to their word.[69] What is crucial, however, is that the insurance policy was entered into in a country in which this clause was not considered as a deviation from the usual behaviour. Had it been entered into in London, it is less clear whether the arbiters would have found for the insured. A few years later, another dispute focusing precisely on the same issue hinged on the fact that the policy, this time executed in London, did not mention the customs of Antwerp as applicable to it.[70] In that case, the unfairness of reneging on the deal was counter-balanced by the unfairness of forcing the insurers to do something perceived as against the usual – and, therefore, correct – way forward.

6.5 Conclusion

The different ways in which the same term "equity" was used in the contexts outlined in this chapter may well depend on different understandings of the word. If that was all, however, there would be little point in this discussion, which would be merely descriptive and of little – if any – significance. Perhaps a more fruitful analysis would be to focus on how the context itself determines, or at least influences, the meaning of the term. Doubtless, early modern English lawyers thought of the concept of "equity" in a different way from that of medieval civil lawyers, and merchants had yet another understanding of the same concept. But was the concept really the same? Arguably, the legal frameworks within which the idea of equity developed in England and on the Continent were remarkably different from each other, and a salient feature of the mercantile world was precisely the absence of any such legal framework. In comparing the different approaches to that same concept, therefore, it becomes necessary to appreciate the "contours" surrounding it – the "shape" of legal institutions, the cultural background, the social and cultural features of a specific place and time, and so on. If, in so doing, the difference between "core terms" and the "landscape" surrounding them might become somewhat blurred, the journey would doubtlessly acquire a deeper meaning.

69 G. Rossi, *Insurance in Elizabethan England* (Cambridge: Cambridge University Press, 2016), 241–242.

70 Rossi, *Insurance*, 242.

References

Primary sources

Manuscripts

British Library, Ms. Additional 48020.
Cambridge University Library Ms. gg 2.31.
Paris, Bibliothèque Nationale, Ms lat. 4546.

Cases

Coke v *Fountaine* (1676) 3 Swanston's Chancery Reports 585.
Earl of Oxford's Case (1615) 1 *Reports in Chancery* 1.
Honywood v *Bennett* (1675), *Lord Nottingham's Chancery Cases*, vol. 2 (D. E. C. Yale ed., London: Selden Society, vol. 73, 1954), 214.

Old prints and incunabula

Accursius: see *Pandectarum Iuris Civilis*, 5 vols., Parhisiis, apud Gulielmum Merlin ... et Gulielmum Desboys ..., ac Sebastianum Niuellum ..., 1566.
Azo, *Summa Codicis*. Paris, 1581.
Bartolus de Saxoferrato. *In Primam Partem Codicis ... Commentaria*. Basileae: ex Officina Episcopiana, 1588.
Bernardus Parmensis: see *Decretales Gregorii noni seu Liber Extra*. Basileae: Sebastianus Brant, 1500.
Decretalium Gregorii IX compilatio. Basileae: Johan Froben, 1500.

Edited sources

Aquinas. *Summa Theologiae*, 61 vols. Paris: Vives, 1925–1972.
Aristotle. *Ethica Nicomachea*, edited by J. Bywater. Oxford: Clarendon Press, 1894.
Bryson, William H. *Cases Concerning Equity and the Courts of Equity, 1550–1660*, vol. 1. London: Selden Society, 2000.
Glanvill: see Hall, George D. G., ed. *The Treatise on the Laws and Customs of the Realm of England Commonly Called Glanvill*. London: Clarendon Press, 1965; reprint, 1993.
Guy, John A., ed. *Christopher St German on Chancery and Statute*. London: Selden Society, 1985.
Scott, Samuel Parsons. *The Civil Law*, vol. 1. Cincinnati: The Central Trust Company, 1932.

Secondary studies

Baker, John H. *Baker and Milsom Sources of English Legal History: Private Law to 1750*. 2nd ed. Oxford: Oxford University Press, 2019.
Baker, John H. "The Common Lawyers and the Chancery: 1616." *Irish Jurist* 4, no. 2 (1969): 368–92.

Barton, John L. "Equity in the Medieval Common Law." In *Equity in the World's Legal System*, edited by Ralph A. Newman, 139–55. Brussels: Bruylant, 1973.

Baker, John H. *An Introduction to English Legal History*. 5th ed. Oxford: Oxford University Press, 2019.

Baker, John H. *The Oxford History of the Laws of England (1483–1558)*, vol. 6. Oxford: Oxford University Press, 2003.

Becker, Markus C. "The Past, Present and Future of Organizational Routines: Introduction to the Handbook of Organizational Routines." In *Handbook of Organizational Routines*, edited by Markus C. Becker, 3–14. Cheltenham and Northampton: Edward Elgar Publishing, 2008.

Behrens, Georg. "An Early Tudor Debate on the Relation between Law and Equity." *Journal of Legal History* 19 (1998): 143–61.

Brand, Paul. "The Equity of the Common Law Courts." In *Law & Equity. Approaches in Roman Law and Common Law*, edited by Egbert Koops and Willem J. Zwalve, 39–53. Leiden: Nijhoff, 2014.

Caron, Pier G. "I fondamenti romanistici e patristici del concetto di "aequitas canonica" dalle origini alla dottrina dei decretisti." *Annali della Facoltà giuridica di Camerino* 34 (1984): 119–80.

Coing, Helmut. "English Equity and the Denunciatio Evangelica of the Canon Law." *Law Quarterly Review* 71 (1955): 223–41.

Cortese, Ennio. "Equité et justice, la dynamique bipolaire du droit au Moyen Age." In *Mélanges en l'honneur d'Anne Lefebvre-Teillard*, edited by Bernard D'Alteroche, Florence Demoulin-Auzary, Olivier Descamps, and Franck Roumy, 299–313. Paris: Éditions Panthéon-Assas, 2009.

Cortese, Ennio. *La Norma Giuridica. Spunti teorici nel diritto comune classico*, 2 vols. Milan: Giuffré, 1962–1964.

Cortese, Ennio. "La Summula Placuit piacentiniana e le aggiunte di Giovanni nel Ms. parigino 4546." In *Scritti*, vol. 1, edited by Italo Birocchi and Ugo Petronio, 233–47. Spoleto: Fondazione Centro italiano di studi sull'alto medioevo, 1999.

Doe, Norman. *Fundamental Authority in Late Medieval English Law*. Cambridge: Cambridge University Press, 1991.

Ellickson, Robert. "The Market for Social Norms." *American Law and Economics Review* 3 (2001): 1–49.

Gambaro, Antonio, Rodolfo Sacco, and Louis Vogel. *Traité de droit compare – Le droit de l'Occident et d'ailleurs*. Paris: LGDJ, 2011.

Haskett, Timothy. "Conscience, Justice and Authority in the Late-Medieval English Court of Chancery." In *Expectations of the Law in the Middle Ages*, edited by Anthony Musson, 151–64. Martlesham: The Boydell Press, 2001.

Henderson, Edith G. "Relief from Bonds in the English Chancery: Mid-Sixteenth Century." *The American Journal of Legal History* 18 (1974): 298–306.

Ibbetson, David J. "A House Built on Sand: Equity in Early Modern English Law." In *Law & Equity. Approaches in Roman Law and Common Law*, edited by Egbert Koops and Willem J. Zwalve, 55–77. Leiden: Nijhoff, 2014.

Kantorowicz, Hermann. *Studies in the Glossators of the Roman Law*. Aalen: Scientia Verlag, 1969.

Klimchuk, Dennis. "Aristotle at the Foundations of the Law of Equity." In *Philosophical Foundations of the Law of Equity*, edited by Dennis Klimchuk, Irit Samet, and Henry E. Smith, 32–51. Oxford: Oxford University Press, 2020.

Klinck, Dennis R. *Conscience, Equity and the Court of Chancery in Early Modern England*. Aldershot: Ashgate, 2010.

Landau, Peter. "'Aequitas' in the 'Corpus Iuris Canonici'." *Syracuse Journal of International Law and Commerce* 20 (1994): 95–104.

Lange, Hermann. "Ius aequum und ius strictum bei den Glossatoren." *Zeitschrift der Savigny-Stiftung für Rechtsgeschichte* 71 (1954): 319–47.

Lefebvre, Charles. *Les pouvoirs du juge en droit canonique*. Paris: Librairie du Recueil Sirey, 1938.

Lefebvre, Charles. "Aequitas canonica et periculum animae dans la doctrine de l'Hostiensis." *Ephemerides Iuris Canonici* 13 (1952): 305–21.

Macino, Francesca. "L'applicazione del principio di aequitas nella prassi giudiziaria dei mercanti (xiv-xv sec.)." In *Les documents du commerce et des marchands entre Moyen Âge et époque moderne (XII-XVII s.)*, edited by Cristina Mantegna and Olivier Poncet, 15–33. Rome: Publications de l'École française de Rome, 2018.

Macnair, Mike. "Coke v Fountaine (1676)." In *Landmark Cases in Equity*, edited by Charles Mitchell and Paul Mitchell, 33–62. Oxford: Hart, 2012.

Maitland, Frederic W. *Equity, Also, the Forms of Action at Common Law*. Cambridge: Cambridge University Press, 1929.

Maniscalco, Lorenzo. *Equity in Early Modern Legal Scholarship*. Leiden: Brill, 2020.

Padoa-Schioppa, Antonio. "Equità nel diritto medievale e moderno: spunti della dottrina." *Rivista di storia del diritto italiano* 87 (2014): 5–44.

Plucknett, Theodore F. T., and J. L. Barton, eds. *St German's Doctor and Student*. London: Selden Society, 1974.

Potts, Timothy C. *Conscience in Medieval Philosophy*. Cambridge: Cambridge University Press, 1980.

Roper, William. *The Lyfe of Sir Thomas Moore, Knight*. Edited by Elsie V. Hitchcock. Bloomington: Indiana University Press, 1935.

Rossi, Guido. *Insurance in Elizabethan England*. Cambridge: Cambridge University Press, 2016.

Rossi, Guido. "Early Modern Maritime Insurance Between Mercantile Customs and Ius Commune. Some Remarks on the Liability of the Shipmaster." In *Le Droit face à l'économie sans travail, vol. 2, L'approche international*, edited by Louisa Brunori, Serge Dauchy, Olivier Descamps, and Xavier Prévost, 241–63. Paris: Garnier, 2020.

Rueger, Zofia. "Gerson's Concept of Equity and Christopher St Germain." *History of Political Thought* 3 (1982): 1–30.

Singer, Samuel W., ed. *The Table-Talk of John Selden*. London: John Russell Smith, 1856.

Thorne, Samuel E. "The Equity of a Statute and Heydon's Case." *Illinois Law Review* 31 (1936): 202–16.

Williams, Ian. "Christopher St German: Religion, Conscience and Law in Reformation England." In *Great Christian Jurists in English History. Law and Christianity*, edited by Mark Hill and Richard H. Helmholz, 69–92. Cambridge: Cambridge University Press, 2017.

7 The Concept of Equity in Austrian Private Law. From the Origins of the Austrian General Civil Code (ABGB) to the Present Day

Kamila Staudigl-Ciechowicz

7.1 Introduction

Alongside justice, freedom, and equality, equity is one of the central and timeless concepts of law. Although equity is generally regarded as "one of the supreme concepts of law"[1] and its relationship to law is seen as one of the "great themes in the history of private law,"[2] it is difficult to define the concept of equity precisely.

Not only the term, but also the difficulty of defining it has existed for centuries. Johann Oldendorp, a German jurist and reformer, dealt with this question at length in his works. Although his thoughts will not be explored in depth here, his words from his work published in 1538, *Formula investigandae actionis*, can be used as an illustrative dictum:

> Everyone uses the term equity, but few understand the concept. Everyone says I will show what is equity and what is right/just.[3]

Oldendorp's assessment may be somewhat exaggerated, but it gets to the heart of the problem: an exact definition of the term "equity" is rarely found, and it was – in contrast – overused. Here, too, the restriction applies that this

1 Christoph Becker, "Billigkeit," in *Handwörterbuch zur deutschen Rechtsgeschichte, 2. Aufl. Bd. I* (Berlin: Erich Schmidt, 2008), 587–592.

2 Franz-Stefan Meissel, "Aequitas austriaca – Zur Billigkeit als Rechtsquelle in der Kodifikationsgeschichte des ABGB," in *Festschrift für Thomas Simon zum 65. Geburtstag. Land, Policey, Verfassung*, ed. Gerald Kohl et al. (Wien: Verlag Österreich, 2020), 167.

3 Original text: "Omnes in ore habent aequitatis verbum, pauci vero percipiunt rem ipsam. Nemo non dicit, praestabo quod aequum et iustum est. Was byllich und recht ist." Johannes Oldendrop, *Formula investigandae actionis per quam unusquisque ius suum in iudicio persequatur* (Köln, 1538), chapter "Quid sit aequvitas, quid strictum ius." (https://www.digitale-sammlungen.de/view/bsb10181509?page=24).

DOI: 10.4324/9781003654131-10

statement applies only to some periods. In this context, Claudieter Schott spoke of a "conglomerate of the most diverse historical deposits."[4]

This chapter deals with the concept of equity from the 18th to the 20th centuries. It examines in-depth the question of which forms of concepts of equity exist today in Austrian civil law, to what extent the term "equity" is explicitly used in the legal text, and what is understood by it in these cases. On the other hand, it also examines whether concepts of equity are anchored in Austrian private law without being mentioned literally, as well as their significance for case law.

It is worth noting that in the legal literature of the 19th century the terms "equity" (*Billigkeit*) and "law" (*Recht*) were also assigned a gender-typical contemporary connotation. In 1874, the Viennese university professor Adolf Exner presented "equity" as a term with feminine connotations at the Juristische Gesellschaft in Vienna. He defined decision-making based on the individuality of a specific case as being based on the principle of equity and explained: "This is how a sensible, sensitive woman will act at any given moment, to whom [...] a [...] legal dispute [is submitted] for arbitration (women are the living voices of equity among us)."[5]

7.2 Single-Case Justice versus Codification?

In the regulations of the 17th century, references to equity were not uncommon.[6] We encounter it as a criterion for the interpretation of unclear provisions, for example, in the *Landtafel für Österreich ob der Enns* of 1616/1629.[7] The *Landtafel* was a draft of land law (*Landrecht*), which included civil procedure, private law, and feudal law. Although never enacted, the draft was nevertheless respected in legal practice.[8] Joseph Ferdinand Holger provides insights into the legal practice of the courts in the 18th century in the context of preparations for the first all-Austrian codification of civil law.[9] According to him, when interpreting the law, the wording had to be analysed first, whereby in case of doubt, the conformity of the wording with the will of the legislature had to be ensured. This intention could be ascertained on the basis of the

4 In the German original he wrote on "Konglomerat verschiedenster historischer Ablagerungen." Clausdieter Schott, *'Rechtsgrundsätze' und Gesetzeskorrektur: Ein Beitrag zur Geschichte gesetzlicher Rechtsfindungsregeln* (Berlin: Duncker & Humblot, 1975), 65.

5 Adolf Exner, "Ueber Recht und Billigkeit," *Zeitschrift für Notariat und freiwillige Gerichtsbarkeit* 8, Beilage (1874): 1.

6 Meissel, "Aequitas austriaca," 171.

7 Meissel, "Aequitas austriaca," 171 for further query.

8 Gunter Wesener, "Zur Bedeutung der österreichischen Landesordnungsentwürfe des 16. und 17. Jahrhunderts für die neuere Privatrechtsgeschichte," in *Festschrift Nikolaus Grass*, eds. Louis Carlen and Fritz Steinegger (Innsbruck: Wagner, 1974), 629.

9 Joseph Ferdinand Holger, "Anmerkungen über das österreichische Recht für das Projekt eines Systema Codicis Theresiani," in *Die ältesten Quellen zur Kodifikationsgeschichte des Österreichischen ABGB*, ed. Christian Neschwara (Wien/Köln/Weimar: Böhlau, 2012), 191.

legislative history. In the absence of a corresponding law, the "general legal doctrine" ("*allgemeine Rechts-Lehre*") could be consulted. In practice, judges used analogy with similar cases ("extending the rights from case to case"), the authority of legal scholars and the use of "natural equity" (*natürliche Billigkeit*) when deciding ("intertwined and doubtful") difficult legal questions.[10] On the one hand, this approach was provided for in various legal sources[11]; at the same time, it was carried out in agreement with the sovereigns (*Landesfürsten*).[12]

The codification movement changed the view of judgements based on equity.[13] The preliminary work on the Codex Theresianus already clearly shows that the use of equity in the application of the law was undesirable, and that stricter rules were even established for interpretation. In his preliminary draft, Joseph Azzoni included a section on interpretation and "natural equity." It stated:

> [2.] That, furthermore, no extension from one case to another, or restriction to certain cases, nor any other interpretation should be permitted; least of all an imaginary equity [eingebildete Billigkeit] contrary to the content of this general right.[14]

Decisions based on equity had to give way to the strict application of the new codified laws. In order to standardise and centralise the law, the monarch, as the unifying link between the absolutist Austrian unions of states (*monarchische Union von Ständestaaten*), exercised equity in the area of legislation as the sole legislative body, on the one hand, and in the area of jurisdiction, on the other. Maria Theresa already referred to this form of equity during the codification work in 1772, with the instruction not to bind the content of the new law to Roman law, "but to base it everywhere on natural equity."[15]

Franz-Stefan Meissel aptly speaks here of "equity as a prerogative of the ruler or legislator."[16] Consequently, the right to decide according to equity was centralised, on the one hand, while, on the other, considerations based on equity flowed into the new codifications, thereby enjoying a generalisation

10 Holger, "Anmerkungen," 191.

11 For example, according to land laws as well as court practice. See Meissel, "Aequitas austriaca," 171.

12 Meissel, "Aequitas austriaca," 171; Holger, "Anmerkungen," 191.

13 Meissel, "Aequitas austriaca," 172–175.

14 Original text: "[2.] Daß ferner keinerleÿ Ausdehnung von einem Fall auf den anderen, oder Einschränckung auf gewiße Fälle, noch sonstige Ausdeitung zugelassen werden solle; am allerwenigsten eine eingebildete Billichkeit entgegen den Inhalt dieses allgemeinen Rechtes vorgeschuzet werden köñe." Joseph Azzoni, "Vorentwurf zum Codex Theresianus, Erster Theil. Erste Abhandlung. Fünfter Abschnitt," in *Die ältesten Quellen zur Kodifikationsgeschichte des Österreichischen ABGB*, ed. Christian Neschwara (Wien/Köln/Weimar: Böhlau, 2012), 106.

15 Moriz Wellspacher, "Das Naturrecht und das ABGB," in *Festschrift zur Jahrhundertfeier des Allgemeinen Bürgerlichen Gesetzbuches*, Bd. 1 (Wien: Manz, 1911), 178.

16 Meissel, "Aequitas austriaca," 172.

from individual cases and could now – regardless of the individual judge's understanding of values – be available to the general public and not just to the individual. At the level of jurisdiction, equity "migrated" from the judges to the monarch himself, who was able to take over and decide every case within the framework of so-called *Machtsprüche* (*decisio vi juris eminentis*), which was, however, frowned upon from the time of enlightened absolutism onwards.[17]

The history of Austrian codification clearly shows how equity not only as a term, but also as a judicial instrument in individual case decisions, was opposed.[18] The work on the Codex Theresianus already shows a clear tendency against the use of equity. The aforementioned preliminary draft by Joseph Azzoni from 1753 declared not only analogous conclusions, but especially equity decisions, to be inadmissible in the application of the law. The final draft of the Codex Theresianus dealt with the issue in detail and also withdrew the power of interpretation from judges, thus preventing them all the more from making equity judgements. Questions of interpretation had to be referred to the monarch and his court, which Meissel refers to as "authoritative interpretation."[19] Judges were forbidden to deviate from the wording of the law and to take into account factors of equity.[20] Only in cases explicitly defined by law could equity be used as a criterion for judgement. Consequently, the monarch was to hold the monopoly on equity.[21]

Although the Codex Thersianus did not come into force, the Josephine Code of 1786[22] essentially provided for only a few changes in this area. The monarch could make equity-based decisions within the framework of extraordinary legal assistance, although the term "equity" (*Billigkeit*) itself did not appear in any relevant legal text. If judges had concerns about equity, they were to turn to the monarch.[23] The later codifications followed this line, albeit with further relaxations.

However, these developments did not go unopposed. There were certain voices that wanted to preserve equity as a concept and, to a certain extent, restore the right to refer to equity in judicial decisions.[24] There were already

17 Meissel, "Aequitas austriaca," 174. Vgl. auch Werner Ogris, "Kabinettsjustiz," in *Handwörterbuch,* Bd. II, 1487–1492; Holger Erwin, "Machtspruch," in: *Handwörterbuch,* Bd. III, 1119–1121.

18 Meissel, "Aequitas austriaca," 172–175.

19 Meissel, "Aequitas austriaca," 172.

20 Codex Theresianus I Cap I § V n. 82, printed in: Philipp Harras v. Harrasowsky, ed., *Der Codex Theresianus und seine Umarbeitungen,* Bd. I (Wien, 1883), 50.

21 Meissel, "Aequitas austriaca," 174.

22 Allgemeines bürgerliches Gesetzbuch (Josephinisches Gesetzbuch) vom 1. November. 1786, Justizgesetzsammlung Nr. 591.

23 Meissel, "Aequitas austriaca," 173f.

24 Harras v. Harrasowsky names explicitly Ferdinand Mana von Goldegg, member of the commission for the drafting of the civil code (*Compilations-Commission*) in 1772, as a supporter of equity. Philipp Harras v. Harrasowsky, ed., *Der Codex Theresianus und seine Umarbeitungen,*

concerns in 1772, as some questions could not be resolved from the wording of the law alone, and, consequently, the authorisation to interpret the law, and to use analogy and "general principles"[25] (*allgemeine Grundregeln*) for judges was demanded.[26] The "general principles" or "natural legal principles" (*natürliche Rechtsgrundsätze*), in particular, were areas where concepts of equity could at least partially flow into the law without the term being used as such.

This strict restriction was relaxed somewhat in the Martini draft from 1796. Although the wording of the law still took precedence in accordance with Section 11, the judge could refer to the "declared meaning" of the law, i.e., the *ratio legis*, in the event of doubts and was also authorised to draw analogous conclusions and to decide in accordance with "the general principles of law" according to Section 12 of the draft. During the review of the draft, the opposing viewpoints of the parties involved became apparent: while the estates of Tyrol and Silesia wanted to give the judge as little room for manoeuvre as possible, the estates in Carinthia and Carniola were more open to an interpretation of the law. The Carinthian estates even wanted equity back, although this was to be granted only to the monarch. The aim was to take account of cases "where it was not possible to observe the letter of the law too closely because this would defeat the ultimate purpose of the law, which the law was actually given to achieve."[27] The Lower Austrian estates also spoke out in favour of strengthening the judge and recommended that he should be allowed "in the event of an apparent difference between the words of the law and the meaning of the same, to behave according to the latter, to deviate in the same way from the literal legal provision and the strictness of the rights contained therein, and rather to give way to natural equity, if this equity is undoubtedly compatible with the meaning of that provision."[28]

The reason given was that "by binding oneself to the letter of the law, one would contradict the will of the legislator, and that if the judge were denied consideration of the requirements of equity, he would only be considered as a mechanical tool."[29] In other words, he would serve purely as a subsumption machine. The impossibility of "providing for all eventualities" by law and the impartiality of judges as "enlightened men" were also put forward as arguments in favour of allowing natural equity in judicial decisions, pointing out that "the decision should only be permitted in accordance with the principles of natural equity to the extent that this corresponds to the meaning of the

Bd. IV (Wien, 1886), 22 fn 17. Later especially the estates of Carinthia and Lower Austria were against the total exclusion of equity. Meissel, "Aequitas austriaca," 174f.

25 Harras v. Harrasowsky, *Der Codex*, Bd. IV, 22 fn 17.

26 Meissel, "Aequitas austriaca," 173.

27 Philipp Harras v. Harrasowsky, ed., *Der Codex Theresianus und seine Umarbeitungen*, Bd. V (Wien, 1886), 10 fn 6.

28 Harras v. Harrasowsky, *Der Codex*, Bd. V, 10 fn 6.

29 Harras v. Harrasowsky, *Der Codex*, Bd. V, 10 fn 6.

[respective] law."[30] In this context, "natural equity" was understood as an outgrowth of natural law based on reason. This link – albeit with a strong emphasis on Christianity – is also clearly evident a hundred years later in the writings of the jurist and theologian Konstantin Hohenlohe-Schillingsfürst.[31]

The prominent jurist and imperial advisor Franz Georg von Keeß took a contrary view during the codification work. He rejected an interpretation that went against the wording of the law. "This would greatly jeopardise the uniformity of the application of the law, and everyone would be tempted to bend the law to their own ends. [...] He also disputed the use of equity as a guideline for judicial decisions."[32] On the other hand, he saw the monarch as obliged "to be guided in his legislation by equity, which distinguishes justice from harshness. In the face of the given law, however, no one should be allowed to evade the legislator's order under the pretext of equity."[33] Keeß also referred to Montesquieu and declared that "some things that seem unfair to the individual are indispensable in the interests of the whole."[34]

The debate was repeated around ten years later during the deliberations on the ABGB. The Revision Commission emphasised that "in order not to give the judges too much leeway for arbitrariness, they should not be allowed to decide according to the (often only imaginary) reasons of the legislator or according to the general principles of law; rather, if the case could not be decided from the natural sense and context of the law, the instruction and decision should be obtained from the lawmaker."[35]

It is striking that in the discussion about the powers of the judge in the area of legal interpretation and analogy, no reference is made to equity. In cases where the wording was not clear enough, three solutions were discussed: first, the use of the principles of common law (*gemeines Recht*) or provincial law; second, "to submit the doubtful case *ex officio* to the superior judge"[36]; or, third, to submit such cases "indirectly to the supreme judicial authority or the monarch as lawmaker."[37] All three proposals were critically examined by the Court Commission for Legal Matters (*Hofkommission in Gesetzessachen*) and recognised as inadequate. This led to the consideration of granting the judge the power of deciding according to natural legal principles within narrow limits but in conjunction with a duty to report to the court commission

30 Harras v. Harrasowsky, *Der Codex,* Bd. V, 10 fn 6.
31 Constantin Hohenlohe, "Die natürlichen Rechtsgrundsätze im Lichte der christlichen Wahrheiten." *Archiv für Rechts- und Wirtschaftsphilosophie* 11 (1917/18): 312–319; 12 (1918): 37–47.
32 Harras v. Harrasowsky, *Der Codex,* Bd. V, 11 fn 6.
33 Harras v. Harrasowsky, *Der Codex,* Bd. V, 11 fn 6.
34 Harras v. Harrasowsky, *Der Codex,* Bd. V, 11 fn 6.
35 Julius Ofner, ed., *Der Ur-Entwurf und die Berathungs-Protokolle des Oesterreichischen Allgemeinen bürgerlichen Gesetzbuches,* Bd. I (Wien: Alfred Hölder, 1889), 22.
36 Ofner, *Der Ur-Entwurf,* 23.
37 Ofner, *Der Ur-Entwurf,* 23.

if no appeal was made. This was justified on the grounds of protection against abuse and the aim that such cases "should also be minimised."[38]

In principle, the commission agreed that a middle way had to be found because, "just as it would be questionable on the one hand to allow judges too much room for manoeuvre, it would be just as questionable and even dangerous for the administration of justice if judges were restricted to the mere letter of the law, as was the case in the Josephinian Code."[39] Ultimately, the obligation to refer to the higher court or the court commission was dropped from the ABGB.[40] The relevant paragraphs on interpretation and analogy are still in force. Judges have a range of options available to them, from the wording of the law and *ratio legis* to analogy and the filling of gaps through natural legal principles.[41]

7.3 Equity in the ABGB

In the ABGB, the principle of equity is explicitly mentioned only in a few places. We find it, for example, in Section 500 in the regulation of grazing rights, in the area of determining the time of contract performance in accordance with Section 904 and in the case of equitable liability in Section 1310, as well as in the case of compensation for pain and suffering in accordance with Section 1325. It is clear that the term "equity" is intentionally avoided. The few legal mentions are exceptions, but the basic principle of the code has moved away from "consideration of individual circumstances in individual cases"[42] towards "predictability and [...] uniformity of decisions."[43] In his commentary on the ABGB from 1811, Franz von Zeiller stated, "It may strike some readers that the judge in the present code is not [...] instructed to take equity into account in his decisions."[44] In this context, we also learn what Zeiller understood by the term "equity":

> Equity (as distinct from justice) is usually understood as the ability to fulfil the duties of love, i.e., to perfect others according to their needs and our powers. If the judge were allowed to make a judgement according to equity in this sense, he would be allowed to favour the poor over

38 Ofner, *Der Ur-Entwurf*, 23.
39 Ofner, *Der Ur-Entwurf*, 24.
40 Meissel, "Aequitas austriaca," 177.
41 See below under 7.4. "Natural legal principles" (*natürliche Rechtsgrundsätze*) as hidden equity?
42 Meissel, "Aequitas austriaca," 179.
43 Meissel, "Aequitas austriaca," 179.
44 Franz v. Zeiller, *Commentar über das allgemeine bürgerliche Gesetzbuch für die gesammten Deutsche Erbländer der Oesterreichischen Monarchie,* Bd. I (Wien, 1811), 69.

> the rich, the less powerful over the more powerful, etc., i.e., he would be allowed to shorten the wealthy in order to do a good deed to the poor.[45]

Consequently, Zeiller saw equity as a moral category rather than a legal one.[46] In the deliberations on the ABGB, Zeiller was particularly opposed to *aequitas cerebrina*, i.e., imaginary equity. He criticised the fact that it "takes the place of positive legislation" and that the "judge [...] elevates himself to the status of legislator."[47] Zeiller saw this as a very worrying development, as he explained in December 1801:

> Thus, the legal judgements would have to turn out extremely differently; and so finally the popular opinion, which has become a proverb but is certainly not uplifting, must arise that the outcome of a trial is just as uncertain as a lucky throw and the leanest settlement is better than the fattest lawsuit.[48]

According to Zeiller, this kind of equity had little to do with justice. Rather, Zeiller saw the justice of the law "in the respect for freedom [...] as well as legal certainty and equality."[49] He thus came to a clear distinction:

> A court of justice is not an authority of beneficence; it is, as the word itself implies, intended to grant justice to everyone (without distinction of class or wealth). The judge can and should, on suitable occasions, draw the attention of the entitled person to the equity of remitting his claim, in whole or in part; he can try to persuade him to make a settlement; but he cannot, without himself giving a public example of injustice, restrict him in the free disposal of his property.[50]

45 Original text: "Unter der Billigkeit (zum Unterschiede von der Gerechtigkeit) versteht man gewöhnlich die Fertigkeit, die Liebespflichten zu erfüllen, d. i. Andere nach Maß ihrer Bedürfnisse und unserer Kräfte zu vervollkommnen. Dürfte der Richter in diesem Sinne nach der Billigkeit den Ausspruch thun, so dürfte er den Armen vor dem Reichen, den minder Mächtigen vor dem Mächtigern u.s.w. begünstigen, d.h. er dürfte den Reicheren verkürzen, um dem Dürftigen eine Wohlthat zu erweisen." Zeiller, *Commentar*, 69ff.

46 On the influence of Kant, cf. Meissel, "Aequitas austriaca," 177ff.

47 Ofner, *Der Ur-Entwurf*, 5.

48 Ofner, *Der Ur-Entwurf*, 5.

49 Meissel, "Aequitas austriaca," 178.

50 Original text: "Ein Gerichtshof ist keine Behörde der Wohltäthigkeit, er ist, wie schon das Wort andeutet, dazu bestimmt, jedem (ohne Unterschied des Standes und Vermögens) sein Recht zuzutheilen. Der Richter kann und soll, bey schicklicher Gelegenheit, den Berechtigten auf die Billigkeit, seine strenge Forderung, ganz oder zum Theil, zu erlassen, aufmerksam machen, er kann ihn zu einem Vergleiche zu bewegen suchen; aber er kann ihn, ohne selbst ein öffentliches Beyspiel der Ungerechtigkeit zu geben, in der freyen Verfügung über sein Vermögen nicht beschränken." Zeiller, *Commentar*, 70.

Where the "inequality of circumstances in civil law" is too strong, Zeiller sees the legislator as being called upon to incorporate concepts of equity into the law in the interests of justice and to explicitly authorise the judge to observe this care (*Fürsorge*), as Zeiller calls it. Zeiller even goes a step further and allows concepts of equity to flow into the area of interpretation:

> But also the judge must, where the expressions of the will (of a testator or contracting party) are doubtful or incomplete, have recourse to the presumption of what the parties acting had intended and what they would have expressly agreed, if they had had the doubtful case in mind, in a legal and equitable way of thinking (to be assumed). Here, therefore, equity consists in a correct (logical) interpretation of the declarations of intent.[51]

In abstract terms, it can be stated that aspects of equity have been included in the legal text, particularly where legal concretisation encounters difficulties *a priori*, for example, because different factors have to be taken into account. Section 500 ABGB can be used as an example here. As already mentioned, this is a provision that deals with grazing rights as a servitude. It regulates how, in the absence of an agreement, the number of livestock covered by the grazing right is to be determined.[52] As one of the relevant aspects, Section 500 of the Austrian General Civil Code (ABGB) mentions "equitable consideration" of "the extent and nature of the pasture."[53] An exact concretisation here would lead to a great deal of casuistry[54] and might still not cover all potential factors. Consequently, equity is introduced as a decision factor, but at the same time subject to the restriction of other principles relevant to the decision, in this case the wintering principle (*Überwinterungsgrundsatz*).[55] According to the wintering principle, "no more cattle were allowed to be kept on the pasture than could be wintered with the fodder produced on the dominant land."[56]

Parallels can be found with the other paragraphs that include the equity factor, for example, in the determination of the time of contract performance

51 Original text: "Aber auch der Richter muß da, wo die Aeußerungen des Willens (eines Erblassers oder vertragmachenden Theils) zweifelhaft oder unvollständig sind, zur Vermuthung Zuflucht nehmen, was die Handelnden zur Absicht gehabt, und was sie, wenn ihnen der zweifelhafte Fall vorgeschwebt hätte, bey einer (vorauszusetzenden) rechtlichen und billigen Denkungsart ausdrücklich verabredet haben würden. Hier besteht also die Billigkeit in einer richtigen (logischen) Auslegung der Willenserklärungen." Zeiller, *Commentar*, 71.

52 For more details, cf. Moritz v. Stubenrauch, *Commentar zum allgemeinen österreichischen bürgerlichen Gesetzbuche*, Bd. II, 3. Aufl. (Wien: Manz, 1876), 102–106.

53 Stubenrauch, *Commentar*, 103.

54 See, for example, the corresponding provisions in the Allgemeines Landrecht für preußische Staaten I 22 §§ 80ff.

55 Cf., on the wintering principle Heinrich Klang, "§ 500," in *Kommentar zum Allgemeinen bürgerlichen Gesetzbuch*, Bd. I/2, ed. Heinrich Klang (Wien, 1931).

56 Klang, "§ 500."

pursuant to Section 904 ABGB. This regulation also permits judges to make decisions based on equity under certain conditions, in particular if performance was promised according to possibility or feasibility (*Möglichkeit oder Tunlichkeit*).[57] This also shows that, instead of considering all potential possibilities, the court is authorised to assess the individual situation accordingly. In contrast to Section 500 ABGB, the Supreme Court has repeatedly dealt with Section 904 ABGB, also with regard to the use of equity.[58]

This shows that equity continued to exist as a corrective measure in a precisely defined area. This raises the question of whether there were other ways of incorporating concepts of equity into a judicial decision, even if equity was not explicitly referred to in the law.

7.4 "Natural Legal Principles" (*natürliche Rechtsgrundsätze*) as Hidden Equity?

As already mentioned, the ABGB standardised the interpretation of the law and the filling of gaps in Section 6 ABGB[59] and Section 7 ABGB.[60] As a last resort, if neither interpretation nor the analogy of the law led to a result, the judge had the option of deciding "based on the diligently gathered and thoroughly considered facts in line with the natural legal principles."[61]

This raises the question of the extent to which the use of natural legal principles can also achieve the purpose of the concepts of equity. In his 1975 paper, Clausdieter Schott saw a certain interchangeability between the "general references to the structure of the legal system," among which he counted the "consideration of *ratio legis*, general principles, natural law and equity."[62] Based on this consideration, it can be questioned to what extent equity continued to appear in the Austrian private law system through the "back door" of natural legal principles. Stanislaus Dniestrzański dealt extensively with the

57 Joseph Kitka, "Zur Erläuterung des § 904 des allg. bürg. Gesetzbuches," *Allgemeine österreichische Gerichts-Zeitung* 6 (1855): 41–42.

58 Cf. Josef Schey, ed., *Das Allgemeine bürgerliche Gesetzbuch*, 23. Aufl. (Wien, 1936), 495ff. See, e.g., Oberster Gerichtshof (herafter: OGH), Judgement 19 April 1882, Z. 3627, *Allgemeine österreichische Gerichts-Zeitung* 34 (1883): 315–316.; OGH, Judgement 13 October 1892, Z. 11671, *Gerichtshalle* 37 (1893): 68–70.

59 Section 6 ABGB: No meaning may be inferred from a law other than the meaning which is evident from the genuine meaning of the words in their context and the clear intention of the legislator. Translation from: Peter Eschig and Erika Pircher-Eschig, eds., *Das österreichische ABGB. The Austrian Civil Code, 2. Aufl.* (Wien: LexisNexis ARD ORAC), § 6.

60 Section 7 ABGB: If a matter can neither be determined by the wording nor by the natural meaning of a law, similar matters which have been regulated by law and the purpose of other related laws must be considered. If the matter still remains ambiguous, it must be decided based on the diligently gathered and thoroughly considered facts in line with the natural legal principles. Translation from: Eschig and Pircher-Eschig, *Das österreichische ABGB*, § 7.

61 Translation from: Eschig and Pircher-Eschig, *Das österreichische ABGB*, § 7.

62 Schott, *'Rechtsgrundsätze' und Gesetzeskorrektur*, 59.

topic of natural legal principles in 1911.[63] There is no explicit link between natural legal principles and equity in his essay, but the aspects he associates with natural legal principles are very similar to those of equity. In his opinion, natural legal principles have a broad field of application. Whenever the interpretation of the relevant ABGB provision and analogy to other laws did not offer a solution, the natural legal principles came into play. Dniestrzański explained: "The natural legal principles therefore form a subsidiary basis for deciding legal cases. In contrast to the Prussian Landrecht, the ABGB is not casuistic, but has a general version throughout, which does not get lost in details; since its enactment, the economic conditions have changed a great deal without the legislation being able to keep pace with the requirements of the same – therefore, there is a lot of room for natural legal principles within the framework of Austrian law."[64] Thus, the use of natural legal principles is a way "for the law to adapt to the respective social and economic conditions."[65] With regard to actual legal practice, Dniestrzański explained that it is incorrect "that the judge under Austrian law is never or only rarely in a position to decide according to natural legal principles. Austrian judges have in fact very often made use of this means without realising it, without invoking it."[66]

Parallels in terms of content to equity without using the term can also be found occasionally in Supreme Court rulings, for example, in a decision of the Supreme Court from 1903,[67] which concerned the legal nature of an alpine cooperative (*Alpengenossenschaft*).[68] In that decision, the Supreme Court stated: "Every legal relationship should be judged according to the concrete situation of the case, and if a case cannot be decided either from the words or from the natural meaning of a law, in particular due to existing abnormal circumstances, then the provisions of Section 7 ABGB must be applied. Accordingly, the judge is not obliged to decide a legal case on the basis of legal norms against the application of which there are important reservations and in favour of which neither the clear wording nor the intention of the legislator speaks."[69] Robert von Mayr sets out the considerations that must guide judges in such a decision in his publication *Die Auslobung* from 1905: "The decision should be made as the legislator would make it at that moment, taking into

63 Stanislaus Dniestrzański, "Die natürlichen Rechtsgrundsätze (§ 7 ABGB)," in *Festschrift zur Jahrhundertfeier des Allgemeinen Bürgerlichen Gesetzbuches, Bd. 2* (Wien: Manz, 1911), 2–35.

64 Dniestrzański, "Die natürlichen Rechtsgrundsätze," 20ff.

65 Dniestrzański, "Die natürlichen Rechtsgrundsätze," 19.

66 Dniestrzański, "Die natürlichen Rechtsgrundsätze," 21.

67 OGH, Judgement of 7 January 1903, Nr. 16.746, GlUNF. 2200.

68 The dispute in this case concerned the question whether the alpine cooperative should be classified as a partnership (*Personengesellschaft*). The courts rejected this categorisation and declared it to be an agricultural company (*Agrargesellschaft*). These were special legal structures resulting from the abolition of the manorial system in 1848.

69 OGH, Judgement of 7 January 1903, Nr. 16.746, GlUNF. 2200.

account the actual circumstances of the particular case, by weighing up the opposing subjective interests in accordance with customary practice in the area of law in question."[70] These elements are certainly reminiscent of aspects of equity; the relationship between the judicial creation process and the legislative creation process justifies the use of the principle of equity in the sense of an equitable law.

The study by Inge Gampl reveals a different picture, stating that natural legal principles seem to have little significance in the case law of the highest courts.[71] An understanding of natural legal principles with explicit reference to equity is sought in vain. A case from 1912 clearly shows that equity arguments were deemed inadmissible by the Supreme Court.[72]

The case in question involved the payment of a reward for helping to find the perpetrators of an attempted robbery and murder committed in 1909. A security guard wanted to claim the reward, but he also admitted that he had acted without knowledge of the reward. At that time, the Austrian General Civil Code did not yet specifically regulate rewards (*Auslobung*), but the court of first instance found that it would be "inequitable" to deny "the plaintiff the reward only because he did not know about the reward when he acted."[73] In a further step, the court of first instance justified the legal principle that a reward also grants a right to receive the reward to people who were not yet aware of the reward at the time of the performance based on natural legal principles pursuant to Section 7 ABGB. This clearly shows the inclusion of equity considerations in the vague form of Section 7 ABGB. The Court of Appeal confirmed the judgement of the court of first instance. The decision of the Supreme Court in 1912 was in complete contrast to this. The Supreme Court dismissed the action and stated that "reasons of equity and legal considerations of a general nature [...] may come into question when enacting a law, but they must be disregarded when assessing whether the contested judgement is legally justified."[74]

70 Robert v. Mayr, *Die Auslobung: Eine zivilistische Untersuchung* (Wien: Manz, 1905), 7ff. A similar idea can be found in Art. 1 of the Swiss Civil Code from 1907: "(1) The law applies according to its wording or interpretation to all legal questions for which it contains a provision. (2) In the absence of a provision, the court shall decide in accordance with customary law and, in the absence of customary law, in accordance with the rule that it would make as legislator. (3) In doing so, the court shall follow established doctrine and case law." (https://www.fedlex.admin.ch/eli/cc/24/233_245_233/en).

71 Inge Gampl, "Die 'natürlichen' Rechtsgrundsätze in der Judikatur der k. k. Höchstgerichte Österreichs," in *Festschrift Heinrich Demelius zum 80. Geburtstag*, eds. Gerhard Frotz and Werner Ogris (Wien: Manz, 1973), 51–60; Inge Gampl, "Die 'natürlichen' Rechtsgrundsätze in der Höchstgerichts-Judikatur der Republik Österreich," in *Ex aequo et bono. Festschrift für Willibald M. Plöchl*, eds. Peter Leisching, Franz Pototschnig, and Richard Potz (Innsbruck: Wagner, 1977), 399–408.

72 OGH, Judgement of 24 July 1912, Rv I 598/12, GlUNF 6011.

73 OGH, Judgement of 24 July 1912, Rv I 598/12, GlUNF 6011.

74 OGH, Judgement of 24 July 1912, Rv I 598/12, GlUNF 6011.

The Supreme Court had already used a similar argument a few years earlier in a case that involved a claim for repayment of a small salary. The Supreme Court stated that the case should be resolved on the basis of the law and "by way of an interpretation in accordance with the provisions of Sections 6 and 7 of the ABGB; however, considerations of equity and expediency, as applied in numerous places in the appeal judgement, cannot be taken into account."[75]

Such differences in deciding cases are, of course, not surprising when it comes to the content of fundamental concepts.[76] Another example is the question of the extent to which the principle of good faith (*Treu und Glauben*) belongs to the "generally recognised or general principles of law."[77] This question has also been answered differently in legal literature and legal practice. While Dniestrzański was clearly in favour of its recognition,[78] Gampl took a much more critical view, referring to Supreme Court case law.[79] At the same time, she gave several examples where the Administrative Court (*Verwaltungsgerichtshof*, VwGH) seemed to categorise the principle of good faith as one of the natural legal principles.[80] These examples clearly show how difficult it is to reach a conclusive opinion on this issue.

7.5 Equity, *Teilnovellen*, and Special Legislation under Private Law

Equity was further taken into account in the *Teilnovellen*. The *Teilnovellen* were three partial amendments, which were the largest changes to the ABGB.[81] After several years of revision work, significant changes were introduced in many parts of the Austrian General Civil Code in 1914, 1915, and 1916 by means of imperial emergency decrees due to the war.[82]

Section 914 of the Austrian Civil Code, for example, was amended as a provision for the interpretation of contracts. The influence of the German Civil Code is clearly recognisable in the parliamentary materials. The wording was changed in the spirit of the German doctrine of *Treu und Glauben* (good faith, Section 242 German BGB). The interpretation of contracts now explicitly did not have to adhere to their literal meaning, but had to take into consideration the intention of the parties and, in case of doubt, the contract was

75 OGH, Judgement of 17 April 1907, Nr. 2350, GlUNF 3750.

76 Cf. Gampl, "Die 'natürlichen' Rechtsgrundsätze in der Judikatur," 59, fn 53.

77 Gampl, "Die 'natürlichen' Rechtsgrundsätze in der Höchstgerichts-Judikatur."

78 Dniestrzański, "Die natürlichen Rechtsgrundsätze," 22.

79 Gampl, "Die 'natürlichen' Rechtsgrundsätze in der Höchstgerichts-Judikatur."

80 VwGH, Judgement of 29 October 1929, A 310/29, Nr. 15.836. Critically – since the term "natural legal principle" is not used by the Administrative Court – Gampl, "Die 'natürlichen' Rechtsgrundsätze in der Höchstgerichts-Judikatur," 400.

81 For the partial amendments, cf. Kamila Staudigl-Ciechowicz, "Die Teilnovellen als letzter Akt der österreichischen Zivilgesetzgebung in Mitteleuropa," *Beiträge zur Rechtsgeschichte Österreichs* 2 (2020): 286–294.

82 RGBl 276/1914; RGBl 208/1915; RGBl 69/1916.

to be understood in accordance with honest commercial practice (*Übung des redlichen Verkehrs*). The explanatory notes clearly show a link between honest practice (*redlicher Verkehr*) and equity. In the case of contractual loopholes, the decisive factor was not "how the transaction is conducted at all, but how a transaction of honest and fair-minded people is conducted."[83] If the judge was unable to resolve the dispute either based on the parties' intentions or the agreement established with the help of the law, he had to "decide the question as the legislator would have decided the legal case if the interests of both parties had been considered in equity. Such a decision meets the requirements of honest commercial practice by adapting to it, following the progressive development of commercial conditions with the development of the law and taking account of the changing and newly arising needs of legal life within the limits of the law."[84] A complete adaptation to the German legal solution was deliberately not carried out, nor was the word pair *Treu und Glauben* (good faith) explicitly adopted as such in the ABGB.[85] According to Josef Schey, a Viennese legal scholar, the amended Section 914 did not actually include anything new, so he stated: "Anyone who knew how to read properly would have already found the interpretation of *Treu und Glauben* in the old ABGB."[86] The old Section 914 ABGB referred explicitly to Section 6 ABGB, a provision that dealt with the interpretation of law. Contemporary scholarship went one step further and also included Section 7 ABGB in the reference – consequently, also the use of natural legal principles was to be taken into account.[87] According to Stanislaus Dniestrzański, good faith was a natural legal principle with regard to the law of obligations.[88]

Equitable considerations were also introduced in other areas with the partial amendments. For example, the new Section 848a of the Austrian General Civil Code[89] regulated the division of a property connected to an easement and instructed the judge to determine the use of the easement in such a way

83 Erläuternde Bemerkungen [Explanatory notes], 29 der Beilagen zu den stenographischen Protokollen des Herrenhauses, XVIII Sess 1907, 120.

84 Erläuternde Bemerkungen [Explanatory notes], 29 der Beilagen zu den stenographischen Protokollen des Herrenhauses, XVIII Sess 1907, 120.

85 Bericht der Kommission für Justizgegenstände, 78 der Beilagen zu den stenographischen Protokollen des Herrenhauses, XXI Sess 1912, 151–154.

86 Zit. nach. Franz Gschnitzer, "§ 914," in *Kommentar zum Allgemeinen bürgerlichen Gesetzbuch,* Bd. II/2, ed. Heinrich Klang (Wien, 1934).

87 Gschnitzer, "§ 914."

88 Dniestrzański, "Die natürlichen Rechtsgrundsätze," 22.

89 Section 848a: If an easement or another encumbrance in rem grants an entitlement to benefits, each entitled party, in the case of the separation of the dominant land, and each obliged party, in the case of the separation of the servient land, can apply for a court order relating to the use. The use has to be agreed considering the nature and purpose of the right as well as the relationship of the size and the economic importance of the individual parts of the land without increasing the burden in a way duly representing all interests. Translation from: Eschig and Pircher-Eschig, *Das österreichische ABGB*, § 848a.

that it reasonably corresponds to the interests of all involved parties, taking into account "the nature and purpose of the right, as well as the relationship of the size and the economic importance of the individual parts of the land [...]." In view of the completely different nature and problems of specific cases, it was necessary to take aspects of equity into account in order to be able to proceed flexibly in individual cases. Only the burden of the easement should not be further increased.[90]

Various special laws under private law provide for equitable decisions. These include the Marriage Act,[91] the Tenancy Act,[92] the Inheritance (*Anerben*) Act,[93] the Emergency Paths (*Notwege*) Act[94] and the Commercial Agents Act.[95] While some of these laws and their equity provisions, such as the Emergency Paths Act, date back to the monarchy, in others the references to equity have been added only in recent decades. Equity was and is, therefore, a central principle of the Austrian legal system.

7.6 Concepts of Equity and the First World War

Finally, a brief look should be taken at the question of the extent to which an extraordinary change of circumstances could lead to the reactivation of equity as a legal corrective measure. This consideration can be outlined using the concept of unaffordability (*Unerschwinglichkeit*).[96] The "logical

90 Heinrich Klang, "§ 848a," *Kommentar zum Allgemeinen bürgerlichen Gesetzbuch,* Bd. II/1, ed. Heinrich Klang (Wien, 1935).

91 Sections 60, 61, 67–69a, 77, 78, 83, 111 Ehegesetz, dRGBl I S 807/1938, idF BGBl I 59/2017. The Marriage Act was enacted in 1938. From the very beginning, sections 60, 61, 67–69, 77, 78, and 111 referred to equity. Section 83 was amended in 1978, and section 69a in 1999. Since then, they have contained the term "equity."

92 Section 37 Mietrechtsgesetz, BGBl 520/1981, idF BGBl I 176/2023. The Tenancy Act goes back to 1981, as does the reference to equity.

93 Section 11 Anerbengesetz, BGBl 106/1958, idF BGBl I 38/2019. The Inheritance (Anerben) Act was passed in 1958 and referred to equity.

94 Sections 24, 25. Notwegegesetz, RGBl 140/1896, idF BGBl I 112/2003. The Emergency Paths Act was passed in 1896 and from the beginning included references to equity.

95 Section 24 Handelsvertretergesetz, BGBl 88/1993, idF BGBl I 29/2016. The Commercial Agents Act was enacted in 1993 and referred to equity from the beginning.

96 Cf. on unaffordability: Wilhelm Schlesinger, "Die vorläufige und endgiltige Nichterfüllung," *Österreichisches Zentralblatt für die juristische Praxis* 44 (1926): 1–26; Kamila Staudigl-Ciechowicz, "Cisleithanien (1867–1918) und Republik Österreich (1918–1938)," in *Leistungsstörungsrecht in Mitteleuropa – Art. 354–359 ADHGB*, eds. Martin Löhnig and Stephan Wagner (Tübingen: Mohr Siebeck, 2024), 87, 108–110, 142ff. A similar concept is the principle of *clausula rebus sic stantibus.* For a distinction between these two concepts, cf. Kamila Staudigl-Ciechowicz, "Zur Entwicklung des Zivilrechts in Österreich 1918–1938," in *Österreichisch-Tschechoslowakische Rechtsbeziehungen 1900–1950* (= BRGÖ 2002/2), eds. Herbert Kalb et al. (Wien: Verlag der Österreichischen Akademie der Wissenschaften, 2022), 323ff.

impossibility" pursuant to Section 1447 ABGB[97] as an "absolute necessity of non-occurrence"[98] was equated by case law and academia with so-called legal impossibility, also known as unaffordability. Unaffordability existed if the performance was not factually impossible, but "due to a change in circumstances [...] cannot be expected of the debtor."[99] As Wilhelm Schlesinger explained in 1926, this was actually an "economic concept of impossibility."[100] The requirements for unaffordability were specified by case law. Many cases were caused by wartime conditions.[101] This new legal construction arose from these exceptional situations; the texts of the decisions also contain references to equity and the principle of good faith (*Treu und Glauben*). In 1922, in the case of a loan agreement (*Darlehn*) for a particular quantity of lead, the Supreme Court stated that Section 1447 of the Austrian General Civil Code could be applied to all debt relationships "only if the debtor is able to demonstrate that, due to a subsequent, unforeseeable, fortuitous change in circumstances, the prices of the goods to be returned have increased to such an extent that the performance cannot reasonably [*billigerweise*] be expected of him and must be equated with a legally impossible one."[102] In 1919, the government stated in retrospect that "basically" the jurisdiction of the Supreme Court with regard to contracts concluded in 1914 "amounted to jurisdiction based on principles of equity."[103]

The importance of equity in an extraordinary change of circumstances becomes even clearer with the establishment of the Einigungsamt (arbitration office) in April 1919.[104] As a consequence of the economic difficulties caused by the war and the enormous burdens on some parties who had concluded a

97 Section 1447 ABGB: The complete destruction of a specific asset by accident terminates all obligations, even those to reimburse its value. This principle also applies to such circumstances in which the satisfaction of the obligation or the payment of a debt is impossible due to any other accident. The debtor must, in any event, return or reimburse everything which he received as performance of the obligation as an honest possessor, however, only in such way that he does not gain a benefit from the other's damage. Translation from: Eschig and Pircher-Eschig, *Das österreichische ABGB*, § 1447.

98 Oskar Pisko, "§ 1447," in *Kommentar zum Allgemeinen bürgerlichen Gesetzbuch*, Bd. IV, ed. Heinrich Klang (Wien, 1935).

99 Armin Ehrenzweig, *System des österreichischen allgemeinen Privatrechts*, Bd. II/1, 2. Aufl. (Wien, 1928), 352.

100 Schlesinger, "Nichterfüllung," 20.

101 Several decisions of the Supreme Court from 1915 deal with unaffordability. Cf. Schey, *Das Allgemeine bürgerliche Gesetzbuch*, 838. For example: OGH, Judgement 7 July 1915, R II 42, *Österreichisches Zentralblatt für die juristische Praxis* 33 (1915): Nr. 418; OGH, Judgement of 21 September 1915, Rv II 465/15, *Allgemeine österreichische Gerichts-Zeitung* 66 (1915): 455–456.

102 OGH, Judgement of 21 February 1922, Ob II 119/22, SZ IV 24.

103 Erläuternde Bemerkungen [Explanatory notes], 86 der Beilagen zu den stenographischen Protokollen der Konstituierenden Nationalversammlung, 11.

104 Gesetz vom 4. April 1919, StGBl 220/1919, über die Errichtung von Einigungsämtern für Streitigkeiten aus bestimmten Lieferungsverträgen.

supply contract during the First World War, the Austrian legislature decided to introduce a protective provision. The Einigungsamt was introduced to "submit to the parties an equity-based settlement appropriate to the circumstances of the individual case." The Einigungsamt did not have compulsory jurisdiction as such, but ordinary legal action could be taken only if both parties waived their right to settle the dispute before the Einigungsamt. The relevant law provided for a "speciality of substantive law."[105] Thus, pursuant to Section 4(1) of this act, the Einigungsamt had to apply the principles of equity in its decisions. In the explanatory notes, the government cited the aspect of equity as one of the key points of the law as the aim was to "liberate the court from the shackles of substantive law."[106] The Einigungsamt was a temporary court of arbitration active until 1922.

7.7 Conclusion

The disappearance of "equity" as a term is evident not the least in textbooks. While Ernest Till's multi-volume textbook on Austrian private law still had a separate, albeit short, chapter on the division of law into *ius strictum* and *ius aequum* ("*O podziale prawa na prawo ścisłe i słuszne*"),[107] you will look in vain for a modern equivalent to this in today's textbooks. The reference work by Rudolf Welser and Andreas Kletečka deals with equity aspects only where they are provided for in the law.[108] The term "equity" has no place in the general explanations, but this does not necessarily mean that the considerations underlying equity are not dealt with.

In conclusion, it can be summarised that equity as a separate source of decision-making disappears with the codification movement in Austria. On the other hand, concepts of equity have survived where they have been explicitly standardised by law. Some of these provisions were passed in recent years. Two areas, in particular, should be mentioned here: the Marriage Act and the law of property. Equitable considerations were taken into account in 1978 with the amendment of Section 83 of the Marriage Act, which deals with the division of marital property in the event of divorce. In 2002, an amendment was made to the Austrian Civil Code, which took equity aspects into account when determining the finder's reward (Section 393(2) ABGB).

105 Erläuternde Bemerkungen [Explanatory notes], 86 der Beilagen zu den stenographischen Protokollen der Konstituierenden Nationalversammlung, 13.

106 Erläuternde Bemerkungen [Explanatory notes], 86 der Beilagen zu den stenographischen Protokollen der Konstituierenden Nationalversammlung, 12.

107 Ernest Till, *Prawo prywatne austriackie*, t. I. *Nauki ogólne [Austrian Private Law, vol. I. General Studies]* (Lwów: Księgarnia Seyfartha i Czajkowskiego, 1892), 90–92. This work is a textbook on Austrian private law in Polish, as the language of instruction in the field of law at Galician universities was Polish.

108 Rudolf Welser and Andreas Kletečka, *Grundriss des bürgerlichen Rechts*, Bd. I, 15. Aufl. (Wien: Manz, 2018).

Ideas of equity can also be found in the cloak of other terms, in particular in questions of interpretation ("honest dealings"/*redlicher Verkehr*), terms that require individualisation and discretionary decisions by judges.[109] This clearly shows that questions of equity are still present, but in a controlled, limited form, in each case where the legislature needs equity as a corrective instrument. This form of equity is part of the difficult relationship with equality and freedom. With "controlled" equity, the legislature can consciously decide when to allow equity as a tool to achieve individualised justice and when the principles of legal certainty, equality, and freedom, which Zeiller saw as being threatened by equity,[110] should take precedence.

On the other hand, equity has survived as a component of interpretation and in some currents of doctrine, although mostly as "equity in disguise," as Franz-Stefan Meissel aptly stated in 2020.[111]

References

Primary sources

<u>*Statutes*</u>

Allgemeines bürgerliches Gesetzbuch (Josephinisches Gesetzbuch) vom 1. November 1786, Justizgesetzsammlung Nr. 591.

Allgemeines bürgerliches Gesetzbuch für die gesammten deutschen Erbländer der Oesterreichischen Monarchie "vom 1. Juni 1811, Justizgesetzsammlung Nr. 946.

Anerbengesetz, Bundesgesetzblatt (BGBl) 106/1958, idF BGBl I 38/2019.

Ehegesetz, Deutsches Reichsgesetzblatt (dRGBl) I S 807/1938, idF BGBl I 59/2017.

Gesetz vom 4. April 1919, Staatsgesetzblatt (StGBl) 220/1919, über die Errichtung von Einigungsämtern für Streitigkeiten aus bestimmten Lieferungsverträgen.

Handelsvertretergesetz, BGBl 88/1993, idF BGBl I 29/2016.

Mietrechtsgesetz, BGBl 520/1981, idF BGBl I 176/2023.

Notwegegesetz, Reichsgesetzblatt (RGBl) 140/1896, idF BGBl I 112/2003.

Kaiserliche Verordnung vom 12. Oktober 1914 über die Teilnovelle zum allgemeinen bürgerlichen Gesetzbuche, RGBl 276/1914.

Kaiserliche Verordnung vom 19. März 1916 über die dritte Teilnovelle zum allgemeinen bürgerlichen Gesetzbuch, RGBl 69/1916.

Kaiserliche Verordnung vom 22. Juli 1915 über die Erneuerung und Berichtigung der Grenzen (zweite Teilnovelle zum allgemeinen bürgerlichen Gesetzbuche), RGBl 208/1915.

Schey, Josef, ed. *Das Allgemeine bürgerliche Gesetzbuch*, 23. Aufl. Wien, 1936.

109 Cf. Josef v. Schey, "Gesetzbuch und Richter," in *Festschrift zur Jahrhundertfeier des Allgemeinen Bürgerlichen Gesetzbuches*, Bd. 1 (Wien: Manz, 1911), 511–527.

110 Ofner, *Der Ur-Entwurf*, 5–7.

111 Meissel, "Aequitas austriaca," 184.

Cases

Oberster Gerichtshof (OGH), Judgement of 19 April 1882, Z. 3627. *Allgemeine österreichische Gerichts-Zeitung* 34 (1883): 315–16.

OGH, Judgement of 7 January 1903, Nr. 16.746, Sammlung von zivilrechtlichen Entscheidungen des k.k. Obersten Gerichtshofes (begründet von Julius Glaser und Josef Unger), Neue Folge (GlUNF) 2200.

OGH, Judgementof7 July 1915, R II 42. *Österreichisches Zentralblatt für die juristische Praxis* 33 (1915): Nr. 418.

OGH, Judgement of 13 October 1892, Z. 11671. *Gerichtshalle* 37 (1893): 68–70.

OGH, Judgement of 17 April 1907, Nr. 2350, GlUNF 3750.

OGH, Judgement of 21 September 1915, Rv II 465/15. *Allgemeine österreichische Gerichts-Zeitung* 66 (1915): 455–56.

OGH, Judgement of 21 February 1922, Ob II 119/22, SZ IV 24.

OGH, Judgement of 24 July 1912, Rv I 598/12, GlUNF 6011.

Verwaltungsgerichtshof (VwGH), Judgement of 29 October 1929, A 310/29, Nr. 15.836.

Parliamentary materials

Bericht der Kommission für Justizgegenstände, 78 der Beilagen zu den stenographischen Protokollen des Herrenhauses, XXI Sess 1912.

Erläuternde Bemerkungen [Explanatory notes], 29 der Beilagen zu den stenographischen Protokollen des Herrenhauses, XVIII Sess 1907.

Erläuternde Bemerkungen [Explanatory notes], 86 der Beilagen zu den stenographischen Protokollen der konstituierenden Nationalversammlung. In *Beilagen zu den stenographischen Protokollen der konstituierenden Nationalversammlung der Republik Österreich 1919*, Bd. I. Wien, 1919.

Other primary sources

Azzoni, Joseph. "Vorentwurf zum Codex Theresianus, Erster Theil. Erste Abhandlung. Fünfter Abschnitt." In *Die ältesten Quellen zur Kodifikationsgeschichte des Österreichischen ABGB*, edited by Christian Neschwara, 95–171. Wien/Köln/Weimar: Böhlau, 2012.

Harras v.Harrasowsky, Philipp, ed. *Der Codex Theresianus und seine Umarbeitungen*, Bd. I. Wien, 1883.

Harras v.Harrasowsky, Philipp, ed. *Der Codex Theresianus und seine Umarbeitungen*, Bd. IV. Wien, 1886.

Harras v.Harrasowsky, Philipp, ed. *Der Codex Theresianus und seine Umarbeitungen*, Bd. V. Wien, 1886.

Holger, Joseph Ferdinand. "Anmerkungen über das österreichische Recht für das Projekt eines Systema Codicis Theresiani." In *Die ältesten Quellen zur Kodifikationsgeschichte des Österreichischen ABGB*, edited by Christian Neschwara, 173–326. Wien, Köln and Weimar: Böhlau Verlag, 2012.

Ofner, Julius, ed. *Der Ur-Entwurf und die Berathungs-Protokolle des Oesterreichischen Allgemeinen bürgerlichen Gesetzbuches*, Bd. I. Wien: Alfred Hölder, 1889.

Oldendrop, Johannes. *Formula investigandae actionis per quam unusquisque ius suum in iudicio persequatur*. Köln, 1538.

Zeiller, Franz v. *Commentar über das allgemeine bürgerliche Gesetzbuch für die gesammten Deutsche Erbländer der Oesterreichischen Monarchie*, Bd. I. Wien, 1811.

Secondary studies

Becker, Christoph. "Billigkeit." In *Handwörterbuch zur deutschen Rechtsgeschichte*, 2. Aufl. Bd. I, 587–92. Berlin: Erich Schmidt, 2008. https://www-hrgdigital-de.uaccess.univie.ac.at/HRG.billigkeit

Dniestrzański, Stanislaus. "Die natürlichen Rechtsgrundsätze (§ 7 ABGB)." In *Festschrift zur Jahrhundertfeier des Allgemeinen Bürgerlichen Gesetzbuches.* Bd. 2, 2–35. Wien: Wiener Juristischen Gesellschaft, 1911.

Ehrenzweig, Armin. *System des österreichischen allgemeinen Privatrechts.*, Bd. II/1, 2. *Aufl.* Wien: Manz, 1928.

Erwin, Holger. "Machtspruch." In *Handwörterbuch zur deutschen Rechtsgeschichte*, 2. Aufl. Bd. III, 1119–21. Berlin: Erich Schmidt, 2016. https://www-hrgdigital-de.uaccess.univie.ac.at/HRG.machtspruch

Eschig, Peter, and Erika Pircher-Eschig, eds. *Das österreichische ABGB. The Austrian Civil Code, 2. Aufl.* Wien: LexisNexis ARD ORAC, 2021.

Exner, Adolf. "Ueber Recht und Billigkeit." *Zeitschrift für Notariat und freiwillige Gerichtsbarkeit* 8, Beilage (1874): 1–6.

Gampl, Inge. "Die 'natürlichen' Rechtsgrundsätze in der Höchstgerichts-Judikatur der Republik Österreich." In *Ex aequo et bono. Festschrift für Willibald M. Plöchl*, edited by Peter Leisching, Franz Pototschnig, and Richard Potz, 399–408. Innsbruck: Wagner, 1977.

Gampl, Inge. "Die 'natürlichen' Rechtsgrundsätze in der Judikatur der k. k. Höchstgerichte Österreichs." In *Festschrift Heinrich Demelius zum 80. Geburtstag*, edited by Gerhard Frotz and Werner Ogris, 51–60. Wien: Manz, 1973.

Gschnitzer, Franz. "§ 914." In *Kommentar zum Allgemeinen bürgerlichen Gesetzbuch* Bd. II/2, edited by Heinrich Klang. Wien: Verlag der österreichischen Staatsdruckerei, 1934.

Hohenlohe, Constantin. "Die natürlichen Rechtsgrundsätze im Lichte der christlichen Wahrheiten." *Archiv für Rechts- und Wirtschaftsphilosophie* 11 (1917/18): 312–319, 12 (1918): 37–47.

Kitka, Joseph. "Zur Erläuterung des § 904 des allg. bürg. Gesetzbuches." *Allgemeine österreichische Gerichts-Zeitung* 6 (1855): 41–42.

Klang, Heinrich. "§ 500." In *Kommentar zum Allgemeinen bürgerlichen Gesetzbuch Bd. I/2*, edited by Heinrich Klang. Wien: Verlag der österreichischen Staatsdruckerei, 1931.

Klang, Heinrich. "§ 848a." In *Kommentar zum Allgemeinen bürgerlichen Gesetzbuch*, Bd. II/1, edited by Heinrich Klang. Wien: Verlag der österreichischen Staatsdruckerei, 1935.

Mayr, Robert v. *Die Auslobung. Eine zivilistische Untersuchung.* Wien: Manz, 1905.

Meissel, Franz-Stefan. "Aequitas austriaca – Zur Billigkeit als Rechtsquelle in der Kodifikationsgeschichte des ABGB." In *Festschrift für Thomas Simon zum 65. Geburtstag. Land, Policey, Verfassung*, edited by Gerald Kohl et al., 167–90. Wien: Verlag Österreich, 2020.

Ogris, Werner. "Kabinettsjustiz." In *Handwörterbuch zur deutschen Rechtsgeschichte*, 2. Aufl. Bd. II, 1487–92. Berlin: Erich Schmidt, 2016. https://www-hrgdigital-de.uaccess.univie.ac.at/HRG.kabinettsjustiz

Pisko, Oskar. "§ 1447." In *Kommentar zum Allgemeinen bürgerlichen Gesetzbuch*, Bd. IV, edited by Heinrich Klang. Wien, 1935.

Schey, Josef v. "Gesetzbuch und Richter." In *Festschrift zur Jahrhundertfeier des Allgemeinen Bürgerlichen Gesetzbuches*, Bd. 1, 498–532. Wien: Manz, 1911.

Schlesinger, Wilhelm. "Die vorläufige und endgiltige Nichterfüllung." *Österreichisches Zentralblatt für die juristische Praxis* 44 (1926): 1–26.

Schott, Clausdieter. *'Rechtsgrundsätze' und Gesetzeskorrektur. Ein Beitrag zur Geschichte gesetzlicher Rechtsfindungsregeln*. Berlin: Duncker & Humblot, 1975.

Staudigl-Ciechowicz, Kamila. "Cisleithanien (1867–1918) und Republik Österreich (1918–1938)." In *Leistungsstörungsrecht in Mitteleuropa – Art. 354–359 ADHGB*, edited by Martin Löhnig and Stephan Wagner, 87-144. Tübingen: Mohr Siebeck, 2024.

Staudigl-Ciechowicz, Kamila. "Die Teilnovellen als letzter Akt der österreichischen Zivilgesetzgebung in Mitteleuropa." *Beiträge zur Rechtsgeschichte Österreichs* 2 (2020): 286–94.

Staudigl-Ciechowicz, Kamila. "Zur Entwicklung des Zivilrechts in Österreich 1918–1938." In *Österreichisch-Tschechoslowakische Rechtsbeziehungen 1900–1950* (= BRGÖ 2002/2), edited by Herbert Kalb et al., 316–29. Wien: Verlag der Österreichischen Akademie der Wissenschaften, 2022.

Stubenrauch, Moritz v. *Commentar zum allgemeinen österreichischen bürgerlichen Gesetzbuche*, Bd. II, 3. *Aufl.* Wien: Manz, 1876.

Till, Ernest. *Prawo prywatne austriackie [[Austrian private law]]*, t. I. *Nauki ogólne*, [Austrian Private Law, vol. I. General Studies] Lwów: Księgarnia Seyfartha i Czajkowskiego, 1892.

Welser, Rudolf, and Andreas Kletečka. *Grundriss des bürgerlichen Rechts, Bd. I, 15. Aufl.* Wien: Manz, 2018.

Wellspacher, Moriz. "Das Naturrecht und das ABGB." In *Festschrift zur Jahrhundertfeier des Allgemeinen Bürgerlichen Gesetzbuches*, Bd. 1, 173–207. Wien: Manz, 1911.

Wesener, Gunter. "Zur Bedeutung der österreichischen Landesordnungsentwürfe des 16. und 17. Jahrhunderts für die neuere Privatrechtsgeschichte." In *Festschrift Nikolaus Grass*, edited by Louis Carlen and Fritz Steinegger, 613–31. Innsbruck: Wagner, 1974.

Part 3

Law & Equality

8 Liberty and Inequality in Cicero's *Oratio Pro Sestio*

Francisco J. Andrés Santos

8.1 Introduction

Justice, *freedom*, and *equality* are three central concepts in the political thought and practice of all ages, and they are permanently interrelated, either in harmony or in opposition. They are interlinked concepts, which no philosophy can do without if it wants to construct a sound theory of the best way to organise social life. However, they are to a large extent open concepts whose meaning can be filled in in many different ways. In any case, how one conceives of any one of them depends, in turn, on how one conceives of the others. They are not conceptually independent categories: the three are linked in a logical relationship of co-dependence. And it is on the basis of the conception of each of these terms that the trends of political philosophy have revolved around from the beginning to the present day. It could be said that there was no political philosophy until the idea of justice burst into Greek thought, with which the notions of freedom and equality are necessarily linked in their context.

Particular attention needs to be paid here to the freedom/equality binomial, as proposed in the title of this chapter.[1] These two notions have appeared as dialectically related concepts since ancient Greece, in terms of both philosophical-political reflection and constitutional practice. The Greek *poleis* were the first known historical expressions in which there was a conscious attempt to construct a political space in which both ideas were combined in such a

1 This chapter starts from concepts of freedom and equality based on the ideas of modern republicanism, especially in the version of the contemporary republican left (authors such as Gerald Allan Cohen, Philippe Van Parijs, Antoni Domènech, Andrés De Francisco, etc.). That is, it starts from a conception of freedom as non-domination (cf. P. Pettit, *Republicanism* (New York: Oxford University Press, 1997), 51–79) and of equality as *quantitative* or *distributive* equality (i.e., a tendency towards a distribution of political powers and social goods as equally as possible among the members of the social group, as far as historical-social and cultural conditions allow), and not so much *relational* (where what belongs to each subject is linked to the social relations he or she has with the other members of the comparative class): cf. E. Anderson, "Equality," in *The Oxford Handbook of Political Philosophy*, ed. D. Estlund (Oxford: Oxford University Press, 2012), 40–57). It is not possible to go into detail here on the justification of this view.

DOI: 10.4324/9781003654131-12

way as to give rise to a certain *just* ordering of the society. The results were very diverse, although for us only the political experience of a few places (in particular, Athens between the 6th and 3rd centuries BCE) is sufficiently well known.

Indeed, Athenian democracy[2] constituted the first sufficiently documented experiment in translating the notions of freedom (*eleutheria*) and equality (*isonomia*, *isegoria*, *isotoimia*, *isopoliteia*, etc.)[3] into an operational constitutional design for a given political community. The constitution of Athenian democracy was the result of a historical process in a very complicated geopolitical context, which underwent numerous ups and downs and restructurings throughout its more than two centuries of development. It is, of course, an irreproducible historical experience in a different historical context. Nevertheless, the testimonies provided directly by some of its protagonists or by the ancient historians who recounted its vicissitudes, and, above all, the profound subsequent reflections of the great Greek philosophers on the subject, produced such an impact that they have been able to provide political models and narratives up to the present day. The ideas of freedom and equality put into practice there (but, above all, the interpretations that have come down to us) have permeated Western political thought over the centuries. At the same time, the critical reflection of philosophers (particularly Plato and Aristotle) on the concrete implementation of these notions of freedom and equality in various *poleis* (again, above all in Athens) gave rise to the formulation of an idea of justice as a regulative ideal of political life. Justice thus appears as a function dependent on the conceptions held about the level of equality that should exist among the members of society and the sphere of individual freedom that can be tolerated without resulting in the dispersion of the social group or its absorption by other, larger communities. The designs for a just society projected by Plato and Aristotle had a significant influence on later Greek thought, and finally on Rome.

After the Athenian experience, the next prominent historical-political model that consciously combined the notions of freedom and equality, and of which a very large body of information has been collected, is Rome. The constitution of the Roman Republic was also the historical product of the

2 On Athenian democracy, see. A.H.M. Jones, *Athenian Democracy* (Oxford: Blackwell, 1983); R. Sealey, *The Athenian Republic: Democracy or the Rule of Law?* (University Park: Pennsylvania State University Press, 1987); F. Rodríguez Adrados, *La democracia ateniense* (Madrid: Alianza, 1988); M. H. Hansen, *The Athenian Democracy in the Age of Demosthenes: Structure, Principles, and Ideology*, trans. J.A. Crook (Oxford, UK–Cambridge, USA: Blackwell, 1991); D.L. Stockton, *The Classical Athenian Democracy* (Oxford: Oxford University Press, 1991); J. Bleicken, *Die athenische Demokratie* (Padeborn: Schöningh, 1995); J. Thorley, *Athenian Democracy* (London: Routledge, 2004); P.J. Rhodes, ed., *Athenian* Democracy (Edinburgh: Edinburgh University Press, 2004); R. Osborne, *Athenian Democracy* (Cambridge: Cambridge University Press, 2023), among others.

3 Note the use of a plurality of technical terms to refer to "equality," as opposed to the uniqueness and univocality of the expression meaning "freedom."

work of many generations, conditioned by its specific geopolitical and environmental circumstances. Nevertheless, the picture that has come down to us is not so much that of its actual historical embodiment (even less so than in the case of Athens), but rather the account of it by the historians and thinkers of antiquity and the early Middle Ages. This account is a narrative that combines history and legend, myth and reality, tradition and self-serving invention. According to the picture provided by the sources, the Roman *res publica* was constituted as an alternative political regime to, and opposed to, the *regnum* (i.e., tyranny), on the basis of the primacy of *libertas*. According to this legendary account, the Republic was founded as a consequence of a popular revolt, led by the patrician nobility, against the despotic power of the last king, Tarquinius Superbus (Tarquin the Proud). The institutions of the *res publica* were designed from the outset, therefore, to preserve *libertas*. The latter was understood as the absence of *regnum*: the citizen (*civis*) was free as long as he was not governed by a *rex*, i.e., by a monocratic political power, not subjected to the control of the citizenry (*civitas*). The *res publica*, therefore, was the government of the *populus* by the *populus* itself.

However, unlike in democratic Athens, in Rome one does not find any feature that points to equality as a central idea of the political system, apart from the fact that all *cives* were equal in the sense that none was a *rex* (i.e., a subject that stands above *civitas*, the political community). Even the mere suspicion of an aspiration to *regnum* on the part of a private individual was punishable by death. But, apart from this structural equality of all *cives*, there was no mechanism in the Roman Republic to introduce elements of equality either in access to political power, or much less in the distribution of social goods and utilities. Quite the contrary - the republican institutions were designed to preserve an inequality of origin among the members of the *civitas* and to avoid the formulation of redistributive policies.

In Rome there was no equivalent for terms like *isonomia*, *isegoria*, *isotimia*, *isopoliteia*, *isotimia*, and the like. Unlike liberty (*libertas*), equality was not among the fundamental values of the Roman political imagination.[4] In the concept of *libertas* the idea of equality did not play any role.[5] *Libertas* was understood in basically negative terms: freedom as opposition to monocratic power, a set of guarantees of *civis* against arbitrary interference of political power, a theoretical capacity to participate in political institutions (but denied in practice by an institutional design that blocked the real capacity for action by the majority of citizens).[6] The notion of *auctoritas*, on the other hand, did

4 Vid., H. Oppermann, ed., *Römische Rechtsbegriffe* (Darmstadt: Wiss. Buchgesellschaft, 1967).

5 The word "equality" (*Gleichheit*) does not even appear in the word index of F. Schulz, *Prinzipien des römischen Rechts* (München and Leipzig: Duncker & Humblot, 1934).

6 Schulz, *Prinzipien*, 95–111; C. Wirszubski, *Libertas as a Political Idea at Rome during the Late Republic and Early Principate* (Cambridge: Cambridge University Press, 1950); H. Koesler, "Libertas," in Oppermann, *Römische Rechtsbegriffe*, 120–172; V. Arena, *Libertas and the Practice of Politics in the Late Roman Republic* (Cambridge: Cambridge University Press, 2012);

play a determining role.[7] It implied that some citizens, because of their origin or social status, were called upon to govern, and the rest to be governed (but always on the basis of their consent, which was qualified through the institutions). Only *aequitas*[8] was a concept that tried to rebalance in some way the rough preestablished distribution of social advantages and burdens, but *aequitas* was not "equality" in the sociopolitical sense that the idea had in Greek thought (at least, as Aristotle reported it to us[9]). Rather, it was a concept of an ethical nature that had a specific and important weight in the sphere of private relations, but which also had a social projection that was asserted through certain political institutions. It was not, however, a core element of the republican constitution, as *libertas* was.

However, despite this persistent absence of the value of equality in the axiological basis of Roman society (except for a strictly juridical-formal aspect linked to the conditions for the exercise of political power), this does not necessarily mean that the notion of equality was completely unknown in the ideological environment of Roman history. After all, after coming into contact with the Greek (and Athenian in particular) cultural sphere, this idea had to be assimilated by the Roman ruling classes as well, and it ended up playing a role in the context of the clashes for political power between the various sectors of society. The aim of the following pages is to analyse this dialectical interplay between the notions of freedom and equality in the context of the ideological discourses of the Roman Republic. In particular, they focus on a work by the great orator Marcus Tullius Cicero which is highly representative of the resistance of a part of the leading Roman elite to any erosion of its political and social power caused by the penetration of dissolving Greek isonomic ideas.

8.2 Cicero Enters the Scene

Only at one specific historical moment did the idea of equality seem to be the driving force behind a certain social-political movement.[10] This was the period of the so-called crisis of the Republic, specifically, the last century of its existence (133–31 BCE).[11] In the proposals for reform of the system due to the

C. Balmaceda, *Libertas and Res Publica in the Roman Republic: Ideas of Freedom and Roman Politics* (Boston: Brill, 2020).

7 Schulz, *Prinzipien*, 112-12.

8 F. Wieacker, *Römische Rechtsgeschichte, vol. 1: Einleitung, Quellenkunde, Frühzeit und Republik* (München: Beck, 1988), 506ff.

9 *Pol.* IV, 4, 6, 9; V, 1, 5; VI, 2-4; *Ath. pol. pass.*

10 Another view, however, in Arena, *Libertas*, 169–243, according to which concerns with equality do not figure at all in the account of the political struggle in the 5th century BCE.

11 On the crisis of the Roman Republic the bibliography is immense: a classic reference is R. Syme, *The Roman Revolution* (Oxford: Oxford University Press, 1939); other more recent contributions of some interest are: E. Betti, *La crisi della repubblica e la genesi del principato in Roma*, ed. G. Crifò (Rome: Pontificia Univ. Lateranensis, 1982); P.A. Brunt, *The Fall of the Roman Republic and Other Essays* (Oxford: Clarendon Press, 1988); J. A. Crook,

Gracchi brothers (133–123 BCE), there was undoubtedly a spirit of equality in the constitutional design of the Republic through a series of measures aimed at a greater distribution of positions of power (especially in favour of the *equites*, i.e., the capitalist sectors), but also of the economic resources of society among the various members of the citizenry hitherto excluded from the benefits that imperial expansion had produced (small peasants, citizens of the allied communities, the mass of the urban *plebs*). These proposals, despite their initial failure, paved the way for a breakdown of the system that would eventually lead to a change of political regime (in which, however, the idea of equality also failed to become a central element of the Roman constitution and social life). This is not so strange considering that the final century of the Republic was precisely the last phase of a social-historical development in which traditional Roman values and principles had been undermined by the extraordinary socioeconomic, political, and cultural transformations that had taken place in the Roman state as a result of imperial expansion between the 4th and 2nd centuries BCE.

Indeed, the history of the Roman Republic fits quite well with the theoretical model of the historical development of the relations between subordinate subjects and the *hegemonic power* of certain ruling groups within a technically advanced society once proposed by Antonio Gramsci.[12] According to this model, the hegemonic power of a society's dominant groups or classes ultimately resides in their leading role and the belief it engenders in their capacity to lead through results or illusions. The first instrument of hegemonic power is undoubtedly the religious-philosophical one, but the most effective and practical way of imposing, not only ideology, but the very power of domination through society, is law, since it justifies power, and also gives it its deepest force, of a psychic nature. In any case, both the religious-moral and the legal apparatus act together to impose a series of dominant social values capable of consolidating and perpetuating the dominant positions of the groups that

A. W. Lintott, and E. Rawson, eds., *The Cambridge Ancient History, vol. 9. The Last Age of the Roman Republic, 146–43 BC* (Cambridge: Cambridge University Press, 1992); F. Pina Polo, *La crisis de la República (133–44 BC)* (Madrid: Síntesis, 1999); E.S. Gruen, *The Last Generation of the Roman Republic* (Berkeley: University of California Press, 2007); C.S. MacKay, *The Breakdown of the Roman Republic: From Oligarchy to Empire* (Cambridge: Cambridge University Press, 2009); K.-J. Hölkeskamp, ed., *Eine politische Kultur (in) der Krise? Die "letzte" Generation der römischen Republik* (München: Oldenburg, 2009); C.E.H. Steel, *The End of the Roman Republic* (Edinburgh: Edinburgh Univ. Press, 2013); E.J. Watts, *Mortal Republic: How Rome Fell into Tyranny* (New York: Perseus, 2020). Exhaustive, but now long outdated, W.K.A. Drumann, *Geschichte Roms in seinem Übergange von der republikanischen zur monarchischen Verfassung, oder Pompeius, Caesar, Cicero und ihre Zeitgenossen nach Geschlechtern und mit genealogischen Tabellen*, 6 vols, ed. P. Groebe (Hildesheim: Olms, 1964) (= 1908–1910).

12 Mainly, A. Gramsci, *Quaderni del carcere*, ed. V. Garrata (Torino: Einaudi, 1975); cf. on this, J. V. Femia, "The Concept of Hegemony," in *Gramsci's Political Thought: Hegemony, Consciousness, and the Revolutionary Process*, ed. J.V. Femia (New York: Oxford University Press, 2010) (= 1987), 23–60.

hold hegemonic power. Such beliefs and values are assumed by the population as a whole as natural structuring elements of the society in question, without which the existence and subsistence of the social group as such is inconceivable. Such principles are usually embedded in the history of social groups according to a combination of power relations of domination and leadership, and usually go through three phases.

The first phase is when the social group or ruling class is in power and the population believes that it is indeed in power. In such a case, the social values that consolidate the ruling class are solid and are not questioned. The law serves to organise coexistence and the achievement of common social goals. The legal-political order manages to rationally orient the means of power to the ends of the whole collectivity, as they are focused by these unquestioned values. It creates patterns of conduct that the population believes to be just, good, and useful, and it defends them against internal and external enemies.

The second phase occurs when the dominant group or class is no longer in power, but the population still believes that it is. In this case, social values and law become more "ideological" (in the sense of masking the underlying reality), but this still gives to this group its deepest psychological force as long as the consciousness of the population is not awakened by the revealing critique of other intellectuals or ideologues. Law becomes more coercive to the extent that it seeks to preserve a decaying form of domination. It is often used to enable groups that hold hegemonic power to defend themselves against each other or to attack each other in order to win back the hegemony that, between them all, is being lost. Sometimes law also serves in this case to remove existing values and try to adapt them to new social conditions in order to stop the loss of hegemonic power.

The third, and last, phase is when the dominant group or class is no longer in power and the population has come to know it. Here values are no longer believed to be indisputable and are openly discussed and alternative values are put forward. Law is now purely an instrument of force and the only thing it organizes is the defence of hegemonic power against the powers of groups or classes that strive to break the domination and replace the ruling class, often even with the use of force (revolution). In this struggle, the two sides often accuse each other of being "enemies of the people" or "subversive agents of the state." Legal rules in such a case increasingly lose their normative effectiveness and are often obeyed but not complied with. Traditional rules are often denounced for the contradictory nature of their outward form and their material content of pure domination. The final result is the dissolution of the legal-political system and its replacement by a new one that constitutes and legalises the changes within society.

The history of the Roman Republic, as I have said, was largely similar to this scheme. In fact, in the first phase (ca. 733–ca. 201 BCE), the ruling class – the patrician aristocracy (supposedly descended from the founding *patres* of the *Urbs*) or, from the end of the strife between the estates (the 5th–mid-3rd centuries BCE), patrician-plebeian *nobilitas* – was firmly established in power and aristocratic values were assumed by the population as a whole by virtue of the bonds of fidelity (*fides*).[13] In the second phase (from the end of the Second Punic War to the rise of the Gracchi in 133 BCE), the ruling class ceased to be truly dominant since other social groups (mainly the *equites*, the knights enriched by the opening up of an international market economy as a result of Rome's imperial expansion throughout the Mediterranean basin, as well as local aristocracies) disputed effective power, although traditional values continued to be socially accepted by the majority of the population and there was no organised protest against the monopoly of political power by this ruling class (the *nobilitas*). The *nobilitas* was, however, increasingly obliged to make use of the law (through state instruments such as the *lex publica* or the *edictum praetorium*) to establish those values and cultural representations that ideologically justified its perpetuation in political power and its access to economic resources. Finally, Rome entered the third phase (from the Gracchi's "revolution" between 133 and 123 BCE and the establishment of the new imperial regime in 27 BCE), in which there was a growing conviction that the nobility (*nobilitas*) was no longer really the ruling class and there was increasingly organised opposition to the continuation of its political and legal monopoly. Traditional values were being challenged, new values were emerging, favoured by economic expansion and the penetration of Greek culture. Social practices were increasingly dissident and the *nobilitas*' desire to perpetuate its power could be enforced only through violence (civil wars, dictatorships, social revolts), which would eventually result in the end of the *res publica* and the establishment of a new political-legal regime. It is not possible here to justify in detail the adequacy of the constitutional moments of the Republic to this historical-philosophical scheme, but it should serve as a frame of reference to contextualise what will be said below.

It is precisely in this last phase of development (the time of the "Roman revolution," in Syme's famous expression),[14] with the contestation of the predominance of traditional aristocratic values that justified the conventional structures of the *res publica* (and where, as has been said, equality did not play any significant role), that the idea that equality should be considered a basic structural element of Roman society, alongside *libertas*, began to be glimpsed for a time in the ideological framework of the republican constitution.[15] This emerged both from the political practice of the time and from ideological representations of the Roman past of the period. In practice, it could be seen in the

13 Wieacker, *Römische Rechtsgeschichte*, 504–508.

14 Syme, *The Roman Revolution*.

15 Although often such a claim to equality is made in the name of *libertas* itself, as an attempt to give effective content to its value: cf. M. Schofield, *Cicero. Political Philosophy* (New York: Oxford University Press, 2021), 36–40.

proposals for political reforms and social measures of the Gracchi brothers,[16] as well as, after their failure, of other, even more radical reformers (Saturninus, Livius Drusus, Catiline, Clodius, etc.) and the social-political programme of the *populares* (on which, however, the sources are rather sparse).[17] On the ideological level, the same was present in the more or less legendary and fantastic accounts of the struggles of the plebeians against the patricians at the beginning of the Republic for the *exaequatio* of rights between the two social orders, which were produced by the historians of the Augustan Age, especially Titus Livy (and which, in turn, were based on the ideological representations of the analysts of the last Republican century). Although there are hardly any explicit references to it, a careful reading of the sources and a pragmatic interpretation of the texts and subtexts suggest that the notion of equality acted as a decisive *idée-force* in the processes and tensions that took place at that historical moment.[18]

Moreover, even in the historical-philosophical reflection of the time, the presence of the idea of equality as a relevant value in the republican political axiology is found only in isolation. This is, of course, the sole case of Marcus Tullius Cicero, probably the first and only theoretician of politics of true philosophical scope in the entire history of Rome. Before Cicero, Roman self-awareness of the meaning of its political constitution had been virtually devoid of any theoretical and conceptual development[19]: there was no theorisation of the *res publica* and the fundamental values that underpinned it (*libertas*, *auctoritas*, *fides*, *dignitas*, *virtus*, *pietas*, *honos*, *gravitas*, *constantia*, etc.) until the famous characterisation of the Roman *res publica* of the 2nd century BCE (precisely in the second phase of development mentioned above) by Polybius in book VI of his *Histories*. But Polybius's work is a representation of the Greco-Hellenistic constitutional theory of the Roman state and an idealisation of its functioning at the height of the Republic (a defensive ideological representation of the leading cadres of the *nobilitas* who were beginning at that time to see their power challenged), not the work of an authentic Roman thinker. The Roman tradition, however,

16 There is a rich literature on them: see especially P. Fraccaro, *Studi sull'età dei Gracchi: La tradizione storica sulla rivoluzione Graccana* (Roma: L'Erma' di Bretschneider, 1967); H.C. Boren, *The Gracchi* (New York: Twayne, 1968); C. Nicolet, *Les Gracques ou crise agraire et révolution à Rome* (Paris: Julliard, 1971); A.H. Bernstein, *Tiberius Sempronius Gracchus: Tradition and Apostasy* (Ithaca, NY: Cornell University Press, 1978); D.L. Stockton, *The Gracchi* (Oxford: Clarendon, 1979); N. Barca, *I Gracchi: Quando la politica finisce in tragedia* (Roma: L'Erma' di Bretschneider, 2019); C. Gabrielli, *Res publica servanda est: La svolta dei Gracchi tra prassi politica e violenza nella riflessione storiografica* (Sevilla: Universidad, 2022).

17 Brunt, *The Fall of the Roman Republic*, 348.

18 Schofield, *Cicero.*

19 Wieacker, *Römische Rechtsgeschichte*, 373ff (with extensive bibliographical references).

shunned all theorising, not only because of the Roman aristocracy's reputed allergy to philosophical thought,[20] but, above all, because during the early stages of development described above it was totally unnecessary. Both the ruling classes and the mass of the *cives* considered the state of the *patres* in its historical representation as a unique case of its kind and not in need of a theoretical foundation. The nobility unabashedly identified their will to dominate and their interests with those of the *patricians*, and in this they met with the broad approval of the majority of the population, who accepted these aristocratic values without questioning, even when the socioeconomic and cultural reality itself resulted in the loss of the ruling class's capacity to lead. Until the last century of the Republic, there was the conviction that the current established order was good, just, and pleasing to the gods, which seemed to be strengthened by the successful course of things and transmitted through the *exempla* and the *mores maiorum*. This conception came into definitive crisis, as has been said, after the "revolution" of the Gracchi. Even before that, however, in spite of the penetration of Hellenistic cultural values and theoretical models within the ruling aristocracy (as the example of the work of Polybius, who was part of the ruling circle of the Scipiones, shows).

Cicero, however, was the only Roman writer capable of giving philosophical form to this new consideration of the state of affairs that opened up with the "revolution." Although imbued with Greek literary and philosophical thought, he was nevertheless able to give his representations of the existing state of affairs and the political requirements of the *res publica* a truly Roman stamp (ideological and self-interested representations, to be sure, but not lacking in real theoretical stature). In Cicero's work, one finds a faithful reproduction of the traditional conceptions of the *patricians*, but at the same time a profound assimilation of the philosophical-political models of the Hellenistic schools, resulting in a conceptual synthesis that was a model for later generations. Cicero's theoretical work also bears witness to the presence of the idea of equality in the Roman society of his time and its structural character in the legal-political system in conjunction with *libertas*. In particular, in his major work of political theory, the dialogue *De re publica*, examples of a reference to egalitarian principles can be found, as Schofield has pointed out.[21] Such is

20 Vid. e. g. Suet. *Nero*, 52, Tac. *Agr.* 4.
21 Schofield, *Cicero*, 40–46.

the case of the passages in *rep.* 1, 47[22], 49[23], 53,[24] and 69[25], among others. Of course, one is dealing here rather with equality in the sense of the Aristotelian *isonomia* than with a strong meaning of equality in the modern republican sense. But the fact that the most important political thinker in the history of Rome, precisely at that moment in history, appealed to these principles is not without significance.

It is, in any case, one of his later works (ca. 51 BCE). In his earlier works, however, there are few theoretical-political reflections (although it is undeniable that Cicero's entire work is invariably permeated by a strong political emphasis from his earliest speeches[26]). The most important exception in this respect is the *Oratio pro Sestio*, a speech in defence of a political ally delivered by Cicero in 56 BCE.[27] In it one finds a historical-sociological *excursus*, but already at a high level of theorisation, which anticipates part of what will be seen later in his major works in the field of political philosophy. It is a testimony of extraordinary value: it offers a fairly elaborated conceptual presentation of the author's political ideas at the time and of the programme of action defended by the "senatorial party" (if one can speak in those terms) which Cicero represented; however, it is also a first-hand expression of that process of

22 (Scipio): "How can liberty be equal (I won't speak about kingship, in which slavery is not even hidden or ambiguous) in those polities in which everyone is free in name only" (trans. by Schofield).

23 "Since law (lex) is the bond of citizen association, and the justice (*ius*) of law is equal (*aequale*), then by what justice can an association of citizens be held together, when the status of citizens is not equal (par)? For even if making financial resources equal (*aequum*) is not appealing, even if everyone's mental capacities cannot be equal, definitely the rights (*iura*) of those who are citizens in the same commonwealth ought among themselves to be equal. For what is a citizen body (civitas) other than an association in justice (*ius*)?" (trans. by Schofield).

24 "For that equality of legal rights (*aequabilitas iuris*) of which free peoples are so fond cannot be maintained (for the people themselves, though free and unrestrained, give very many special powers to many individuals, and create great distinctions among men and the honours granted to them), and what is called equality is really most inequitable. For when equal honour is given to the highest and the lowest – for men of both types must exist in every nation – then this very 'fairness' (*aequabilitas*) is most unfair (*iniquissima*); but this cannot happen in States ruled by their best citizens" (trans. by Keyes). It has been pointed out that in this passage there is perhaps some confusion between *aequabilitas* and *aequitas* in Cicero's view (Schofield, *Cicero*, 57 fn. 60).

25 "For there should be a supreme and royal element in the State, some power also ought to be granted to the leading citizens, and certain matters should be left to the judgment and desires of the masses. Such a constitution, in the first place, offers in a high degree a sort of equality (*aequabilitatem quandam magnam*), which is a thing free men can hardly do without for any considerable length of time, and, secondly, it has stability" (trans. by Keyes).

26 *Pro Sextus Roscius Amerinus (*80 BCE), *orationes in Verrem (*70 BCE), *pro Cluentius (*66 BCE): see. H. Ottmann, *Geschichte des politischen Denkens, vol. 2.1. Die Römer* (Heidelberg: J.B. Metzler, 2002), 84–88.

27 The last extensive commentary on this speech is by R.A. Kaster, ed., *Marcus Tullius Cicero: Speech on Behalf of Publius Sestius* (Oxford: Clarendon Press, 2006) (with exhaustive bibliographical references).

historical transition in which the current system was challenged and traditional values and principles were being called into question. Ciceronian discourse represented that defensive programme which the dominant class, which had lost its hegemonic power, ideologically sustained in order to preserve its position with respect to emerging groups. Rather than a defence of egalitarian principles, it was a strengthening of aristocratic values and the conviction that power should be in the hands of the social group which is *naturally* called to it, but with the consent and conviction of the rest of the social strata. A discourse which, despite its initial success, was destined to fail historically, as Cicero himself would see not much later. The following pages of this chapter are dedicated to trying to understand this issue.

8.3 Political Situation in Rome after Cicero's Consulship

The year of his consulship (63 BCE) was for Cicero the high point of his life, to which he often and proudly turned his gaze afterwards.[28] On the one hand, he was elected consul by the unanimous vote of all the *centuriae*; on the other hand, he had achieved a goal that he, a *homo novus* (upstart, *arriviste* from the equestrian order[29]), was envied for by the most prominent *optimates*: entry into the exclusive circle of the *principes civitatis* (leading politicians).[30] He also had great success in his office: he managed to maintain the united front

28 Cicero, *pro Sulla*, 30; *pro Archia*, 28; *p. red, cum populo*, 16; *de domo sua*, 99; *pro Sestio*, 49; *in Vatinium*, 7; *pro Pisone*, 4–7, 67; Appianus, *bell. civ.* 2, 1–7; Plutarchus, *Cicero*, 10–24; Dio Cassius, 26–42. On Cicero's consulship, see S. Kurczyk, *Cicero und die Inszenierung der eigenen Vergangengenheit: Autobiographisches Schreiben in der späten Römischen Republik* (Köln: Böhlau, 2006), 326ff; cf. M. Gelzer, *Cicero: Ein biographischer Versuch* (Wiesbaden: Franz Steiner, 1969), 71–104; K. Kumaniecki, *Cicerone e la crisi della repubblica romana* (Roma: Centro di Studi Ciceronani, 1972), 181–233; J. Guillén, *Héroe de la libertad: Vida política de Cicero*, vol. 1 (Salamanca: Universidad Pontificia, 1981), 169–288; P. Grimal, *Cicero*, trans. Ana Escartín Arilla (Madrid: Gredos, 2013), 145–171; K. Tempest, *Cicero: Politics and Persuasion in Ancient Rome* (London: Bloomsbury, 2011), 85–100; S. Castán, "Cicerón entre el fragor de las luchas políticas: El consulado del 63 a. C. y el debate en torno a la legalidad del senatus consultum ultimum," *Revista Internacional de Derecho Romano* 16 (2016): 270–330, among many others.

29 On the concept of "*homo novus,*" see Ch. Meier, "Cicero's Consulat," in *Cicero, ein Mensch seiner Zeit*, ed. G. Radke (Berlin: De Gruyter, 1968), 62.

30 It should be borne in mind that access to the highest magistracy, especially for a *homo novus*, was extremely complicated: only twenty quaestors were elected each year, of whom only fourteen could reach the next level in the *cursus honorum* (tribune or aedile); and of these only eight could go on to the next stage (praetor), and of these only two could become consuls (i.e., only 10% of those who reached the first magistracy of their career); it is not unusual, therefore, that the great consular families did everything possible to prevent people from outside their ranks from gaining access. The case of Cicero is even more exceptional since he also took all the magistracies of the *cursus honorum* at the minimum age (*legitimo anno* or *suo anno*), and on the first attempt: cf. C. Habicht, *Cicero the Politician* (Baltimore/London: The Johns Hopkins University Press, 1990), 24ff.

of the Senate and the *equites* (*concordia ordinum*)[31] against the coup machinations of Catiline and his supporters and, with cunning and good fortune, to uncover Catiline's conspiracy and to obtain in the Senate the execution of the Catilinarians arrested in the city.[32] With his enthusiasm for his successes, Cicero nourished the hope that he had won the eternal gratitude of his fellow citizens and thus also secured his decisive influence on the course of politics in the future.

However, that hope was misguided. When on 10 December 63 the new tribunes of the plebs took office, two of them, L. Calpurnius Bestia and Q. Caecilius Metellus Nepos, immediately began to stir up agitation against him for having Roman citizens executed without first consulting the people.[33] When on 29 December, the last day of his consulship, Cicero wanted to speak to the people about the exercise of his office, both tribunes vetoed his plan. He could only swear the traditional oath that he had saved the state and the people.[34] It soon became clear to him that the *concordia ordinum*, which had come about under the pressure of a threatening situation and which suited his personal situation as well as his inner conviction and which corresponded to his desire for harmony and balance, could not last long because of the divergence of interests between the Senate and the equestrian order. On 5 December 61, he wrote to Atticus that the "cohesive unity" he had created during his consulship no longer provided him with sufficient cover, and that he hoped to find it in Pompey.[35]

31 On the concept of *concordia ordinum*, a classic study is H. Strasburger, *Concordia ordinum: Eine Untersuchung zur Politik Ciceros* (Leipzig: Universitätsverlag von Robert Noske, 1931).

32 The execution took place on 5th December 63 BCE; cf. Sallustius, *Catilinae*, 55, 1; Plutarchus, *Cicero*, 22. On Cicero's actions at this juncture the literature is immense: see, for example, C. M. Odahl, *Cicero and the Catilinarian Conspiracy* (New York: Routledge, 2010). Cf. also fn below.

33 Cicero was branded a *tyrannus* (see Cicero, *pro Sulla*, 30; Plutarchus, *Cicero*, 23, 1). Cicero had indeed had the arrested conspirators executed under cover of the *senatusconsultum ultimum*, which had been issued to put an end to the conspiracy and restore order. However, this action was openly contrary to the legislation in force at the time (*lex Valeria de provocatione*, a. 300 BCE; *leges Porciae de provocatione*, 2nd century BC; *lex Sempronia de capite civis*, a. 123/122 BCE), which provided that no citizen could be executed by order of a magistrate without the prior trial of the people with all due process of law (*iudicium populi*). This right to appeal to the ultimate judgement of the people (*provocatio ad populum*) was considered a cornerstone of the republican *libertas* (the analytical tradition traces it back to the very origins of the Republic, by a *lex Valeria* of 509 BCE; reiterated by a *lex Valeria Horatia* of 449 BCE, but both laws are of doubtful existence), so it could not be rendered ineffective by a mere *senatusconsultum*. On this fundamental right and its historical evolution, see B. Santalucia, *Diritto e processo penale nell'antica Roma*, 2 ed. (Milano: Giuffrè, 1998), 29ff, 52ff, 70ff (with extensive lit. on pp. 32–33 fn 9, and pass.). On the discussion of the legality of Cicero's actions, see A. Dremmond, *Law, Politics, and Power: Sallust and the Execution of the Catilinarian Conspirators* (Stuttgart: Steiner, 1995); Castán, "Cicerón entre el fragor," 308–324.

34 Cicero, *ad familiares*, 5, 2, 7.

35 Cicero, *ad Atticum*, 1, 17, 10.

Pompey, after nearly six years' absence, had returned to Italy towards the end of the year 62. He had accomplished great feats[36]: he had extinguished the plague of pirates at sea, conquered numerous kingdoms, enlarged the sphere of Roman dominion by the conquest of new countries, excellently ordered the administration of those territories, and won a high regard for his generosity, benevolence, and the creation of a lasting peace among men in the East. It might be expected, therefore, that in view of such achievements, his legitimate claims – the granting of a triumph, the recognition of his dispositions in the East, and the provision of land to his veterans[37] – would be granted without difficulty in Rome. There, however, he soon fell into the maelstrom of the game of political intrigue, which he believed he was above, having been elevated to his preeminent position outside the usual course of succession in the magistracies.[38] He could exert no pressure to get what he wanted since he had discharged his soldiers upon arrival in Brundisium (Brindisi) in Italy, and thereby deprived himself of the only means of putting pressure on the Senate. It did grant him his third triumph (over the East, after the previous ones over Africa and Hispania),[39] but the aristocratic majority of the Senate refused to grant his other demands. It is therefore no surprise that Pompey yielded to Caesar's wooing. Caesar managed to reconcile Pompey and Crassus and win them both over to form a three-way alliance aimed at ensuring that nothing in Roman politics would be undertaken that would displease any of the three.[40] Caesar, during his consulship, fulfilled the wishes of Pompey and Crassus and secured himself a springboard to power by having himself granted the province of Gaul, together with Illyricum, by a plebiscite proposed by Vatinius.[41] Caesar, and above all Pompey, who was on friendly terms with Cicero, also tried to win him over to the triumvirate. It was clear to Cicero that he would thereby gain a defence against the danger of being held accountable for his behaviour against the Catilinarians, but he believed that on moral grounds he should refuse since he saw in Caesar the best representative of popular methods, and the acceptance of his proposal would contradict his political

36 Cicero, *pro Sestio*, 67; cf. Plutarchus, *Pompeius*, 26–42; Dio Cassius, 36, 37–54; 37, 1–9, 20–23.

37 Appianus, *bell. civ.* 2, 9; Dio Cassius, 37, 23.

38 Because of his services to senatorial policy with his extraordinary command (suppression of Lepidus's insurrection in Italy and Sertorius's in Hispania, as well as the annihilation of fugitive slaves in 71 BCE), Pompey obtained the consulship in 70 BCE, even though he had neither reached the age legally established for it (45 years, and he was only 35) nor fulfilled the other requirements of Silan legislation (having completed the *cursus honorum* of the ordinary magistracies), in addition to not being able to be present in Rome at the time of the elections, as was mandatory: cf. Pina Polo, *La crisis de la república*, 144.

39 Cicero, *pro Sestio*, 129. Pompey had won two triumphs for his victories in Hispania in 71; the third he received in 62, after his victories against the pirates and in Asia, see Plutarchus, *Pompeius*, 43; Dio Cassius, 37, 21.

40 Suetonius, *Caesar*, 20, 21.

41 On this character, see *infra* fn 62.

convictions and his programme of unity among the *ordines* (social classes). To exert pressure on Cicero, Caesar then used as a weapon a man whose passionate hatred Cicero had attracted: Clodius.

8.4 The Tribunate of Clodius and His Hostility towards Cicero

Publius Clodius Pulcher[42] was initially a friend of Cicero, but then a complete rift arose between them because of Clodius's sacrilege against *Bona Dea* (a female deity and the guardian of motherhood).[43] In December 62 (on the night between the 4th and 5th), Clodius, disguised as a harp dancer, sneaked into a *Bona Dea* cult party reserved for women, in order to approach Caesar's wife Pompeia. He was discovered and prosecuted under a senatorial decree, but he was acquitted by bribed judges.[44] Cicero testified against him and, once Clodius was acquitted, he lashed out at him with all his eloquence in the Senate, thereby attracting his bitterest enmity.[45] In order to be able to proceed better against his enemy, Clodius decided to become a tribune of the people. Cicero's refusal to join the triumvirs, or at least to remain silent, furthered his intentions. In the year 59, on the very day when at noon Cicero, in defence of his former colleague in the consulship C. Antonius, expressed himself with the strongest invectives against the new political course, Caesar presented at three o'clock in the afternoon a *lex curiata* by which the patrician Claudius was adopted by a plebeian (and thus changed his name to the plebeian form of Clodius). With the support of the triumvirs, Clodius then became tribune of the people.[46] As soon as he entered the tribunate (10 December 59), he introduced four laws to remove the obstacles to radical popular methods.[47]

42 There is a vast amount of literature on Clodius: see H. Benner, *Die Politik des P. Clodius Pulcher: Untersuchungen zur Denaturierung des Clientelwesens in der ausgehenden römischen Republik* (Stuttgart; Franz Steiner 1987); W. Will, *Der römische Mob. Soziale Konflikte in der späten Republik* (Darmstadt: Wissenschaftliche Buchgesellschaft, 1991); W.J. Tatum, *The Patrician Tribune: Publius Clodius Pulcher* (Chapel Hill/London: University of North Carolina Press, 1999), among others.

43 These were the nocturnal feasts in honour of this divinity held by the vestals and some Roman matrons (men were excluded and it was a secret and state ritual, for the well-being of the Roman people): they took place at the beginning of December and were hosted by the wife of a magistrate *cum imperio* (in this case, Caesar's wife, at the time consul of that year). The nickname (because the name was not mentioned) of *Bona Dea* was given to an Italic divinity of fertility worshipped especially in Rome and Latium; she was the daughter or wife (according to different versions) of the god Faunus: see Plutarchus, *Caesar,* 9, 4–8; *Quaest. Rom.*, 20; cf. C.V. Daremberg and E. Saglio, *Dictionnaire des antiquités grecques et romaines* (Graz: Akademische Druck, 1969) (reprint), s. v. "Bona dea."

44 Cicero, *pro Sestio*, 89; Dio Cassius, 37, 45.

45 Plutarchus, *Cicero*, 29–30.

46 Cicero, *pro Sestio*, 16; Dio Cassius, 38, 12.

47 A. M. Suárez Piñeiro, *La crisis de la República romana (133–44 a. C.): La alternativa política de los populares* (Verín-Santiago: Ed. Lóstrego, 2004), 157–164. During his tribunate, Clodius passed no less than twelve laws: cf. G. Niccolini, *I Fasti dei tribuni della plebe* (Milano:

The first law (*lex frumentaria*) stipulated that the distribution of wheat to the people should be free of charge.[48] The second (*lex de iure et tempore legum rogandarum*) prohibited, with the repeal of the *lex Aelia et Fufia*,[49] the *obnuntiatio*, i.e., a consultation of the auspices on election days and the right to veto the holding of assemblies and the adoption of bills in case of unfavourable signs.[50] The third (*lex de collegiis restituendis novisque instituendis*) reauthorised the political clubs (*collegia*), banned in 64, and allowed the foundation of new ones.[51] This removed the limits that had been set on the formation of political bands in order to prevent insidious machinations. And the fourth (*lex de censoria notione*) forbade the censors to impose a note of infamy and expel someone from their estate without having been formally accused and found guilty by both magistrates.[52]

Giuffrè 1934), 286–298; T.R.S. Broughton, *The Magistrates of the Roman Republic*, vol. 2 (Cleveland (Oh.): The American Philological Association, 1968); J.M. Arbizu, *Res publica oppressa: Política popular en la crisis de la República* (Madrid: Ed. Complutense, 2000), 253.

48 Cicero, *pro Sestio*, 55; *pro domo sua*, 25; Asconius, 8 C; Dio Cassius, 38, 13; *Scholia Bobbensia*, 132 St.

49 On this *lex*, see G. Rotondi, *Leges publicae populi Romani* (Hildesheim: Georg Olms, 1962), 393ff.

50 Cicero, *pro Sestio*, 33 and 56; *p. red. in senatu*, 11; *de haruspicum responso*, 58; *in Vatinium*, 18; *de provinciis consularibus*, 46; *in C. Pisonem*, 46. According to Cicero's version, this law abolished the *lex Aelia et Fufia* altogether, but, in reality, it seems only to have modified it, in order to better control the practice of *obuntiatio*, by requiring it to be performed in person and not at a distance, with a view to avoiding permanent obstructions, such as that which had been exercised by the consul Bibulus against Caesar's legislation: cf. Asconius, 8 C; Dio Cassius, 38, 13.

51 Cicero, *pro Sestio*, 34 and 55; *p. red. in senatu*, 33; *pro domo sua*, 129; *in C. Pisonem*, 9; *ad Atticum*, 3, 15, 4; Asconius, 7–8 C; Dio Cassius, 38, 13. Religious and professional *collegia* had been forbidden by a *senatusconsultum* of 64 BCE (*adversus rem publicam videbantur ese constituta*: Asconius, *in Pisonem*, 6–7). Clodius's *rogatio* allowed the foundation of new *collegia*, even with political leanings, and the holding of *ludi compitalici* without restriction. It has been much discussed to what extent these *collegia* could be considered remedies of modern political parties: see A. Torrent, "Partidos políticos en la República tardía: From the Gracchi to Caesar (133–44 BC)," *Revista Internacional de Derecho Romano* 8 (2012): 19–82. In any case, following the bloody street clashes between the gangs of Clodius and Milon, *collegia* of a political nature were again banned by a *senatusconsultum* of 56 BCE (*ut sodalitates de curiatique discederent lexque de iis ferretur, ut qui discedissent ea poena quae est de vi tenerentur*: Cicero, *ad Quintum fr.*, 2, 3).

52 Cicero, *pro Sestio*, 55; *de provinciis consularibus*, 46; Ascon. 8 C; Dio Cassius, 38, 13; 40; 57; *Scholia Bobbensia*, 132 St. Cicero considered that by this law the very institution of censorship had been eliminated (*vetus illa magistra pudoris et modestiae censura sublata est*: *in C. Pisonem*, 10; cf. *de haruspicum responso*, 58). In reality, the law was limited to a modification of the procedure for imposing the censorial note, in order to alleviate the difficulties suffered at that time by the *lectio senatus* due to the abuse of censorship in recent times: see Suárez Piñeiro, *La crisis de la República romana*, 159.

The consuls of that year 58, Gabinius and Piso,[53] were won over by Clodius with an agreement that they would obtain the provinces of their choice with an abundant financial and military endowment.[54] After these measures were carried out, Clodius undertook more serious attacks.[55] One of them was the bill presented at the end of January 58 (*lex de capite civis Romani*), which said that whoever had caused a Roman citizen to be killed without judicial process was to be subject to proscription (*aqua et igni interdictio*).[56] Cicero was not named in the proposed law, but it was clear that the proposal was directed against him.[57] He dressed in mourning and turned to the people for help, but wherever he appeared, he was mocked and threatened by Clodius's gangs. Thousands of people, especially of the equestrian order (*equites*), dressed in mourning clothes like Cicero. A delegation went to the Senate. Piso was not present at the senatorial session, being indisposed, and Gabinius rudely refused to do anything on Cicero's behalf. Only the tribune of the people, L. Ninius, spoke about the political situation, and the Senate decided to wear mourning clothes as well.[58] Gabinius immediately called a *contio* (popular meeting), at which he declared that no one should believe that the Senate had anything to say and threatened the *equites* with revenge for the 5th of December 63 (execution of the Catilinarians). As a warning, by an edict he banished L. Aelius Lamia, who had taken a particularly strong stand in favour of Cicero, 200 miles from Rome.[59] The consuls also immediately ordered the senators to resume their customary dress.[60] In his *contiones* Clodius declared again and again to be acting in collusion with Pompey, Crassus, and Caesar.[61] None of these had publicly opposed him; nevertheless, Cicero expected something from Pompey, who had so often promised his help.[62] The latter tried to avoid a decision that would be troublesome to him by retiring to his estate. The reason, as Cicero points out,[63] was that his enemies had spread the rumour to

53 Aulus Gabinius (ca. 101–48/47 BCE): see RE 7/1, coll, 424-430; DKP 2, coll. 652–654. Lucius Calpurnius Piso Caesoninus (101–ca. 43 BCE): see RE 3/1–2, coll. 1376–1378; DKP 1, coll. 1020–1021 (Abbreviations: RE: G. Wissowa, ed., *Paulys Realencyklopädie der classischen Altertumswissenschaft* (Stuttgart: J. B. Metzler, 1893–1980), 83 vols.; DKP: *Der kleine Pauly* (Stuttgart: Druckenmüller, 1964–1975), 5 vols.).

54 Cicero, *pro Sestio*, 24, 33.

55 Dio Cassius 38, 14ff.

56 Cicero, *ad Atticum*, 3, 15, 5; *pro Sestio*, 25 and 53–54; *in C. Pisonem*, 16 and 30; *pro domo sua*, 50; 54; 62; 110; Veleius Pat, 2, 45, 1; Asconius, 46 C; Plutarchus, *Cicero*, 30–31; *Cato minor*, 35, 1; *Pompeius*, 48, 6; *Caesar*, 14, 9; Appianus, *bell. civil.*, 2, 15; Dio Cassius, 38, 14–17; Livius, *periocha*, 103; *Scholia Bobbensia*, 130; 147; 168 St.

57 Cf. *supra* fn 6.

58 Cicero, *pro Sestio*, 25ff.

59 Cicero, *pro Sestio*, 28ff.

60 Cicero, *pro Sestio*, 32.

61 Cicero, *pro Sestio*, 39ff.

62 Cicero, *pro Sestio*, 15.

63 Cicero, *pro Sestio*, 41.

Pompey that his life was threatened by Cicero's supporters. To give his action a semblance of legality, Clodius called a popular assembly in which he urged the consuls and Caesar to express their opinion on Cicero's consulship.[64] Gabinius declared that he would condemn in the strongest terms the execution of citizens without proper judicial procedure, Piso said that he was no friend of cruelty, and Caesar referred to his position on 5th December 63 (for everyone knew that he had not then approved of the execution[65]), but did not consider it right to pass a law with retroactive effect. Abandoned by the powerful, Cicero, on the advice of his friends – in order, he later explained by way of justification,[66] to avoid a bloody civil war and to preserve his life for the benefit of the state and the younger generation – left Rome at night in the first third of March 58. The next day Clodius's law was passed, Cicero's house on the Palatine was burnt down, his house in Tusculum destroyed, and his patrimony plundered and handed over to the consuls. The very next day and at the same hour the consuls received – as agreed with Clodius – the provinces of Syria and Macedonia.[67] Since by his flight Cicero had escaped legal proceedings, Clodius proposed a new law, according to which Cicero was to be outlawed because he had caused a forged *senatusconsultum* to be signed and had had Roman citizens killed without a court sentence; all his property was to be confiscated and any proposal to repeal this law was to be forbidden.[68] Cicero was to move 500 miles away from Rome and went to Thessalonica. After Cicero, Cato, the ringleader of senatorial politics with Cicero, was also removed from Rome, but under an honourable pretext.[69]

8.5 Conflict in Rome during Clodius's Tribunate

Clodius seemed to feel himself master of Rome. With his armed followers, he went out to meet any resistance that opposed him. In his audacity, he even went so far as to snub Pompey by helping the young Tigranes of Armenia, who had been taken to Rome as a prisoner by Pompey.[70] He sold a most sacred sanctuary to the Galatian Brogitarus, a very immoral man. Brogitarus was the son-in-law of Deiotarus, tetrarch of Galatia, and both were illegally proclaimed kings by Clodius.[71] Pompey himself no longer felt safe from Clodius's attacks, so he no longer dared to show himself in public.[72] Clodius even went so far as to launch attacks against Caesar at the end of his tribunate, disputing the

64 Dio Cassius, 38, 16ff.
65 Sallustius, *Catilinae*, 51.
66 Cicero, *pro Sestio*, 43ff.
67 Cicero, *pro Sestio*, 53ff.
68 Cicero, *pro Sestio*, 65, 69.
69 Cicero, *pro Sestio*, 56ff, 60ff.
70 Cicero, *ad Atticum*, 3, 8, 3.
71 Cicero, *pro Sestio*, 56.
72 Cicero, *pro Sestio*, 15, 69.

validity of his laws. This defiant attitude led the *potentes* to drop their opposition to Cicero's return to the homeland. When on 1 January 57 the consul P. Lentulus Spinther addressed the Senate for the first time, he introduced Cicero's return as an item on the agenda. His colleague Q. Metellus Nepos, while expressing his personal enmity towards Cicero, agreed to the item being dealt with in the session. The first to be called upon to express his opinion was the consular L. Aurelius Cotta, who said that a simple *senatusconsultum* was sufficient since, in his opinion, the *lex Clodia* had no legal value. Pompey, on the other hand, called for a decision by the people since otherwise the popular opponents of the measure could not be silenced. This was supported by the rest of the Senate. Only the tribune of the people, Sextus Atilius Serranus, asked for a day of reflection and prevented an agreement in the following days of the January session by imposing his veto.[73] Eight tribunes of the people well disposed towards Cicero, led by Q. Fabricius, undertook a new initiative: they put forward a proposal to recall Cicero, which was to be put to the vote on 23 January. The night before, Clodius, with armed slaves and the gladiatorial troop of his brother, the praetor Ap. Claudius Pulcher, occupied the forum and dispersed the popular assembly. Quintus, Cicero's brother, was driven from the tribune of orators with fists.[74] Clodius dominated the streets without restrictions, and the magistrates and the Senate found no effective means to oppose him.[75]

Thus, the tribune Milo decided to break Clodius' reign of terror with his own troops, after having tried in vain to neutralise him in court by means of a criminal prosecution de vi (for use of violence).[76] His example was followed by his colleague Sestius, after he was almost killed in an assault by Clodius' henchmen.[77] At the beginning of July, Lentulus again submitted Cicero's return to the Senate for debate. Pompey read out a written proposal. The Senate was determined not to tolerate any further delay in the matter: if a decision of the plebs was not reached, Cicero should return with the permission of a comitia (public assembly).[78] Lentulus and Pompey spoke on Cicero's behalf before the people at a meeting in the Campus Martius (Field of Mars). On 4 August 57, the comitia centuriata met with a large turnout and the law was passed.[79] Cicero's immediate return to Rome took the form of an impressive triumphal procession.[80]

Clodius had suffered a defeat, but, after a few weeks of calm, he was by no means willing to allow Cicero to enjoy a sense of triumph. So, he began

73 Cicero, *pro Sestio*, 72ff.
74 Dio Cassius 39, 7.
75 Cicero, *pro Sestio*, 76ff, 85.
76 Cicero, *pro Sestio*, 86ff.
77 Cicero, *pro Sestio*, 79ff, 90ff.
78 Cicero, *pro Sestio*, 129.
79 Cicero, *pro Sestio*, 109; 112.
80 Cicero, *pro Sestio*, 131.

to harass him wherever he could. He blamed him for a famine that was then looming, in order to cause disturbances, and he chased away the workmen who were working on the reconstruction of his house on the Palatine Hill. Milo tried to neutralise Clodius again by an accusation de vi, but had to refrain from the accusation by a resolution of the Senate.[81] After Clodius was elected aedile curule, the tables were turned, and it was he who accused Milo de vi.[82] He also tried to confront the other man who had taken a strong stand in favour of Cicero's return, P. Sestius.[83]

8.6 The Trial against Sestius

On 10 February 56,[84] at the instigation of Clodius, charges *de ambitu* (for electoral corruption) and *de vi* were brought against Sestius at the same time.[85] The *de vi* trial took place at the beginning of March and ended on the 11th with a unanimous acquittal.[86] The prosecution accused Sestius of having recruited and equipped a band of armed men for the exercise of violence,[87] and brought as witnesses L. Aemilius Paulus, the Clodian Gellius Publicola, half-brother of the consul of 56,[88] and, above all, P. Vatinius, one of Caesar's closest allies.[89] Sestius was defended by four of Rome's greatest orators of the time: Q. Hortensius, M. Crassus, L. Licinius Calvus, and, lastly, Cicero.[90]

Cicero's defence of Sestius can be summarised briefly and concisely in rhetorical terms: how can a man who for a long time had behaved peacefully in the face of Clodius's terrorist machinations be accused *de vi*? Just because this man, after he had been attacked by Clodius's gangs in the forum in the exercise of his duties and only by chance saved his life, dared to organise a troop for his defence? It was sheer necessity that drove Sestius to such a measure

81 Cicero, *pro Sestio*, 95.
82 Cicero, *pro Sestio*, 95.
83 On the figure of P. Sestius and his oscillating relations with Cicero, see J. Cousin, *Introduction to Cicéron, Discours, t. 14. Pour Sestius. Contre Vatinius* (Paris: Les Belles Lettres, 1965), 21–30.
84 For precise dates, cf. Cicero, *ad Quintum fr.*, 2, 3, 5 and 2, 4, 1.
85 The accuser *de ambitu*, whom Cicero does not name in his speech, was a certain Nerio, and *de vi*, M. Tullius Albinovanus (cf. Cicero, *ad Quintum fr.*, 2, 3, 5): the former considered Sestius's behaviour during the election campaign for his tribunate to be intimidating towards the electors; the latter considered Sestius's constitution of a bodyguard to be violence. Of the first accusation and the corresponding trial (if there was one) we do not know the details. For the trial *de vi*, M. Tullius Albinovanus and T. Claudius were orators of the accusation. The tribunal (*quaestio perpetua de vi*) was presided over by M. Aemilius Scaurus.
86 Cicero, *ad Quintum fr.*, 2, 4, 1.
87 Cicero, *pro Sestio*, 78; 84; 90; 92.
88 Cicero, *pro Sestio*, 110ff.
89 Cicero, *pro Sestio*, 32ff. On Vatinius, see RE 8A/1, coll. 495-520; DKP 5, coll. 1148 f.; J. Cousin, *Introduction*, 225–233 (with lit.); furthermore, G. Bellardi, "Un mostro partorito dalla parola: P. Vatinio nella interrogario di Cicerone," *Atene & Roma* 17 (1972): 1–20.
90 Cicero, *pro Sestio*, 63.

since the institutions and the law had proved impotent.[91] So much for the line of defence adopted by Cicero. But, if one looks at the speech in its entirety, one is confused by the abundance of the topics discussed. First, the person of Sestius and the judicial investigation are dealt with, but in only a small part of the speech.[92] Second, a large space is occupied, on the other hand, by the precedents of Cicero's exile and return.[93] And, third, in a more theoretical part, he sets out his own political programme.[94] It is the real ideological nerve centre of the speech, which concludes with an appeal to the Roman youth to take seriously the doctrines set out in it[95]; to this are added the *proemium* (preface)[96] and an *excursus* (discussion) interspersed with an energetic invective against the main witness for the prosecution, P. Vatinius,[97] from whom came the malicious expression of the "caste of the *optimates*" (*natio optimatium*).[98] Already in antiquity Cicero was criticised because he "*extra causam vagatus est*,"[99] i.e., he spoke little of the cause. From this, it has been concluded that "the published speech ... would hardly have had anything in common with the one actually delivered in court."[100] This conclusion has been contradicted in more recent times (notably by Boyancé, lately by Kaster[101]), but, in any case, it is relevant that, as has been rightly stated, the speech, despite the parts apparently remote from the subject, nevertheless constitutes a closed unit.[102] In this sense, it addresses the problems raised in the discourse. The first is the problem regarding the part that has been inappropriately called an *excursus*, i.e., the part that contains the considerations on the *optimates* (aristocrats) and represents Cicero's political convictions.[103]

91 Cicero, *pro Sestio*, 79ff.

92 Cicero, *pro Sestio*, 6–14; 75–95; 144–147.

93 Cicero, *pro Sestio*, 15–74; 127–131.

94 "Manifiest für die innere Politik," O. Plasberg calls it in *Cicero in seinen Werken und Briefen* (Leipzig, 1926. Reprint: Darmstadt: Wissenschaftliche Buchgesellschaft, 1962); "manifesto politico del partito conservatore," says L. Perelli, *Il pensiero politico di Cicerone: Antologia dagli scritti politici* (Torino: Petrini, 1972), 165.

95 Cicero, *pro Sestio*, 96–126; 136–143.

96 Cicero, *pro Sestio*, 1–5.

97 This testimony gave rise to a speech which has been independently transmitted, the *Interrogatio in Vatinium testem*; see edition and commentary in L.G. Pocock, *A Commentary on Cicero in Vatinium* (Amsterdam: Hakkert 1967).

98 Cicero, *pro Sestio*, 32–135.

99 *Schol. Bobbiensia* 125 Stangl.

100 E. Meyer, *Caesars Monarchie und das Prinzipat des Pompeius* (Stuttgart: Cotta, 1963), 135, n. 2. This opinion is followed by a large part of the critics.

101 P. Boyancé, "Otium cum dignitate," *Revue d'Études Antiques* 43 (1941): 172–191; Kaster, *Marcus Tullius Cicero*, 31–37.

102 Boyancé, "Otium," 175; M. Fuhrmann, "Cum dignitate otium: Politisches Programm und Staatstheorie bei Cicero," *Gymnasium* 67 (1960): 481–500.

103 Cicero, *pro Sestio*, 96ff.

8.7 *Optimates* vs. *Populares*: The Programme of Cicero in the Sestiana: "*otium cum dignitate*"

Provoked by the accuser's malicious question as to what kind of men the *optimates* are, Cicero develops what he means by *optimates*. He starts from the clear distinction between two political orientations on the Roman stage. The leaders of one of these orientations are the *populares*, and those of the other, the *optimates*.[104] The *optimates* are men who do not seek to please the masses with their words and deeds, but whose policy is to seek the approval of all the good people (*optimus quisque*). The good people are those who are moderate, reasonable, and who live in orderly economic relations of all strata. The equating of *optimates* with *optimus quisque* gives Cicero the possibility to extend the concept beyond the usual interpretation: all these good and respectable people – so to speak, the entire Roman people apart from some perverse and fanatical adventurers – are also *optimates*, even the freedmen.[105] The political goal of the *optimates* leaders is designated by Cicero with the synthetic and somewhat vague formula "*cum dignitate otium*."[106]

104 The *optimates* and the *populares* are not parties in the modern sense with a fixed political programme and a homogeneous militancy. Thus, the *populares* are not democrats since for them it was not a question of democratisation of constitutional institutions, although certain actions were characteristic of it (e.g., agrarian legislation, the demand for a secret ballot, etc.). The concepts of *optimates* and *populares* do not designate various political groups, but individual politicians, senators who pursued their goals with the support of the Senate or the people – especially the *plebs urbana* or parts of it, the *plebs contionalis* – and the popular assembly. Thus, the *via optimas* or the *via popularis* were, above all, different methods by which a politician could achieve his goals. Cf. on this subject s. v. *optimates*, in: RE 18,1, coll. 773–778, and *populares*, in: RE 10, coll. 549–615. On the "political parties" in Rome, see *supra* fn 51.

105 Cicero, *pro Sestio*, 97.

106 On the meaning of this syntagma there is a rich literature: see E. Rémy, *Dignitas cum otio*, 32 Musée Belge 1928, 113 127; Boyancé, "Otium"; A. Grilli, "Otium cum dignitate," *Acme* 4 (1951): 227–240; C. Wirszubski, "Cicero's cum dignitate otium – A reconsideration," *Journal of Roman Studies* 44 (1954): 1–13; Fuhrmann, "Cum dignitate otium"; J.P.V.D. Balsdon, "Auctoritas, Dignitas, Otium," *Classical Quarterly* 10, no.1 (May 1960): 43–50; A. Magariños, "Enseñanzas y problemas políticos en el "Pro Sestio" de Cicerón," *Cuadernos de la Fundación Pastor* 3 (1961): 79–97; W.K. Lacey, "Cicero, Pro Sestio 96–143," *Classical Quarterly* 12 (1962): 67–71; J. André, *L'otium dans la vie morale et intellectuelle romaine* (Paris: PUF, 1966), 295ff; A. Weische, "Philosophie Grecque et Politique Romaine Dans La Partie Finale Du pro Sestio," *Bulletin de l'Association Guillaume Budé: Lettres d'Humanité* 29 (4): 483–488; K. Adomeit, "'Rechts' und 'links' bei Cicero," in *De iustitia et iure: Festgabe für Ulrich von Lübtow zum 80. Geburtstag*, eds. M. von Hareder und G. Thilman (Berlin: Duncker & Humblot, 1980), 81–91; U. von Lübtow, "Cicero's Rede für Publius Sestius," in *Sodalitas: Scritti in onore di Antonio Guarino*, vol. 1, ed. V. Giuffrè (Napoli: Jovene, 1984–1985), 177–201; J. Christes, "Cum dignitate otium (Cic. Sest. 98): Eine Nachbereitung," *Gymnasium* 95 (1988): 303–315; T. Takahata, "Politik – Philosophie – Rhetorik in cum dignitate otium Ciceros," *Classical Studies* 16 (1999): 60–97; J. Dalfen, "Ciceros 'cum dignitate otium': Einiges zur (nicht unproblematischen) Freizeitkultur grosser Römer," in *Otium – Negotium: Beiträge des Interdisziplinären Symposions der*

Dignitas does not correspond to our concept of "dignity."[107] Dignity, in our linguistic usage, is an absolute value that applies to all human beings. The Roman word *dignitas*, on the other hand, does not affirm the equality of human beings, but their inequality. It highlights social differences since it designates the value recognised by society, the position of primacy that one assumes by virtue of one's birth or one's own merit. *Otium* is the opposite of *negotium*,[108] and therefore of the activities that fill the life of the common Roman citizen: financial and commercial business, but above all public activity in the military or political sphere. *Otium* designates everything that belongs to the private sphere, whether it is just a break from strenuous activity or a conversation with friends or occupation with art and science, literature and philosophy. In the language of politics, *otium* is often identical with peace and tranquillity, especially in the internal sphere, and it is often used with *pax*, *concordia*, and *salus*, or also with *quies* and *tranquillitas*, as opposed to *novae res*, *seditio*, *discordia*, and *tumultus*. *Dignitas* and *otium* are concepts that can be used in relation to individuals as well as collective groups and institutions. Thus, it is possible to speak of the *dignitas* and *otium* of a person,[109] but also of the *dignitas* of a group[110] or of an institution.[111] Likewise, the term "*otium*" is often used to designate a situation of public tranquillity and security.[112]

This state of public tranquillity and security (one of the senses of *otium*) can be enjoyed by the Roman people only if the leadership of the state is entrusted to the best individuals, that is, to the *optimates*, to whom the highest rank

Sodalitas zum Thema Zeit, Carnuntum, 28.–30. 8. 1998, ed. E. Sigot (Vienna: Ed Praesens, 2000), 169–187; F. Materiale, "L'ideale politico di Cicerone nella Pro Sestio," in *Cicerone e la politica*, ed. F. Salerno (Napoli: Satura Ed., 2004), 145–153; Kaster, *Marcus Tullius Cicero*, 31–37; T. Nótári, "Cum dignitate otium: Remarks on Cicero's Speech in Defence of Sestius," *Fundamina* 22, no. 2 (2016): 99–115; A. Bragova, "The Concept cum dignitate otium in Cicero's Writings," *Studia Antiqua et Archeologica* 21, no. 1 (2016): 45–49 (with further references); C. Codoñer, "Dignitas en Cicerón: Otium cum dignitate," *Studia Philologica Valentina* Anejo 2 (2021): 69–85

107 See H. Wegehaupt, "Die Bedeutung und Anwendung von dignitas in den Schriften der republikanischen Zeit" (PhD diss., Friedrich-Wilhelms-Universität zu Breslau, 1932); Balsdon, "Auctoritas, Dignitas, Otium"; Codoñer, "Dignitas en Cicerón."

108 On the Roman concept of *otium*, see J. André, *L'otium dans la vie morale*; Dalfen, "Ciceros 'cum dignitate otium'"; D. Hanchey, "Otium as a Civic and Personal Stability in Cicero's Dialogues," *Classical Quarterly* 106 (2013): 171–197; F. C. Eickhof, *Der lateinische Begriff "otium"* (Tübingen: Mohr Siebeck, 2021); H. Mouritsen, *The Roman Elite and the End of the Republic: The Boni, The Nobles and Cicero* (Cambridge: Cambridge University Press, 2022), 124–141.

109 E.g., of Cicero's *dignitas*, which he lost for the duration of his exile (Cicero, *pro Sestio*, 125; 128; 129) or during Caesar's dictatorship (Cicero, *de off.* 3,1,2) and of Scipio's and Cicero's *otium* (Cicero, *de off.* 3,1).

110 E.g., the *dignitas* of the senatorial aristocracy (Cicero, *pro Sestio*, 104), which had been postponed by the power of the triumvirate (Cicero, *ad familiares*, 1,8,4).

111 E.g., *dignitas imperii* or *rei publicae (*Cicero, *pro Sestio*, 1).

112 E.g., *salus communis atque otium* (Cicero, *pro Sestio*, 15); *bonorum statum otiumque* (*ibid.* 46); *otium* del *populus* (*ibid.* 104).

(*dignitas*) corresponds, which enables them to advocate in their actions for the *otium* and *dignitas* of the state (sc. *rei publicae*; cf. *universae rei publicae gloria*).[113] *Cum dignitate otium* or, as Cicero also says, *otiosa dignitas*,[114] can be achieved only by men who preserve, protect, and defend the traditional order of the state and the foundations and institutions on which it is based. Cicero names as such institutions the sacred order, the organs of the state, the legal system and justice, foreign relations, the military system and the financial administration.[115] This order is, in his opinion, doubly endangered: on the one hand, by troublemakers and political adventurers; on the other hand, by individuals who are concerned with only one of two ends: those who seek *dignitas* without regard for *otium* and, on the other hand, those who are content with *otium* and renounce *dignitas*.[116] Above all, Cicero sees a great danger in the indifference of the latter, who, in case of threat, would be called upon to defend the order of the state: they do not realise that when they are content with *otium*,[117] they lose both (*dignitas* and *otium*).[118] In the history of Rome there are many examples of the correct behaviour of true *propugatores rei publicae* (champions of the state), who, in their fight against the troublemakers of the popular party, spared no effort and avoided no danger and showed that *dignitas*, *laus*, and *gloria* were the guidelines of their way of thinking and acting.[119] In those cases it was risky to oppose the popular actions in the first place since the popular policy then corresponded to the wishes of the masses, whereas the people now, after serious disturbances and clashes, longed for peace and tranquillity (*otio suo*) and declared themselves to be in line with the policy of the *optimates*. While the previous great popularly oriented leaders met with the approval of the masses (such as Tiberius Gracchus or Saturninus), the present occasional leaders of the *plebs* in their *contiones* rely on only paid rabble.[120] The real unanimous opinion of the people (*verus populus*)[121] and the sudden change of opinion in favour of the *optimates* is shown in public expression, in the *contiones*, the elections, in the theatre, and in the gladiatorial games, and, above all, also in the spontaneous manifestations of sympathy

113 Cicero, *pro Sestio*, 104.
114 Cicero, *pro Sestio*, 98.
115 Cicero, *pro Sestio*, 98.
116 His voluntary departure into exile was clearly seen by Cicero as a bearable compromise: he did not allow himself to be led to forget the general *otium* with regard to his *dignitas* and to run the risk of a bloody civil war, but, at the same time, he did not forget to take care of his call to return and the recovery of his *dignitas* (Cicero, *pro Sestio*, 45ff).
117 This tendency was clearly widespread in the camp of the *optimates*: see G. Achard, *Pratique rhétorique et idéologie politique dans les discours "optimates" de Cicéron* (Leiden: Brill, 1981), 25ff.
118 Cicero, *pro Sestio*, 98ff.
119 Cicero, *pro Sestio*, 101ff.
120 Cicero, *pro Sestio*, 101ff.
121 Cicero, *pro Sestio*, 108; 114.

for Cicero (decidedly a *homo non popularis*[122]), in the aforementioned activities and in his return from exile.[123] *Optimate* politics is therefore the only way to glory (*laus*), consideration (*dignitas*), and fame (*honour*). It is based on recognition by the "good" (*boni*)[124] and acceptance of the constitutional order created by the forefathers with such great wisdom, in which the Senate is responsible for the direction of the state. The magistrates are subject to the authority of the Senate, which protects the dignity of the other estates and the freedom of the people and their interests. Although the *optimates* have had to take upon themselves a great deal of effort and danger since they have to fight against the *audaces*, the *improbi*, and occasionally also against the *potentes*, access to this body is open to all virtuous citizens.[125] But history teaches that those enemies who have disregarded the decrees of the Senate, the will of the good, the institutions and legal procedures, and have wanted to please the ignorant or the agitated multitude have almost all succumbed. That is why Cicero proposes imitating the conduct of the many great men of history, namely, "to love our country, to obey the Senate and to help the good."[126]

Cicero addresses this appeal above all to the young people who turn their gaze to *dignitas*, *res publica*, and *gloria*,[127] and he repeatedly states that his reflections on the nature of the *optimates* should provide the younger generation with doctrine and guidance.[128] He fears that, in view of the terrible events of recent times, especially in view of his own fate and the accusation against Sestius, no one will be found to assume political responsibility and defend the common good.[129] That is why he recalls that he had to go into exile, but he was soon recalled and restored to his former rank (*dignitas*).[130] This is precisely how other defenders of *optimate* politics, who were mainly victims of attacks by the *populares*, fared: they were all rehabilitated again by the people, except for one, Lucius Opimius.[131]

8.8 Sestius's Lines of Defence to the Prosecution

The programmatic reflections on the *optimates*, who base the salvation of the *res publica* on a state order committed to tradition, undoubtedly go beyond what the defence of Sestius required, but they are closely linked to this case

122 Cicero, *pro Sestio*, 122.
123 Cicero, *pro Sestio*, 106–131.
124 See Mouritsen, *The Roman Elite*, pass.
125 About these oppositions, see Mouritsen, *The Roman Elite*, 105–123.
126 Cicero, *pro Sestio*, 136-143.
127 Cicero, *pro Sestio*, 51.
128 Cicero, *pro Sestio*, 96; 102; 119; 136.
129 Cicero, *pro Sestio*, 1; 49; 93; 95.
130 Cicero, *pro Sestio*, 51.
131 Cicero, *pro Sestio*, 140. Lucius Opimius (*consul unicus* in 121 BCE) was accused of killing Gaius Gracchus, but he was actually condemned in 110 for having accepted certain "favours" from Jugurtha in the matter of the succession of Numidia.

and the main part of the speech, as Cicero himself underlines.[132] Sestius belonged to the *optimates*: he always showed exemplary behaviour, not only in his family life,[133] but also in his political activity.[134] He not only defended Cicero, a deserving fellow citizen, but also at the same time the Senate, the whole of Italy, and the state.[135] Right at the beginning, Cicero stresses that, like Milo[136] and others, in the struggle for the established order of the state and the freedom of all (*pro statu civitatis et pro communi libertate*), Sestius sided with the Senate and all good people[137] against some perverse subjects whom he characterises as troublemakers, traitors, and destructive and fanatical adventurers, among other things, and which he attacks with stinging mockery.[138] Cicero, who in the final part of the speech identifies the *optimates* with all the *boni*, emphasises already in the first part that almost the whole of the Roman people are on the side of those who take a stand in favour of the values handed down and the traditional state order. Thus, both the Senate and the equestrian order, the whole of Italy, and, in short, the citizens of all estates were extremely worried when the tribune of the people Clodius and the consuls Gabinius and Piso joined together to the detriment of the state.[139] After Clodius had presented his proposal directed against Cicero, the Senate and the citizenry mourned, and all the cities and corporations expressed themselves in favour of the persecuted.[140] When Cicero left Rome to go into exile, all the good people mourned.[141] When on 1st January 57 his return was discussed, the Senate met *en masse*, the people were full of hope, and delegations from all over Italy flocked to him.[142] At stake in this struggle between these two enemy groups were the traditional values and the proven foundations of the constitution, which Cicero regarded as the basis of the *otiosa dignitas*: the sacred order, the executive power of the magistrates, the authority of the Senate, the legal system and jurisprudence, international relations, military organisation, and financial administration.[143] None of these state institutions had been spared abuse and mistreatment in recent times. Thus, according to him, in 58 the *lex Aelia* and the *lex Fufia*, which gave the magistrates the right to ask for auspices and, in case of unfavourable forecasts, to veto the holding

132 Cicero, *pro Sestio*, 96.
133 Cicero, *pro Sestio*, 6ff.
134 Cicero, *pro Sestio*, 8–14.
135 Cicero, *pro Sestio*, 15; 83.
136 Cicero, *pro Sestio*, 87ff.
137 Cicero, *pro Sestio*, 1 s.
138 See especially the caricatured description of the consuls Piso and Gabinius in §§ 18ff of the speech.
139 Cicero, *pro Sestio*, 25.
140 Cicero, *pro Sestio*, 32; 36.
141 Cicero, *pro Sestio*, 53.
142 Cicero, *pro Sestio*, 72.
143 Cicero, *pro Sestio*, 99.

of popular assemblies and the passing of laws, were repealed.[144] Cicero states that the repeal of these laws, which in his opinion constituted a dam against machinations against the state, had destroyed all the correct rules of worship, the auspices, the powers of the magistrates, and thus, in practice, the entire constitution.[145] The magistrates' power was paralysed. They were corrupt and abused their office, and they paralysed all political initiative.[146] The repression of the censors, the important judgement of a person invested with the most honourable office, was set aside by the Clodian law.[147] When, in the exercise of his power as tribune of the people, Sestius used a veto to combat the consul's abuse of his office, he was so beaten by the Clodius's thugs that he was left almost dead and was lucky to survive.[148] The authority of the Senate was repeatedly rendered contemptible or outright disregarded.[149] Law and order were no longer worth anything; their most serious contravention is seen by Cicero in his own exile,[150] and there was no longer any retreat even in the face of an abuse of justice.[151] Foreign relations, which had been the domain of the Senate, were used by Clodius to enrich his allies by poisoning relations with foreign nations.[152] Rome's military honour was tarnished[153] and its finances ruined.[154] The means by which the political confrontations were conducted are described by Cicero in concrete scenes from the year 57: stonings, beatings, and assaults.[155] State power was no longer strong, pre-state relations dominated: as in the state of nature, it was not law (*ius*) but brute force (*vis*) that reigned.[156]

8.9 Conclusion: Cicero's Convictions and the Fate of the Republic

One can easily see that Cicero's speech in defence of Sestius, despite dealing with such varied topics, nevertheless constitutes a closed totality: it is a masterly example of "how a critical situation leads to fundamental knowledge, to

144 But, in reality, there was probably no such derogation: cf. *supra* fn 50.
145 Cicero, *pro Sestio,* 33; 56.
146 Cicero, *pro Sestio,* 32ff; 42; 55.
147 Cicero, *pro Sestio,* 55.
148 Cicero, *pro Sestio,* 59.
149 Cicero, *pro Sestio,* 25ff; 42; 44; 75, among others.
150 Cicero, *pro Sestio,* 53; 65; 73.
151 Cicero, *pro Sestio,* 2; 29; 89.
152 Cicero, *pro Sestio,* 64ff; 93ff.
153 Cicero, *pro Sestio,* 73ff.
154 Cicero, *pro Sestio,* 55; 66.
155 Cicero, *pro Sestio,* 75ff.
156 Cicero, *pro Sestio,* 91ff.

the attempt to give a new guideline for an action that had become insecure through a return to the principles of politics and the State."[157]

The *Sestiana* shows that Cicero believed that the state could be renewed on the basis of the traditional constitutional order, in which the Senate is in charge. He did not see – nor certainly did all his contemporaries, perhaps with the exception of Caesar – that the Senate and the magistrates were no longer equal to the task of handling the military and technical-administrative functions that corresponded to the times of imperialism. Rome could no longer govern an urban-based order since it had become a world empire. The *Sestiana* also shows that Cicero was of the opinion that successful political action and crisis management of the state depended above all on good convictions, *concordia ordinum*, and *consensus omnium bonorum*[158] (even Caesar, Pompey, and Crassus are *boni*[159]). He was undoubtedly convinced that such unity, which had come about during his consulship due to a special political situation, could and should be a lasting alliance for all situations. Reality quickly taught him otherwise: in April of the same year – shortly after the successful outcome in the trial of Sestius – the triumvirate of Caesar, Pompey, and Crassus met in Lucca and renewed their alliance. It was the end of the *libera res publica* and of political activity linked to it on the basis of "*cum dignitate otium.*"[160] A few years later, Cicero dedicated to the fallen *res publica* an imperishable monument in his work *De re publica*,[161] and he renewed and reconstructed the *Sestiana*'s ideas in a theoretical and political reflection of principles. In the place of *dignitas* and *otium* there appear *ius* (*iustitia*) and *utilitas communis*, law and common utility,[162] and in the place of the oligarchic system, the mixed

157 M. Fuhrmann, "Rede für Sestius," in *Marcus Tullius Cicero, Sämstliche Reden*, vol. 5, ed. M. Fuhmann (Düsseldorf-Zurich: Artemis und Winkler, 2000), 285.

158 The *consensus omnium bonorum* alluded to a much broader agreement than the simple *concordia ordinum* between senators and *equites* for the defence of their interests against the popular masses (as had resulted from the coalition against Catiline's conspiracy), since it also included the local elites (*decurions*), as well as wealthy sectors of the urban *plebs* desirous of a state of public order, social peace, and balance of power.

159 Cicero, *pro Sestio*, 52.

160 Cicero, *ad familiares*, 1, 8, 3 f.; *de re publica*, 5, 2; *de officiis*, 3, 1ff; among others.

161 The dialogue *De re publica* was published between 54 and 51 BCE. It consisted of six books, of which only fragments have been left to us (especially a very long one in the last book, traditionally entitled "Scipio's Dream"). It is a fictitious dialogue between several Roman intellectuals on the model of the ideal state, which took place in the days of the *feriae Latinae* shortly before the death of Scipio Aemilianus (129 BCE), the real protagonist of the work and spokesman for Cicero's ideas.

162 Cicero, *de re publica*, 1, 39:... *Est igitur, inquit Africanus, res publica res populi, populus autem non omnis hominum coetus quoquo modo congregatus, sed coetus multitudinis iuris consensu et utilitatis communione sociatus. eius autem prima causa coeundi est non tam inbecillitas quam naturalis quaedam hominum quasi congregatio; non est enim singulare nec solivagum genus hoc, sed ita generatum ut ne in omnium quidem rerum affluen<tia>.*

constitution.[163] However, as pointed out above,[164] *De re publica* is a work of maturity, at a time when Cicero's expectations have been frustrated and he has been forced to withdraw from active politics. Therefore, it constitutes an account which, while idealising the republican system of the *patres*, is nevertheless more open to the demands of the new political situation.

In short, the Ciceronian programme in this *oratio* (and in the rest of his political-theoretical work) is that of an elitist, profoundly unequal republic. The idea was to defend at all costs the traditional oligarchic political system of Rome, in which government and decision-making power should remain in the hands of a qualified minority, represented by the senators, while the uneducated plebs should play a passive role of trusting obedience to the designs emanating from the Senate because, in his opinion, the *dignitas* of the Roman citizen consists in each person accepting his or her rightful place in society for only then does stability and harmony reign and the state becomes strong. The *consensus omnium bonorum* is nothing more than a call for coordinated action by all those who would take up this conservative republican programme[165]: a great coalition of property owners to defend, by means of an iron grip on political power, their private interests against the increasingly insistent social demands of the lower classes. The aim was to unite the socioeconomic power-holding minority to ensure the survival of the political system that underpinned their domination and the social and economic inequalities on which it was based. Their reluctance to accept any meaningful reform that might solve, or at least attenuate, some of the major problems that beset Roman society at the time meant that various social groups were excluded from this social consensus: the urban and rural *plebs*, of course, but also important sectors of the elite, such as a large part of the local Italic aristocracies and businessmen, who saw in the *populares* a possibility of opening the way to a reform programme that would provide them with their longed-for political and economic promotion in line with their economic rise under the protection of Roman expansionism. The inability of an important section of the Roman aristocracy, including Marcus Tullius Cicero himself, to accept institutional, political, and social changes in the traditional organisation of the *res publica* led to the entrenchment of certain problems and fuelled confrontation within society so that, paradoxically, this was one of the main factors in the final disintegration of the republican regime, which they wanted to preserve at all costs.

163 See in this regard F.J. Andrés Santos, "Cicero y la constitución mixta: Un enfoque crítico." *Cuadernos electrónicos de Filosofía del Derecho* 27 (2013): 1–30.

164 Cf. *supra Introduction* at the end.

165 A. Rivera García, "El republicanismo de Cicerón: retórica constitución mixta y ley natural en De republica," *Doxa: Cuadernos de Filosofía del Derecho* 29 (2006): 367–386.

References

Primary sources

Kaster, Robert A., ed. *Marcus Tullius Cicero. Speech on Behalf of Publius Sestius.* Oxford: Clarendon Press, 2006.

Secondary studies

Achard, Guy. *Pratique rhétorique et idéologie politique dans les discours "optimates" de Cicéron.* Leiden: Brill, 1981.

Adomeit, Klaus. "'Rechts' und 'links' bei Cicero." In *De iustitia et iure. Festgabe für Ulrich von Lübtow zum 80. Geburtstag*, edited by Manfred von Hareder und Georg Thilman, 81–91. Berlin: Duncker & Humblot, 1980.

Anderson, Elisabeth. "Equality." In *The Oxford Handbook of Political Philosophy,* edited by David Estlund. Oxford: Oxford 2000University Press, 2012.

André, Jean-Marie. *L'otium dans la vie morale et intellectuelle romaine.* Paris: PUF, 1966.

Andrés Santos, Francisco J. "Cicero y la constitución mixta: un enfoque crítico." *Cuadernos electrónicos de Filosofía del Derecho* 27 (2013): 1–30.

Arbizu, José M. *Res publica oppressa. Política popular en la crisis de la República.* Madrid: Ed. Complutense, 2000.

Arena, Valentina. *Libertas and the Practice of Politics in the Late Roman Republic.* Cambridge: Cambridge University Press, 2012.

Balsdon, J. P. V. D. "Auctoritas, Dignitas, Otium." *Classical Quarterly* 10, no. 1 (May 1960): 43–50.

Balmaceda, Catalina. *Libertas and* Res Publica *in the Roman Republic: Ideas of Freedom and Roman Politics.* Boston: Brill, 2020.

Barca, Natale. *I Gracchi: quando la politica finisce in tragedia.* Roma: L'Erma' di Bretschneider, 2019.

Bellardi, Giovanni. "Un mostro partorito dalla parola. P. Vatinio nella interrogario di Cicerone." *Atene & Roma* 17 (1972): 1–20.

Benner, Herbert. *Die Politik des P. Clodius Pulcher. Untersuchungen zur Denaturierung des Clientelwesens in der ausgehenden römischen Republik.* Stuttgart: Franz Steiner, 1987.

Bernstein, Alvin H. *Tiberius Sempronius Gracchus: Tradition and Apostasy.* Ithaca, NY: Cornell University Press, 1978.

Betti, Emilio. *La crisi della repubblica e la genesi del principato in Roma.* Edited by Giuliano Crifò. Rome: Pontificia University Lateranensis, 1982.

Bleicken, Jochen. *Die athenische Demokratie.* Padeborn: Schöningh, 1995.

Boren, Henry C. *The Gracchi.* New York: Twayne, 1968.

Boyancé, Pierre. "Otium cum dignitate." *Revue d'Études Antiques* 43 (1941): 172–91.

Bragova, Arina. "The concept cum dignitate otium in Cicero's writings." *Studia Antiqua et Archeologica* 21, no. 1 (2016): 45–49.

Broughton, T. Robert S. *The Magistrates of the Roman Republic*, vol. 2. Cleveland, OH: The American Philogical Association, 1968.

Brunt, Peter A. *The Fall of the Roman Republic and Other Essays.* Oxford: Clarendon Press, 1988.

Castán, Santiago. "Cicerón entre el fragor de las luchas políticas: el consulado del 63 a. C. y el debate en torno a la legalidad del senatus consultum ultimum." *Revista Internacional de Derecho Romano* 16 (2016): 270–330.

Christes, Johannes. "Cum dignitate otium (Cic. Sest. 98): eine Nachbereitung." *Gymnasium* 95 (1988): 303–15.

Codoñer, Carmen. "Dignitas en Cicerón. Otium cum dignitate." *Studia Philologica Valentina* Anejo 2 (2021): 69–85.

Cousin, Jean. *Introduction to Cicéron, Discours, t. 14. Pour Sestius. Contre Vatinius.* Paris: Les Belles Lettres, 1965.

Crook, John A., Andrew W. Lintott, and Elizabeth Rawson, eds. *The Cambridge Ancient History, vol. 9. The Last Age of the Roman Republic, 146–43 BC.* Cambridge: Cambridge University Press, 1992.

Dalfen, Joachim. "Ciceros 'cum dignitate otium': einiges zur (nicht unproblematischen) Freizeitkultur grosser Römer." In *Otium – Negotium: Beiträge des Interdisziplinären Symposions der Sodalitas zum Thema Zeit, Carnuntum, 28–30. 8. 1998*, edited by Ernst Sigot, 169–87. Vienna: Ed Praesens, 2000.

Daremberg, Charles V., and Edmond Saglio. *Dictionnaire des antiquités grecques et romaines, vol. I.* Graz: Akademische Druck, 1969 (reprint).

Dremmond, Andrew. *Law, Politics, and Power: Sallust and the Execution of the Catilinarian Conspirators.* Stuttgart: Steiner, 1995.

Drumann, Wilhelm K. A. *Geschichte Roms in seinem Übergange von der republikanischen zur monarchischen Verfassung, oder Pompeius, Caesar, Cicero und ihre Zeitgenossen nach Geschlechtern und mit genealogischen Tabellen*, 6 vols. Edited by Paul Groebe. Hildesheim: Olms, 1964 (=1908–1910).

Eickhof, Franziska C. *Der lateinische Begriff* "otium". Tübingen: Mohr Siebeck, 2021.

Femia, Joseph V. "The Concept of Hegemony." In *Gramsci's Political Thought: Hegemony, Consciousness, and the Revolutionary Process*, edited by J. V. Femia, 23–60. New York: Oxford University Press, 2010 (=1987).

Fraccaro, Plinio. *Studi sull'età dei Gracchi: la tradizione storica sulla rivoluzione Graccana.* Roma: L'Erma' di Bretschneider, 1967.

Fuhrmann, Manfred. "Cum dignitate otium. Politisches Programm und Staatstheorie bei Cicero." *Gymnasium* 67 (1960): 481–500.

Fuhrmann, Manfred. "Rede für Sestius." In *Marcus Tullius Cicero, Sämtliche Reden*, vol. 5, edited by M. Fuhrmann, 281–85. Düsseldorf-Zurich: Artemis und Winkler, 2000.

Gabrielli, Chantal. *Res publica servanda est: la svolta dei Gracchi tra prassi politica e violenza nella riflessione storiografica.* Sevilla: Universidad, 2022.

Gelzer, Matthias. *Cicero: Ein biographischer Versuch.* Wiesbaden: Franz Steiner, 1969.

Gramsci, Antonio. *Quaderni del carcere*, 4 vols. Edited by V. Garrata. Torino: Einadudi, 1975.

Grilli, Alberto. "Otium cum dignitate." *Acme* 4 (1951): 227–40.

Grimal, Pierre. *Cicero.* Translated by Ana Escartín Arilla. Madrid: Gredos, 2013.

Gruen, Erich S. *The Last Generation of the Roman Republic.* Berkeley: University of California Press, 2007.

Guillén, José. *Héroe de la libertad. Vida política de Cicero*, vol. 1. Salamanca: Universidad Pontificia, 1981.

Habicht, Christian. *Cicero the politician.* Baltimore and London: The Johns Hopkins University Press, 1990.

Hanchey, David. "Otium as a Civic and personal stability in Cicero's Dialogues." *Classical Quarterly* 106 (2013): 171–97.

Hansen, Morgen H. *The Athenian Democracy in the Age of Demosthenes: Structure, Principles, and Ideology*. Translated by John A. Crook. Oxford and Cambridge: Blackwell, 1991.

Hölkeskamp, Karl-Joachim, ed. *Eine politische Kultur (in) der Krise? Die "letzte" Generation der römischen Republik*. München: Oldenburg, 2009.

Jones, Arnold H. M. *Athenian Democracy*. Oxford: Blackwell, 1983.

Der kleine Pauly, 5 vols. Stuttgart: Druckenmüller, 1964–1975.

Koesler, Heinrich. "Libertas." In *Römische Rechtsbegriffe*, edited by Hans Oppermann, 120–72. Darmstadt: Wiss. Buchgesellschaft, 1967.

Kumaniecki, Kazimierz. *Cicerone e la crisi della repubblica romana*. Roma: Centro di Studi Ciceronani, 1972.

Kurczyk, Stephan. *Cicero und die Inszenierung der eigenen Vergangengenheit: autobiographisches Schreiben in der späten Römischen Republik*. Köln: Böhlau, 2006.

Lacey, Walter K. "Cicero, Pro Sestio 96–143." *Classical Quarterly* 12 (1962): 67–71.

Lübtow, Ulrich von. "Cicero's Rede für Publius Sestius." In *Sodalitas: Scritti in onore di Antonio Guarino*, vol. 1, edited by Vincenzo Giuffrè, 177–201. Napoli: Jovene, 1984–1985.

MacKay, Christopher S. *The Breakdown of the Roman Republic: From Oligarchy to Empire*. Cambridge: Cambridge University Press, 2009.

Magariños, Alberto. "Enseñanzas y problemas políticos en el 'Pro Sestio' de Cicerón." *Cuadernos de la Fundación Pastor* 3 (1961): 79–97.

Materiale, Francesco. "L'ideale politico di Cicerone nella Pro Sestio." In *Cicerone e la politica*, edited by Francesco Salerno, 145–53. Napoli: Satura Ed., 2004.

Meier, Christian. "Cicero's Consulat." In *Cicero, ein Mensch seiner Zeit*, edited by Gerhard Radke, 62. Berlin: De Gruyter, 1968.

Meyer, Eduard. *Caesars Monarchie und das Prinzipat des Pompeius*. Stuttgart: Cotta, 1963.

Mouritsen, Henrik. *The Roman Elite and the End of the Republic: The Boni, The Nobles and Cicero*. Cambridge: Cambridge University Press, 2022.

Niccolini, Giovanni. *I Fasti dei tribuni della plebe*. Milano: Giuffrè 1934.

Nicolet, Claude. *Les Gracques ou crise agraire et révolution à Rome*. Paris: Julliard, 1971.

Nótári, Tamás. "Cum dignitate otium. Remarks on Cicero's Speech in Defence of Sestius." *Fundamina* 22, no. 2 (2016): 99–115.

Odahl, Charles M. *Cicero and the Catilinarian Conspiracy*. New York: Routledge, 2010.

Oppermann, Hans, ed. *Römische Rechtsbegriffe*. Darmstadt: Wiss. Buchgesellschaft, 1967.

Osborne, Robin. *Athenian Democracy*. Cambridge: Cambridge University Press, 2023.

Ottmann, Heiner. *Geschichte des politischen Denkens, vol. 2.1. Die Römer*. Heidelberg: J. B. Metzler, 2002.

Perelli, Luciano. *Il pensiero politico di Cicerone. Antologia dagli scritti politici*. Torino: Petrini, 1972.

Pettit, Phillip. *Republicanism*. New York: Oxford University Press, 1997.

Pina Polo, Francisco. *La crisis de la República (133–44 BC)*. Madrid: Síntesis, 1999.

Plasberg, Otto. *Cicero in seinen Werken und Briefen*. Leipzig, 1926. Reprint: Darmstadt: Wissenschaftliche Buchgesellschaft, 1962.

Pocock, Lionel G. *A commentary on Cicero in Vatinium*. Amsterdam: Hakkert 1967.
Rémy, Émile. "Dignitas cum otio." *Musée Belge* 32 (1928): 113–27.
Rhodes, Peter J., ed. *Athenian Democracy*. Edinburgh: Edinburgh University Press, 2004.
Rivera García, Alberta. "El republicanismo de Cicerón: retórica constitución mixta y ley natural en De republica." *Doxa: Cuadernos de Filosofía del Derecho* 29 (2006): 367–86.
Rodríguez Adrados, Francisco. *La democracia ateniense*. Madrid: Alianza, 1988.
Rotondi, Giuseppe. *Leges publicae populi Romani*. Hildesheim: Georg Olms, 1962.
Santalucia, Bruno. *Diritto e processo penale nell'antica Roma*. 2nd ed. Milano: Giuffrè, 1998.
Schofield, Malcolm. *Cicero. Political Philosophy*. New York: Oxford University Press, 2021.
Schulz, Fritz. *Prinzipien des römischen Rechts*. München and Leipzig: Duncker & Humblot, 1934.
Sealey, Reginald. *The Athenian Republic: Democracy or the Rule of Law?* University Park: Pennsylvania State University 1987.
Steel, Christopher E. H. *The End of the Roman Republic*. Edinburgh: Edinburgh University Press, 2013.
Stockton, David L. *The Classical Athenian Democracy*. Oxford: Oxford University Press, 1991.
Stockton, David L. *The Gracchi*. Oxford: Clarendon, 1979.
Strasburger, Heinrich. *Concordia ordinum. Eine Untersuchung zur Politik Ciceros*. Leipzig: Universitätsverlag von Robert Noske, 1931.
Suárez Piñeiro, Ana M. *La crisis de la República romana (133–44 a. C.): La alternativa política de los populares*. Verín-Santiago: Ed. Lóstrego, 2004.
Syme, Ronald. *The Roman Revolution*. Oxford: Oxford University Press, 1939.
Takahata, Tadashi. "Politik – Philosophie – Rhetorik in cum dignitate otium Ciceros." *Classical Studies* 16 (1999): 60–97.
Tatum, William J. *The Patrician Tribune. Publius Clodius Pulcher*. Chapel Hill and London: The University of North Carolina Press, 1999.
Tempest, Kathryn. *Cicero. Politics and Persuasion in Ancient Rome*. London: Bloomsbury, 2011.
Thorley, John. *Athenian Democracy*. London: Routledge, 2004.
Torrent, Armando. "Partidos políticos en la República tardía. From the Gracchi to Caesar (133–44 BC)." *Revista Internacional de Derecho Romano* 8 (2012): 19–82.
Watts, Edward J. *Mortal Republic: How Rome Fell into Tyranny*. New York: Perseus, 2020.
Wegehaupt, Hans. "Die Bedeutung und Anwendung von dignitas in den Schriften der republikanischen Zeit." PhD diss., Friedrich-Wilhelms-Universität zu Breslau, 1932.
Weische, Alfons. "Philosophie Grecque et Politique Romaine Dans La Partie Finale Du pro Sestio." *Bulletin de l'Association Guillaume Budé: Lettres d'Humanité* 29 (4): 483–88.
Wieacker, Franz. *Römische Rechtsgeschichte, vol. 1: Einleitung, Quellenkunde, Frühzeit und Republik*. München: Beck, 1988.
Will, Wolfgang. *Der römische Mob. Soziale Konflikte in der späten Republik*. Darmstadt: Wissenschaftliche Buchgesellschaft, 1991.

Wirszubski, Chaim. "Cicero's cum dignitate otium - A reconsideration." *Journal of Roman Studies* 44 (1954): 1–13.
Wirszubski, Chaim. *Libertas as a Political Idea at Rome during the Late Republic and Early Principate.* Cambridge: Cambridge University Press, 1950.
Wissowa, Georg ed. *Paulys Realencyklopädie der classischen Altertumswissenschaft*, 83 vols. Stuttgart: J. B. Metzler, 1893–1980.

9 Equity and Equality in Richard Francis's *Maxims of Equity*[1]

Jan Halberda

The OA publication was funded by the Faculty of Law and Administration of the Jagiellonian University granted within the Priority Research Area Heritage under the program "Excellence Initiative—Research University" at the Jagiellonian University in Krakow.

This chapter presents various patterns of using the term "equity" in Richard Francis's book entitled *Maxims of Equity*[2] and its affinity with both law and equality. The initial part of this chapter, primarily addressed to the reader not educated in a common law jurisdiction, presents the specific features of equity law in England (1). The next section lists the maxims of equity as found by Richard Francis (2). The focus is then directed to those cases in which that author considered equality issues (3). The fourth part of the text indicates the meanings of Francis's use of the term "equity" (4) and is followed by conclusions (5).

The book's author, Richard Francis (1698/1700–1742) was born in Dublin, Ireland, of Anglo-Irish descent. He studied law in Dublin (Trinity College) and London (the Middle Temple). After being called to the bar in 1724, he practiced law in London. Then he moved to Virginia in the 1730s, where he practiced law in Williamsburg. His masterpiece *Maxims of Equity* proved highly successful, with four English editions from 1727 to 1812 and a final one – the "Americanised" edition – in Richmond, Virginia, in 1823. Apart from being the author of *Maxims of Equity*, Francis is not known to legal history.[3]

The book's first edition, published in 1727, abounds with many different and inconsistently applied meanings of equity. There are common footprints of Aristotle's *epieikeia*, on the one hand, of natural justice, on another, not to

1 The author would like to thank Professor James R. Gordley (Tulane Law School) and Professor John H. Langbein (Yale Law School) for their comments on the draft of this article.

2 Richard Francis, *Maxims of Equity: Collected From and Proved by Cases, Out of the Books of the Best Authority in the High Court of Chancery. To Which is Added the Case of the Earl of Coventry, Concerning the Defective Execution of Powers. Lately Adjudged in the High Court of Chancery*, London: In the Savoy: printed by E. and R. Nutt, and R. Gosling (assigns of E. Sayer, Esq) for J. Stephens, 1727.

3 William H. Bryson, "Francis, Richard," in *Oxford Dictionary of National Biography*, vol. 20 (Oxford: Oxford University Press, 2004), 748; Zechariah Chafee, Jr., "Coming into Equity with Clean Hands I," *Michigan Law Review* 47 (1949): 880.

DOI: 10.4324/9781003654131-13

mention references to equity as a set of rules applied in courts.[4] What is striking is Francis's use of that term in an *aequitas*-like pattern and his focus on the aspect of equality.

9.1 What Is Equity?

The English word "equity" can be juxtaposed with various meanings of this term that have emerged throughout history. The list most often begins with a number of concepts of *epieikeia*, by which Aristotle specified, among others, a way for rectification of law. As the law provided general solutions for the majority of cases, there were others where a ruling had to be adjusted to fit particular features of a case according to the lawmaker's intention. The Aristotelian concept of equity, transfused by the intermediation of Thomas Aquinas and Jean Gerson, was publicised in the 16th century in England by Christopher St German's dialogue *Doctor and Student*.[5] At that time, equity law and the Court of Chancery had been developing for a long time.

Back in the ancient world, Roman jurists developed the concept of *aequitas*, which meant equality and emphasised the need to decide like cases alike and thus to treat individuals equally: to give to each his own (*suum cuique tribuere*, D.1.1.10pr). In the words of Fortier, *aequitas* implied "evenness, equality, sameness, justice and fairness." This meaning was known to medieval lawyers. It is worth noting that equity is indeed an anglicised term for *aequitas*, i.e., equality.[6]

On the other hand, medieval canon lawyers employed a notion of *aequitas canonica*, which stood for the power to show clemency in certain circumstances. In Antiquity as well as during the Middle Ages, the term *aequitas* was also referred to in another context as a prerogative of a Roman or medieval emperor (or later in canon law: a pope) to impose unwritten law in place of the wording of written law.[7] In the end, the notion of equity was used to describe

4 While the most prominent one was the Court of Chancery, it was not the only court that administered equity, another example being the "equity side" of the Court of Exchequer.

5 Alan Cromartie, "Epieikeia and Conscience," in *The Oxford Handbook of English Law and Literature, 1500–1700*, ed. Lorna Hutson (Oxford: Oxford University Press 2017), 320ff; Mark Fortier, *The Culture of Equity in Early Modern England* (Burlington, VT: Ashgate, 2005), 17–19, 61–63; Stephen Humphreys, "Equity before 'Equity,'" *Modern Law Review* 86, no. 1 (2022): 89–90; Lorenzo Maniscalco, *Equity in Early Modern Legal Scholarship* (Leiden: Brill 2020), 33–34.

6 Cromartie, "Epieikeia," 321, 324; Fortier, *The Culture of Equity*, 3; Humphreys, "Equity before 'Equity,'" 86ff; Marek Kuryłowicz, "Aequitas i iustitia w rzymskiej praktyce prawnej [Some Reflections on Aequitas and Iustitia in Roman Jurists' Concepts]," *Annales Universitatis Mariae Curie-Skłodowska Sectio G* 66 (2019): 179–180.

7 Cromartie, "Epieikeia," 324; Fortier, *The Culture of Equity*, 7; Humphreys, "Equity before 'Equity,'" 87, 103; Maniscalco, *Equity*, 28.

precepts of natural justice. The multiplicity of these meanings was known to some English lawyers at the time Francis's book was published.[8]

Despite painstaking efforts of scholars, it is difficult to grasp a proper definition of equity in English law. Most often, authors describe only how it applies and where it originated. Thus, many still refer to Maitland's classic work that reduced equity to "that body of rules which is administered only by those Courts which are known as Courts of Equity" with the caveat that after the Judicature Acts of 1873–1875 the past tense should be substituted in place of the present.[9]

Until that time, a dual system of administration of justice was in place in England, with courts of law and of equity acting separately. To some extent, this was also the case in other common law jurisdictions.[10] Although reforms led to the fusion of court organisation and procedure, they did not reach the level of substantive law everywhere, and, therefore, the division between law and equity is still recognised.[11]

9.1.1 Common Law Writs and Chancery

Common law developed in the Westminster courts starting in the 12th and 13th centuries. Proceedings could begin before those courts provided that an original writ was issued by the chancery. Each writ was applicable only to a particular set of typical facts and triggered a formalised procedure that *a priori* prescribed how parties should exchange their arguments and prove the

8 Fortier, *The Culture of Equity*, 7–8, 67–69 (William West's *Symboleography* from the 16th century); David Ibbetson, "A House Built on Sand: Equity in Early Modern English Law," in *Law & Equity. Approaches in Roman Law and Common Law*, eds. E. Koops and W.J. Zwalve (Leiden: Brill, 2014), 76–77; Maniscalco, *Equity*, 4–6.

9 Frederic W. Maitland, *Equity, also the Forms of Action at Common Law: Two Courses of Lectures* Cambridge: Cambridge University Press, 1910), 20. Joshua Getzler, "Patterns of Fusion," in *The Classification of Obligations*, ed. P. Birks (Oxford: Clarendon Press, 1997), 157, 164; Jamie Glister and James Lee, *Hanbury & Martin Modern Equity*, 22nd ed. (London: Sweet & Maxwell, 2021), 4; Humphreys, "Equity before 'Equity,'" 87; Mike Macnair, "Equity and Conscience," *Oxford Journal of Legal Studies* 27 (2007): 680; Willem J. Zwalve and Egbert Koops, "Introduction: The Equity Phenomenon," in Koops and Zwalve, *Law &* Equity, 5.

10 The Supreme Court of Judicature Act 1873, c. 66, the Supreme Court of Judicature Act (1873) Amendment Act 1875, c. 77. In the United States, reforms were initiated even earlier: Kellen Funk, "The Union of Law and Equity: The United States, 1800–1938," in *Equity and Law: Fusion and Fission,* eds. J. Goldberg, H. Smith, and P. Turner (Cambridge: Cambridge University Press, 2019), 46ff. Australia followed suit at the turn of the 19th century: Roderick P. Meagher, John D. Heydon, Mark J. Leeming, *Meagher, Gummow and Lehane's Equity, Doctrines, and Remedies* (Chatswood, NSW: LexisNexis Butterworths, 2002), 1–17.

11 There are, however, ongoing disputes over this issue between supporters of equity separateness (Glister and Lee, *Hanbury & Martin*, 14, 18–23; Meagher, Heydon, and Leeming, *Meagher*, 52–54; Henry E. Smith, "Equity as Meta-Law," *The Yale Law Journal* 130 (2021): 1150ff; Graham Virgo, *The Principles of Equity and Trusts* (Oxford: Oxford University Press, 2023), 8, 27) and its alignment with law (Getzler, "Patterns of Fusion," 158, 191). The latter view holds sway in the United States.

relevant facts. Dozens of specific writs were developed in the chancery's work, but, at the end of the 13th century, the catalogue of writs became closed. In cases that fell outside it, would-be plaintiffs were not deprived of justice, but they had to file their suit in another (local, feudal, or ecclesiastical) court.

Still, there were cases where the royal writs did not fit and there were no prospects of obtaining effective protection in another court. A recurring scenario was that local courts were often corrupted or biased.[12] In such hopeless instances, a petitioner could beg the king to dispense justice as an act of grace. These requests were actually entrusted to the chancellor, who "became keeper of the king's conscience."[13] His activity in this regard already had a recognised status at the end of the 14th century and led in the next one to the development of the Court of Chancery wherein equity – then still known under the name of "conscience" – was applied.[14]

9.1.2 Chancellor Picks Up the Call

One might consider an analogy between the way the Westminster courts and the chancellor worked in the matrix of medieval writs, on the one hand, and the modus operandi of a modern customer call center service, on the other.

Today, in order to get things done when a problem arises, one calls customer service. After a while, an AI bot orders the caller to dial a certain digit, depending on the purpose of the customer's call. If one's case doesn't fit into any of the preassigned subjects, nothing will be accomplished. It was the same with the medieval court applying writ procedures. If today's customer's case indeed fits into one of the set categories, then he/she has to communicate very precisely, using specific phrases, which will be understood by the AI protocol. Again, that was just like in the medieval writ procedure, where parties had to follow strict rules of pleading that organised the communication between them and a court. Moreover, in order to prove facts, they had to comply with specific models of proof. By calling a customer service number today, one can usually solve only one problem. Common law likewise recognised the single-issue principle: a litigant could not dispute both facts and law at the same

12 Francis noted that that prompted equity's intervention (Francis, *Maxims of equity*, 24–26 [cases no. 1, 2, 5]).

13 William Blackstone, *Commentaries on the Laws of England*, v. 3 (Oxford: Clarendon Press 1765–1769), 47.

14 Blackstone, *Commentaries*, 51–52. John H. Baker, *An Introduction to English Legal History*, 5th ed. (Oxford: Oxford University Press, 2019), 110–114; J. Baker, *The Oxford History of the Laws of England. Volume VI, 1483–1558* (Oxford: Oxford University Press, 2003), 40; Ibbetson, "A House Built on Sand," 55; John H. Langbein, Renee Lettow Lerner, and Bruce P. Smith, *History of the Common Law: The Development of Anglo-American Legal Institutions* (Austin, New York: Wolters Kluwer Law & Business, Aspen Publishers, 2009), 105, 272–281; Mike Macnair, "Arbitrary Chancellors and Problem of Predictability," in Koops and Zwalve, *Law & Equity*, 82–83; Macnair, "Equity and Conscience," 670. Cf. Guido Rossi's contribution in this book.

time. The idea was that a legal argument had to be resolved by a court, while a dispute over facts was resolved by an ordeal, a duel, a compurgation, or by a trial by jury. Contacting customer service and dealing with an AI bot to solve problems is often a nightmare. An unfortunate plaintiff may have had the same feeling with common law procedure in the Middle Ages. Today the bright side is that at least sometimes a customer can dial zero and connect directly with an operator, who is still a human being. In the past, the chancellor was such an "operator" and was able to resolve hopeless cases if a plaintiff still wanted to avoid local or feudal court.

The procedure applied in the Court of Chancery differed significantly from the common law procedure in the Westminster courts. The chancellor – like an operator today – could "step outside the box." To begin with, he didn't need an original writ – a "bill in equity" was sufficient. He could resolve questions of law and fact at the same time. He could, to a much greater extent than other judges, determine what were the facts of a case. He could also, by means of a "subpoena," examine parties or witnesses and order them to deliver documents or written submissions. This way of proving facts and therefore this knowledge was unavailable to judges sitting in other courts. This, in turn, allowed the Court of Chancery to arrive at sounder decisions because they were based on real facts. This court's procedural advantages allowed it to decide cases on the basis of facts that could not be proven through the strict channels of common law procedure. The knowledge gathered by these means was thus the chancellor's private knowledge that, in turn, prompted frequent contemporary references to his conscience as the basis of the decision-making. According to Macnair, the conscience-based adjudication characteristic of equity was – as indicated above – procedural in nature.[15]

9.1.3 Chancery under Siege

If a case was pending or had already been decided before any other court, the chancellor was able to stay it (or its enforcement) by an injunction.[16] This power led to conflict with other judges, which culminated in the Earl of Oxford's Case (1615). That ruling determined that the Court of Chancery could trump the Westminster courts and hijack some of their cases.[17]

15 Blackstone, *Commentaries*, 436ff. Baker, *An Introduction*, 110–112; Baker, *The Oxford History*, 41–42, 48; Getzler, "Patterns of Fusion," 176–177, 191; Ibbetson, "A House Built on Sand," 59–60; Langbein, Lerner, and Smith, *History of the Common Law*, 289–295, 320–328; Macnair, "Equity and Conscience," 659, 672–678.

16 *Some observations in the practice of the Court of Chancery under the late Ordinance of Regulation*, London, 1653–1658, 14. Francis, *Maxims of equity*, 3 (c. 5), 4 (c. 8), 72 (c. 17).

17 *Earl of Oxford's Case* (1615) 1 *Reports in Chancery* 1. Much later the prevalence of equity law over common law was recognised by the Supreme Court of Judicature Act 1873 (s. 25, 11). Blackstone, *Commentaries*, 53–54; Baker, *An Introduction*, 117, 123; Getzler, "Patterns of

Undoubtedly, the Chancery had its own flaws. The innovative procedural devices failed in practice. A report advocating the reform of the Court of Chancery pointed out that witness's hearings were conducted by "examiners' deputies" who were so poorly paid that they subsisted solely on voluntary donations from litigants, which obviously could affect the outcome of hearings. Proceedings were not transparent. Like other institutions, this court was affected by notorious bribery of clerks.[18]

Ultimately, the chancellor's one-man adjudication was also perceived as suspect. Chancellor was accused of acting arbitrarily, which resulted in uncertainty of law and unpredictability of decisions: his rulings were not based on a clear set of rules but on his own unspecified "conscience." Thus, each time a change in the chancellor's office took place, a change in decision-making followed ("either the Humor of the Judge, or the Judge himself being changed").[19]

9.2 Fourteen Maxims of Equity

These criticisms stand out clearly in the preface of *Maxims of Equity.*[20] Francis's work seems to be an answer to these charges, which he proclaimed as straightforward lies.[21] The book is very concise and laconic[22] and demanding laborious reading. Perhaps the material that made up this book was collected as part of Francis's own studies of the law – it could be a student's book. It shows how unsystematic and chaotic judge-made law was before the era of Blackstone.

Fusion," 182; Ibbetson, "A House Built on Sand," 56–60, 74; Langbein, Lerner, and Smith, *History of the Common Law*, 329–335.

18 *Some observations*, 1-22.

19 Cf. fn 20. Baker, *An Introduction*, 118; Langbein, Lerner, and Smith, *History of the Common Law*, 316; Macnair, "Arbitrary Chancellors," 83–92.

20 Francis, *Maxims of Equity*, 1 (preface): "It is a common Objection against our Courts of Equity, that their Power being absolute and extraordinary, their Determinations must consequently be uncertain and precarious: That not being bound by any established Rules or Orders, nor circumscribed within the Limits of positive Laws, the unhappy Suitor must enter into a Court of Equity with Doubts and Fears; and if he has succeeded once, 'tis great Chance but he may fail upon a Second Trial, either the Humor of the Judge, or the Judge himself being changed; and that this is true in Fact, for that after the most solemn arguing of Causes in all their Niceties and Circumstantials, Decrees made thereon have been frequently reversed by the same, and more often by succeeding Chancellors."

21 Francis, *Maxims of Equity*, 1 (preface): "It is Pity that Englishmen, who are so wont to boast of that invaluable Blessing of Freedom of Property, should be heard to give themselves so broad a Lye, as to say, that those Courts of Justice, where Matters of Property of the greatest Value are daily determined, are arbitrary and precarious in their Determinations."

22 The book is 112 pages in total and consists of: a preface (5 pages), list of maxims (1 page), main text (72 pages), index (12 pages), and the Case of the Earl of Coventry (22 pages). Note that pagination starts anew in the main text, and, again, but only from its third page, anew in the Case of the Earl of Coventry. The index is not paginated.

Francis discussed each maxim in separate chapters by presenting case studies that illustrated circumstances in which the Court of Chancery would or would not intervene. He did not directly give names of cases, but they can be identified by his references to the reports (e.g., Salkeld's *Reports*, or Vernon's *Cases* printed in Dublin). An extremely succinct presentation of facts was followed by an equally concise commentary on the rulings. Arguments in favor of a given decision were sometimes presented in glosses, which often rephrased and clarified the main text. Most of the chapters consist of from four to twelve cases, with the exception of the three plausibly most important ones: the maxim "Equality is Equity" is scrutinised by 21 cases, while "Where Equity is equal, the Law must prevail" by 18, and "Equity suffers not Advantage to be taken of a Penalty or Forfeiture, where Compensation can be made" by 15. These three maxims consumed 40% of all examples used by the author.[23]

The timing is of particular interest because the book was published in 1727 and thus in the middle of equity's transformation. It was at that time that, in order to refute the charges of their critics, the chancellors attempted to formalise equity and started following their own precedents.[24] The publication of the book was probably a result of this transformation rather than its cause or catalyst. Between the end of the 17th century (Lord Nottingham) and the beginning of the 19th century (Lord Eldon), equity crystalised into a set of rules.[25] Francis attempted to show his reader, a law student, what were the foundations of equity.[26] For the purpose of justifying its presence alongside common law[27] and countering the charges of unprincipled arbitrariness shown in the book's preface,[28] he resorted to the maxims of equity, citing extensively Bacon's *The elements of the common lawes of England*.[29]

23 In total, Francis presented 137 cases.

24 As evidenced in one of the cases: Francis, *Maxims of Equity*, 64 (c. 8): "It was strongly insisted, at the Bar, that this (…) was in Truth a Thing against Conscience, and contradictory to many established Rules of Law and Equity. But Lord Keeper declared he would not change the Rule, that so long prevailed in this Case". Nevertheless, the binding force of precedent was not absolute before the Court of Chancery, see Francis, *Maxims of Equity*, 3 (preface): "the Court of Law, rigidly adheres to its own established Rules, be the Injustice arising from thence, ever so apparent; whereas the Court of Equity will not adhere to its own most established Rules, if the least Injustice arises from thence."

25 Blackstone, *Commentaries*, 55. Baker, *An Introduction*, 118–119; Getzler, "Patterns of Fusion," 175–176, 185; Langbein, Lerner, and Smith, *History of the Common Law*, 316–317, 351–355; Macnair, "Arbitrary Chancellors," 95ff; Meagher, Heydon, and Leeming, *Meagher*, 1–11; Smith, "Equity as Meta-Law," 1060.

26 Francis, *Maxims of Equity*, 4 (preface): "Some of the Principal of those Rules of Equity, are attempted to be shown in the following Work. If the Imperfectness of it should be objected; to that it is answered, that the Intent was only to lead the young Student into a proper Method of his Enquiries into this Science of Equity."

27 Cf. fn 55 and text above it.

28 Cf. fn 20, fn 21.

29 Francis, *Maxims of Equity*, 4 (preface): "That he could not confer so profitable an Addition unto the Science of the Law, as by collecting the Rules and Grounds, dispersed throughout

Although maxims had already appeared in earlier works (such as St German's *Doctor and Student* or in Bacon's *The elements of the common lawes of England*, which he quoted in the preface), Francis's book was the first to refer to maxims of equity in its very title.[30] As his work was created in the period of equity transformation, that was also the time when these maxims began to emerge. Their particular wording was not used before. Many of them were coined by him, in particular "Equality is equity," which is still recognised today.[31] On the other hand, he did not refer to several others because they were not yet known.[32]

Modern scholars are divided over their relevancy today. Some take maxims seriously, as significant guidelines either for the application of equitable doctrines in practice or for teaching equity in law schools.[33] There are others who approach them with tongue in cheek.[34] Francis highlighted fourteen maxims of equity, which are listed below, in order according to their supposed relevance today:

the Body of the same Laws; …to see more profoundly into the Reason of such Judgments and ruled Cases…; so that the Incertainty of Law, which is the principal and most just Challenge that is made to the Laws of our Nation at this Time, will by this new Strength laid to the Foundation, be somewhat the more settled and corrected."

30 On the collection of maxims as a genre in English legal literature, see Alfred W. B. Simpson, "The Rise and Fall of the Legal Treatise: Legal Principles and the Forms of Legal Literature," *University of Chicago Law Review* 48 (1981): 644–651.

31 The maxim "equality is the highest Equity" can be found in *Ward v Lant* (1701), a case printed in *Precedents in Chancery* published in 1733, and thus after Francis's book. *Precedents in Chancery, being a collection of cases, argued and adjudged in the High Court of Chancery; from the year 1689, to 1722*, London: In the Savoy: printed by E. and R. Nutt, and R. Gosling (assigns of Edward Sayer, Esq) for Arthur Bettesworth, and Charles Hitch, at the Red-Lyon in Pater-Noster Row, 1733.

32 However, among those omitted by Francis was also the maxim "Equity follows the law," which was in legal circulation even before his time. Chafee, Jr., "Coming into Equity," 880–881; Roscoe Pound, "On Certain Maxims of Equity," in *Cambridge Legal Essays*, eds. P.H. Winfield and A.D. McNair (Cambridge: W. Heffer, 1926), 262–275.

33 Francis himself explicitly referred to this teaching goal – cf. fn 26. Gino E. Dal Pont, *Equity and Trusts in Australia* (Pyrmont, NSW: Lawbook Co., 2023), 14; Meagher, Heydon, and Leeming, *Meagher*, 85; Sham Qayyum, "Some New Maxims of Chancery: 'Explicated for the More Facile Introduction of Such as Are Studiously Addicted to That Noble Profession,'" *Trusts & Trustees* 27, nos. 1–2 (2021): 91; Smith, "Equity as Meta-Law," 1058, 1130 ("They are, after all, at the heart of equity"); Virgo, *The Principles*, 29–30. There is a correlation between the notion of separateness of law and equity and the emphasis on maxims of equity: Meagher, Heydon, and Leeming, *Meagher*, 52–54 (they refer to "fusion fallacy"); Smith, "Equity as Meta-Law," 1058.

34 Roger Young, Stephen Spitz, "SUEM – Spitz's Ultimate Equitable Maxim: In Equity, Good Guys Should Win and Bad Guys Should Lose," *South Carolina Law Review* 55 (2003): 175–177. Ben McFarlane, "The Maxims of Equity," in *Snell's Equity*, ed. John McGhee and Steven Elliott (London: Sweet & Maxwell, 2020), 91–92 ("limited utility of maxims"). Chafee, Jr., "Coming into Equity," 877ff, 1065ff, analysed English and American case law on "clean hands" and found this maxim useless.

"Equity suffers not a Right to be Without a Remedy" (No. 6) – the sixth on his list; recognised today by the majority, often in rephrased form with "right" replaced by "wrong" (Hanbury; Meagher; Smith).[35]

"Equality is Equity" (No. 3) – with two variants of its wording conveying similar meaning, one with the original word order (Smith) and one reversed, "Equity is equality" (Hanbury; Meagher; Virgo).

"He that will have Equity done to him, must do it to the same person" (No. 1) – today in rephrased wording: "He who seeks equity must do equity."[36]

"He that hath committed Iniquity, shall not have Equity" (No. 2) – significantly rephrased with the focus on "clean hands": "He who comes to equity must come with clean hands."

"Equity regards not the Circumstance, but the Substance of the Act" (No. 13) – today rephrased as: "Equity looks to the intent rather than to the form."

"Equity suffers not Advantage to be taken of a Penalty or Forfeiture, where Compensation can be made" (No. 12) – no longer referred to by the majority, with some exceptions (Pound; Smith).[37]

"Where Equity is equal, the Law must prevail" (No. 14) – still recognised today in slightly rephrased wording.[38]

"Equity regards Length of Time" (No. 10) – this maxim is caught today by another one "Where there are equal Equities the first in time shall prevail" (Hanbury; Smith) or by various others (Hanbury: "Delay defeats equities"; Meagher: "Equity assists the diligent, not the tardy"; Virgo: "Equity assists the diligent").

"It is Equity that should make Satisfaction, which received the Benefit" (No. 4); "It is Equity that should have Satisfaction, which sustained the Loss" (No. 5); "Equity relieves against Accidents" (No. 7); "Equity prevents Mischief" (No. 8); "Equity prevents Multiplicity of Suits" (No. 9)[39]; "Equity will not suffer a double Satisfaction to be taken" (No. 11) – these six are no longer referred to today. In turn, modern scholars have added several other maxims, in particular: "Equity follows the law"; "Equity acts in personam"; "Equity regards that as done which ought to be done"; and "Equity imputes an intention to fulfil an obligation."[40]

35 Some authors (Virgo) find this maxim obsolete as it no longer distinguishes equity from law.

36 Smith, "Equity as Meta-Law," 1126 (referring to the feminine gender: "She who seeks equity must do equity").

37 Pound, "On Certain Maxims," 259, and Smith, "Equity as Meta-Law," 1119 ("Equity abhors a forfeiture").

38 Not listed by Virgo.

39 That one is listed by Smith, "Equity as Meta-Law," 1123 ("Equity delights to do justice and not by halves").

40 The last one is not listed by Virgo, who, in turn, (invents and) adds several others. Dal Pont, *Equity and Trusts*, 15–20; Glister and Lee, *Hanbury & Martin*, 23–27; Meagher, Heydon, and Leeming, *Meagher*, 85–121; Smith, "Equity as Meta-Law," 1115–1127; Virgo, *The Principles*, 29–43.

9.3 Cases on Equality

From the perspective of this book's theme, the chapter on the maxim "Equality is equity" is particularly interesting. Reading Francis's work allows one to conclude that the scope of this maxim's application in the 18th century was significantly different from what it is today.[41] The scope's breadth emphasises one of the ways in which equity was understood: like the Roman notion of *aequitas.*

Francis gathered two categories of cases. The first one, which I would call "Equality between Parties," consists of cases that focus strictly on equality in relations between parties. Like parties should be treated alike (thus equally), but they would not be so treated but for the chancellor's intervention because of the lack of an adequate remedy at law. The foregoing shows that the concept of equality was behind yet another maxim: "Equity suffers not a Right to be Without a Remedy," which resulted in the belief that a lack of adequate remedy at common law should not prevent a petitioner from protecting his rights if his position was similar to that of an individual having such a remedy. In such instances, equity was to step in as a safety net of the administration of justice. This category fits into the modern understanding of what is covered by the maxim "Equality is equity." The meaning it conveyed is a tendency of equity law to treat equally those who acquired rights or assumed liability together. A presumption follows that, in equity, co-owners' or co-sureties' respective rights or duties are equal. A number of Francis's case studies referred to the contribution between co-debtors that was required in order for them to participate equally in liability.[42] There were other cases which dealt with equality if the payment of estate debts was affected by the insufficiency of funds to cover them all.[43] Nowadays, the focus on equality also leads to a preference for "tenancy in common" over "joint tenancy." In the former type of co-ownership, a right of survivorship is excluded, under which a co-owner's death results in an incremental increase in the rights of the other co-owners.[44] One could find such cases also in Francis's book.[45]

The second category of cases, which could be called "Equality against Windfall," seems at first glance to be a heterogeneous group and includes the remainder of Francis's cases illustrating that maxim. The common denominator emerging from these cases, though, was a prevention of windfall. Equity

41 On the other hand, such issues as (in)equality depending on citizenship, religion, race, ethnicity, and non-marital origin were outside the scope of Francis's interest.

42 Francis, *Maxims of Equity*, 14–16 (c. 12, 14, 16, 18).

43 Francis, *Maxims of Equity*, 10–14 (c. 5-9, 11, 13; c. 11: "For a Debt without Specialty, is as much a Debt Jure Naturali, and in Conscience, as a Debt by Specialty; and there shall be Equality where Conscience is the Judge").

44 Glister and Lee, *Hanbury & Martin*, 25–26; Meagher, Heydon, and Leeming, *Meagher*, 103–106; Virgo, *The Principles*, 42–43.

45 Francis, *Maxims of Equity*, 16 (c. 19: "The Advantage of Survivorship is against Equity").

attempted to intervene if as a result of a fortuitous event (an accident),[46] or in consequence of an opportunistic act of a party, that party would gain a benefit at the expense of the other in unjustifiable circumstances, or, to paraphrase, such a gain or loss was against conscience.[47]

Thus, cases illustrating the maxim involved an "insider" who entered into a transaction concerning an asset belonging to the estate of a deceased person in order to obtain a benefit at the expense of other stakeholders. The Court of Chancery, guided by the precept of "Equality is equity," sought (proportional) equality between them.[48]

This category also accommodated contract law cases dealing with a change of circumstances as we would call it today.[49] Here, equality was intended to even out the legal consequences of actual facts with a hypothetical situation that would occur unless the litigant against whom equity was sought to be applied did not act in an opportunistic way (causing or utilising certain facts). The "accident" that disturbed the balance between litigants might be the death of one of the parties to a contract or third parties taking over a piece of real property that was subject to a tenancy. In that latter case, equity, following the maxim "Equality is equity," demanded a proportional reduction in rent.[50] Again, the intervention of equity, applied as a safety net, provided an exception to the law.

Of particular importance is a case in which the chancellor's authority to check the correctness of a trustee's distribution of funds from an estate (or a trust) was acknowledged. There have been cases in which a trustee was to divide assets among beneficiaries (often the trustor's children) according to either their merits or their needs. This may at first glance seem noncontroversial because the trustor had empowered the trustee with full discretion to allocate funds among beneficiaries. Nevertheless, in the case cited by Francis,[51] it was resolved that the distribution could be controlled, and amended, if necessary, by the Court of Chancery ensuring that the trustee's powers were exercised properly. One might wonder whether the trustee's power was abused in that specific case and that fact caused equity to step in.

46 The maxim in question could operate in tandem with the maxim "Equity relieves against Accidents" in this type of case. It seems that in others the same could be said of maxims: "It is Equity that should make Satisfaction, which received the Benefit" (No. 4), "It is Equity that should have Satisfaction, which sustained the Loss" (No. 5), "Equity will not suffer a double Satisfaction to be taken" (No. 11), and "Equity suffers not Advantage to be taken of a Penalty or Forfeiture, where Compensation can be made" (No. 12).

47 Cf. fn 61.

48 Francis, *Maxims of Equity*, 9–10 (c. 1-3): "for the taking away one Man's Gain, to make up another's Loss, is making them both equal." The facts of c. 1 are similar to the one reported as anon. (1707) 1 Salkeld 155.

49 While only a minor number of Francis's cases on "Equality is equity" involved contract cases, many more of them are to be found in other chapters of his work.

50 Francis, *Maxims of Equity*, 13 (c. 10), 15 (c. 15).

51 Francis, *Maxims of Equity*, 17 (c. 20).

The discussed maxim was also consulted in the context of jettison. Indeed, if goods were thrown off a ship in "Stress of Weather, or in Danger or just Fear of Enemy" in order to save a ship and the remainder of the cargo, then a contribution had to be made between the shipowner and all merchants who had their cargo onboard. In a gloss on this point, Francis presented a case in which a contribution was not allowed, however. Expecting to be hijacked by enemy forces, a shipmaster ordered that the more valuable part of the cargo (silks) be unloaded (and presumably hidden) on the coast. The ship, along with the remaining cargo (olive oil), was seized and lost. Still, the chancellor refused to grant a bill in equity that would allow the oil merchants to demand a contribution from the silk merchants because (to paraphrase) the olives did not save the silks and the salvage of the silks did not cause the loss of the olives.[52] One might wonder whether the maxim "Equality is equity" should not be applied here as well.

9.4 What, After All, Is Equity?

Although most frequently the term "equity" was used by Francis inconsistently[53] and in an ambiguous way,[54] there are several patterns of its usage in his book. In the preface, he presented law and equity as sets of rules that were applied, respectively, by various courts operating in full symbiosis. He seemed to be touched by it: "the Beauty of this Contrivance, whereby Justice is produced from such jarring Jurisdictions; and what neither strict Form and Order or absolute Latitude in judging, can separately produce, is effected by the excellent Temperature of both together. This hath been judiciously compared to the mingling of two Herbs, which of themselves are Poison, but together make a wholesome Medicine." This herbal comparison came from Lord Ellesmere (*Arguments proving from antiquity the dignity, power and jurisdiction of the Court of Chancery*), who, as Fortier indicates, had borrowed it from William Lambarde's *Archeion* from the late 16th century.[55]

Francis continued by stating that judges who sit in the Westminster courts were resolving disputes according to the strict rules of law and were not given any discretion.[56] However, it was not possible to introduce *ex ante* rules that

52 Francis, *Maxims of Equity*, 18 (c. 21). Cf. Roman doctrine of *lex Rhodia de iactu*.

53 The inconsistency of that use was a common pattern in the past: Fortier, *The Culture of Equity*, 60, 77; Ibbetson, "A House Built on Sand," 55, 76–77; Maniscalco, *Equity*, 219; Macnair, "Equity and Conscience," 661, 671; Willem J. Zwalve, *The Equity of the Law: Law and Equity since Justinian*, in Koops and Zwalve, *Law & Equity*, 30–31.

54 Francis, *Maxims of Equity*, 1 (c. 1: "to pray Equity against"), 3 (c. 6: "there is no Equity, that his Security should be enlarged"), 3 (c. 6: "that relief (...) was not proper in Equity"), 26 (c. 5: "If a Man hath Cause to complain In Equity"). Maxims nos. 10 and 13 might be added here as well.

55 Francis, *Maxims of Equity*, 3 (preface). Fortier, *The Culture of Equity*, 80.

56 Francis, *Maxims of Equity*, 2 (preface): "The Judges in our Courts of Law, are bound by their Oaths to observe the strict Rules of Law; and therefore as upright Judges, they must deter-

would fit all cases that might arise.[57] A court of law was bound by its own rules even if they led to injustice, while a court of equity was not. Thus, it was the Court of Chancery where the rigors of the law were mitigated. This sounded like a direct reference to Aristotle's *epieikeia*. The need to adjust (to rectify) general laws to the circumstances of a case was a safety net of the administration of justice. It created space for the chancellor's "equitable" intervention.[58]

An analysis of the case studies reveals that often the use of the term "equity" indeed bore the hallmarks of Aristotle's thought. Although it may not have been directly apparent from the literal content, the legal context of cases indicated it. The recurring pattern of these cases was that a petitioner's interests would be violated if general law (i.e., common law) was applied, but equity rectified the law and protected the petitioner.[59] This was the meaning conveyed by the term in a number of verb phrases,[60] which could also be seen as indicating another meaning (equity as a set of rules), as discussed below.

Francis objected to charges of arbitrariness, stating that the chancellor was directed by "Conscience"[61] (capitalised) and "guided by an infallible Monitor within his own Breast." He was adjudicating disputes according to the "original and eternal Rules of Justice."[62] Was it, though, a call for deciding cases on the basis of natural justice? The answer seems to be affirmative.

Equity as an equivalent of justice was to be found in the majority of Francis's maxims (Nos. 1–6, 11, 12, 14), in particular in: "He that will have Equity

---

mine according to the known Customs and Statutes of the Realm, although they are sensible, that even is so judging, they do an Act of manifest Injustice."; 3: "the Court of Law, rigidly adheres to its own established Rules, be the Injustice arising from thence, ever so apparent; whereas the Court of Equity will not adhere to its own most established Rules, if the least Injustice arises from thence."

57 Francis, *Maxims of Equity*, 2 (preface): "human Providence is too weak, to make Laws, which shall prove just in all Cases."

58 Francis, *Maxims of Equity*, 3 (preface): "On the other Hand the Judge in a Court of Equity, is bound not to suffer an Act of Injustice to prevail, tho' it be warranted by the Forms and Proceedings of Law; and therefore he moderates the Rigour of several Penalties; relaxes the strict Ties of unreasonable Conditions; aids against unavoidable Losses, clandestine Frauds and the like; and thence it is, that Judgment shall be given in the same Case against a Man on one Side of Westminster-Hall, and quite contrary for him on the other; and yet both these agreeable to Justice."

59 Francis, *Maxims of Equity*, 15 (c. 14: "Sureties shall be compelled in Equity to contribute"), 51 (c. 12: "dismissed the Bill, as containing no Equity"), 17 (case 20: "Equity will in many Cases controul the unequal Distribution"), 53 (c. 1: "But Equity seems not much regard the Consideration"), 55 (c. 2: "Even mistakes in Deeds are amended in Equity").

60 Francis, *Maxims of Equity*, 11 (c. 5: "Equity will place"), 15 (c. 15: "Equity will apportion"), 11 (c. 5) and 16 (c. 19: "Equity will decree"), 34 (c. 11: "Equity will bind"), 52 (c. 15: "Equity will relieve"), 53 (c. 1: "Equity will enforce").

61 There were other references to this notion which show grammatical similarity in the use of both equity and conscience: Francis, *Maxims of Equity*, 6 (c. 2: it would be "against Conscience to insist upon it"), 55 (c. 2: "shall be compelled in Conscience"), 17 (Case of the Earl of Coventry: "bound in conscience").

62 Francis, *Maxims of Equity*, 1–5 (preface).

done to him, must do it to the same person" (No. 1); "He that hath committed Iniquity, shall not have Equity" (No. 2); "It is Equity that should make Satisfaction, which received the Benefit" (No. 4). As the context of the preface indicated, the expression "Courts of Justice" used there referred to the Court of Chancery and those other courts where equity was applied as well.[63] In the Case of the Earl of Coventry, which was annexed to the book, both Baron Gilbert and Baron Parke indicated that the inconsistency of common law with natural justice triggered the intervention of the court.[64] In the preface, Francis drew attention to the injustice that might result from strict observance of the law.[65] Both terms "Equity" and "Justice" (in capital letters) were set as equivalents in the case studies: "It is the constant Justice of a Court of Equity" and, most plausibly: "ought in Equity and Justice to be esteemed a Marriage."[66]

Francis rarely used negations of the terms "equity" and "equitable," but, when he did, they ("iniquity" and "iniquitous" instead of "unequitable") referred to either an unacceptable act or the status quo: "he shall not have it, because he has committed Iniquity" or to such feature of, for instance, an agreement: "unreasonable and iniquitous."[67] One could find negation in the maxim "He that hath committed Iniquity, shall not have Equity" as well. This usage provokes again the thought that the equity Francis was referring to had to be understood as justice.

While the notion of equity law was not yet used, the term "equity" frequently referred to a set of rules: "Rules of Equity."[68] These provided for particular doctrines of a substantive or procedural nature[69] that were applied in the Court of Chancery, which was – at this time – referred to circularly as the

63 Francis, *Maxims of Equity*, 1 (preface).

64 Francis, *Maxims of Equity*, 3–9 (Case of the Earl of Coventry).

65 Francis, *Maxims of Equity*, 2–5 (preface: "an act (manifest) of Injustice"; "Temper of Justice" jeopardised by strictness of law).

66 Francis, *Maxims of Equity*, 2 (preface: "Rules of Equity ... never been found to be unjust"), 26 (c. 5: "failure of justice" if equity do not step in), 60 (c. 4), 62 (c. 2). Note that in the herbal comparison (see text above fn 55) justice was to be achieved by the cooperation of law and equity. By the way, explicit references to the term "fairness" are scarce: Francis, *Maxims of Equity*, 4 (c. 7: "such Bargains may be fair"), 37 (c. 4: "a fair Claim"), 53 (c. 1: "not obtained with all imaginable Fairness").

67 Francis, *Maxims of Equity*, 4 (c. 7), 6 (c. 2: "For that would be to decree Iniquity"; "the Iniquity of the Bargain"; "the Bargain is plainly iniquitous").

68 Francis, *Maxims of Equity*, 3–4 (preface), 6 (c. 2 "The Doubtfulness of Equity may be here objected since no Rule is settled"; "common Equity to decree Specifick Performances of Agreements"), 15 (c. 14: "Sureties shall be compelled in Equity to contribute"), 17 (c. 20: "case proper and relievable in Equity"), 23 (c. 7: "sued in Equity"), 31 (c.2: "otherwise (...) Equity would do a Mischief"), 47 (c. 7: "Shall not be relieved in Equity"), 53 (c. 1: "deviseth the lands, they pass in Equity"; "But Equity seems not much regard the Consideration"), 58 (c. 3: "shall be good in Equity"), 68 (c. 13: "shall be executed in Equity").

69 Francis, *Maxims of Equity*, 1 (c. 1: "Rebutter in Equity", "Equity of Redemption"), 11 (c. 5: "Equity will place"), 13 (c. 9: "Bill in Equity"), 25 (c. 2: "Remedy in Equity"), 26 (c. 5: "Cause to complain in Equity"), 28 (c. 7: "Relief in Equity").

"Court of Equity."[70] To this category one can add the maxims "Equity relieves against Accidents" (No. 7); "Equity prevents Mischief" (No. 8); "Equity prevents Multiplicity of Suits" (No. 9); as well as the repeated use of active verb phrases such as "Equity will relieve," forecasting what the chancellor is going to do in a given case.[71] Very rarely, this meaning was conveyed in an adjective form, as in the index: "Feme, her equitable Estate," where the focus was on the protection of wives' interests that was provided particularly in equity as a set of rules applicable in the Court of Chancery.[72] In multiple cases, that usage allowed equity to be juxtaposed with common law ("Rules of Law and Equity").[73]

What is striking is that there are many cases where the term "equity" strongly emphasised the need to treat parties equally.[74] The book's index is stocked with items on who with whom had or did not have "equal Equity."[75] This usage recalls that the English noun "equity" comes from the Latin *aequitas*. In Antiquity, Roman lawyers emphasised the need to decide like cases alike and to treat individuals equally. As indicated above, Francis's elaboration on the maxim "Equality is equity" was the longest in his work and used the highest number of cases as an illustration. While the maxim itself "Equality is equity" drew attention to *aequitas*, which is Latin for "equality,"[76] the phrase "Science of Equity"[77] recalled Roman jurist Celsus's statement that law is the art of the good and the equitable (*Ius est ars boni et aequi*, D.1.1.1pr).

Besides the references to equity as a measure allowing like cases to be treated alike, there were others where equity would be weighed as a measure

70 Francis, *Maxims of Equity*, 1ff.

71 Francis, *Maxims of Equity*, 4 (c. 1: "Equity will relieve"), 11 (c. 5), 16 (c. 19) and 21 (c. 1: "Equity will decree"), 14 (c. 12: "Equity will make the Tenant pay"), 15 (c. 15: "Equity will apportion"), 26 (c. 6: "Equity gives Aid"), 34 (c. 11: "Equity will bind"), 53 (c. 1: "Equity looks upon Articles"; "Equity will enforce"). Though cf. text *supra* fn 60.

72 Francis, *Maxims of Equity*, 50 (c. 12: "equitable Excuses"), 11 (Case of the Earl of Coventry: "equitable interest").

73 Francis, *Maxims of Equity*, 51 (c. 12: "both in Law and Equity"), 55 (c. 2: "For if the Assurance is bad, and yet there is Remedy in Equity, to what purpose is the Common Law?"), 62 (c.2) and 65 (c. 9: "he shall not account in Equity otherwise than at Law"), 68 (c. 8: "Rules of Law and Equity"), 71 (c. 17: "the Surety who was not liable in Law, should be liable in Equity").

74 Francis, *Maxims of Equity*, 1 (c. 1: "the same Equity for the Mortgagee to have both debts be paid to him"), 11 (c. 6: "there is the same Equity in case of younger Children"), 22 (c. 2: "there is the same Equity if the Purchaser takes"), 53 (c. 1: "equal Equity with either of them").

75 "Heir, has not equal Equity with a Jointress";"...with a Purchaser"; "...with a Creditor"; "...with younger Children"; "Heir, has equal Equity with a Volunteer."

76 There are other concepts of this maxim's background. Cf. Pound, "On Certain Maxims," 265 (Aristotelian origin); Smith, "Equity as Meta-Law," 1125 ("This maxim sounds in fairness").

77 Francis, *Maxims of Equity*, 4 (preface).

for assessing (valuing) a person's rights, in particular vis-à-vis the other litigant ("Consideration to give the Grantor greater Equity than the Heir").[78]

9.5 Conclusion

The procedural advantages of equity over common law often become obvious when one analyses Francis's cases.[79] Because of them, the chancellor was able to scrutinise thoroughly the multifaceted context of a case and investigate relations between all involved stakeholders. Thus, equity as a set of rules emerged in the course of the exercise of his powers allowing him to use extraordinary methods of fact-finding.[80] By these means, the Court of Chancery was capable of making decisions which, judged from either a moral or common sense perspective, were sounder than those of other courts.

The chancellor assessed cases from a *post factum* perspective. As a result, the Court of Chancery was more likely to reach fair decisions than other courts which resorted to *a priori* programmed, straightforward (and thus clumsy) rules of common law. While the latter applied general law, equity came to rectify it – as Aristotle would understand it. Equity law and common law were (and are) designed to perform various functions in the legal system with equity being a meta-law,[81] or a safety net that could be employed to provide exceptions to the law wherever needed.

Francis referred to equity in various ways and one can only wonder whether he was aware of that diversity and, if so, of the sources of particular usages. While in the preface the traces of Aristotle's *epieikeia* prevailed, on the one hand, in the main body of the book equity most often meant either justice or a set of rules applied in the Court of Chancery, on the other. What strikes civil lawyers is the *aequitas*-like pattern that is found occasionally in the *Maxims* and that draws attention to Roman law heritage. At this stage, one can only wonder whether it was a coincidence or a lingering subconscious leftover brought into the Chancery long ago by university teaching when chancellors were still clergymen?

78 Francis, *Maxims of Equity*, 68 (c. 13).

79 Francis, *Maxims of Equity*, 7 (c. 5), 33 (c. 7), 53-54 (c. 1), 72 (c. 17), 17 (Case of the Earl of Coventry).

80 Although at a certain stage in the 17th century the Westminster courts also began to apply these methods, the Court of Chancery's jurisdiction over a certain spectrum of cases was never surrendered.

81 Smith, "Equity as Meta-Law," 1054 ("Equity is law about law, or meta-law"), 1125.

References

Primary sources

<u>*Statutes*</u>

The Supreme Court of Judicature Act 1873, c. 66.
The Supreme Court of Judicature Act (1873) Amendment Act 1875, c. 77.

<u>*Cases*</u>

Earl of Oxford's Case (1615) 1 *Reports in Chancery* 1.
Ward v Lant (1701).
Anon. (1707) 1 Salkeld 155.

<u>*Old prints*</u>

Blackstone, William. *Commentaries on the Laws of England.* Oxford: Clarendon Press, 1765-1769.

Francis, Richard. *Maxims of Equity: Collected From and Proved by Cases, Out of the Books of the Best Authority in the High Court of Chancery. To Which is Added the Case of the Earl of Coventry, Concerning the Defective Execution of Powers. Lately Adjudged in the High Court of Chancery.* London: In the Savoy: printed by E. and R. Nutt, and R. Gosling (assigns of E. Sayer, Esq) for J. Stephens, 1727.

Precedents in Chancery, Being a Collection of Cases, Argued and Adjudged in the High Court of Chancery; from the Year 1689 to 1722. London: In the Savoy: printed by E. and R. Nutt, and R. Gosling (assigns of Edward Sayer, Esq) for Arthur Bettesworth, and Charles Hitch, at the Red-Lyon in Pater-Noster Row, 1733.

Some Observations in the Practice of the Court of Chancery under the Late Ordinance of Regulation. London, 1653–1658.

Secondary studies

Baker, John H. *An Introduction to English Legal History.* 5th ed. Oxford: Oxford University Press, 2019.

Baker, John H. *The Oxford History of the Laws of England. Volume VI, 1483–1558.* Oxford: Oxford University Press, 2003.

Bryson, William H. "Francis, Richard." In *Oxford Dictionary of National Biography*, vol. 20, Oxford: Oxford University Press, 2004.

Chafee, Zechariah Jr. "Coming into Equity with Clean Hands I." *Michigan Law Review* 47 (1949): 877–906.

Cromartie, Alan. "Epieikeia and Conscience." In *The Oxford Handbook of English Law and Literature, 1500–1700*, edited by Lorna Hutson, 320–36. Oxford: Oxford University Press,, 2017.

Dal Pont, Gino E. *Equity and Trusts in Australia.* Pyrmont, NSW: Lawbook Co., 2023.

Fortier, Mark. *The Culture of Equity in Early Modern England.* Burlington, VT: Ashgate, 2005.

Funk, Kellen. "The Union of Law and Equity. The United States, 1800–1938." In *Equity and Law: Fusion and Fission*, edited by J. Goldberg, H. Smith, and P. Turner, 46–69. Cambridge: Cambridge University Press, 2019.

Getzler, Joshua. "Patterns of Fusion." In *The Classification of Obligations*, edited by P. Birks, 157–92. Oxford: Clarendon Press, 1997.

Glister, Jamie, and James Lee. *Hanbury & Martin Modern Equity*. 22nd ed. London: Sweet & Maxwell, 2021.

Humphreys, Stephen. "Equity before 'Equity'." *Modern Law Review* 86, no. 1 (2022): 85–121.

Ibbetson, David. "A House Built on Sand: Equity in Early Modern English Law." In *Law & Equity. Approaches in Roman Law and Common Law*, edited by E. Koops and W. J. Zwalve, 55–77. Leiden: Brill, 2014.

Kuryłowicz, Marek. "Aequitas i iustitia w rzymskiej praktyce prawnej [Some Reflections on aequitas and iustitia in Roman Jurists' Concepts]." *Annales Universitatis Mariae Curie-Skłodowska Sectio G* 66 (2019): 173–88.

Langbein, John H., Renee Lettow Lerner, and Bruce P. Smith. *History of the Common Law. The Development of Anglo-American Legal Institutions.* Austin, New York: Wolters Kluwer Law & Business, Aspen Publishers, 2009.

Maitland, Frederic W. *Equity, also the Forms of Action at Common Law: Two Courses of Lectures*. Cambridge: Cambridge University Press, 1910.

Maniscalco, Lorenzo. *Equity in Early Modern Legal Scholarship*. Leiden: Brill, 2020.

McFarlane, Ben. "The Maxims of Equity." In *Snell's Equity*, edited by John McGhee and Steven Elliott. London: Sweet & Maxwell, 2020.

Macnair, Mike. "Arbitrary Chancellors and Problem of Predictability." In *Law & Equity. Approaches in Roman Law and Common Law*, edited by E. Koops and W. J. Zwalve, 79–104. Leiden: Brill, 2014.

Macnair, Mike. "Equity and Conscience." *Oxford Journal of Legal Studies* 27 (2007): 659–81.

Meagher, Rodrick P., John D. Heydon, and Mark J. Leeming. *Meagher, Gummow and Lehane's Equity, Doctrines, and Remedies.* Chatswood, NSW: LexisNexis Butterworths, 2002.

Pound, Roscoe. "On Certain Maxims of Equity." In *Cambridge Legal Essays*, edited by P. H. Winfield and A. D. McNair, 259–77. Cambridge: W. Heffer, 1926.

Qayyum, Sham. "Some New Maxims of Chancery: 'Explicated for the More Facile Introduction of Such as Are Studiously Addicted to That Noble Profession'." *Trusts & Trustees* 27, no. 1–2 (2021): 90–107.

Simpson, Alfred W. B. "The Rise and Fall of the Legal Treatise: Legal Principles and the Forms of Legal Literature." *University of Chicago Law Review* 48 (1981): 632–79.

Smith, Henry E. "Equity as Meta-Law." *The Yale Law Journal* 130 (2021): 1050–1144.

Virgo, Graham. *The Principles of Equity and Trusts.* Oxford: Oxford University Press, 2023.

Young, Roger, and Stephen Spitz. "SUEM - Spitz's Ultimate Equitable Maxim: In Equity, Good Guys Should Win and Bad Guys Should Lose." *South Carolina Law Review* 55 (2003): 175–89.

Zwalve, Willem J. "The Equity of the Law: Law and Equity since Justinian." In *Law & Equity. Approaches in Roman Law and Common Law*, edited by E. Koops and W. J. Zwalve, 15–37. Leiden: Brill 2014.

Zwalve, Willem J., and Egbert Koops. "Introduction: The Equity Phenomenon." In *Law & Equity. Approaches in Roman Law and Common Law*, edited by E. Koops and W. J. Zwalve, 1–13. Leiden: Brill, 2014.

Index

Note: 'n' denotes footnote numbers

Index of Items

Note: Page numbers in **bold** represent tables, while 'n' denotes footnote numbers

FSC
www.fsc.org
MIX
Papier | Fördert gute Waldnutzung
FSC® C083411

Kolibri 360 GmbH
Ferdinand-Jühlke-Straße 7
99095 Erfurt, Deutschland
produktsicherheit@kolibri360.de